Configuring SAP Asset Accounting

SAP S/4HANA Finance

Narayanan Veeriah

Configuring SAP Asset Accounting
SAP S/4HANA Finance

ISBN: 9798653831157
© Narayanan Veeriah
1st Edition, 2020

Acknowledgements

I acknowledge the understanding and adjustments made by my family, especially my wife, for all the encouragement and letting me concentrate working on this book, as with previous other books. I thank Narayanan Krishnan, who helps in checking out the content for its correctness.

Preface

As with my other books on SAP, this book also follows a case-study approach to make your learning easy. Efforts have been taken, throughout the book, to guide you step-by-step in understanding how to configure your SAP system, to meet your exact business needs. Each configuration activity has been discussed with appropriate screen shots (from an SAP system) and illustrations to help you 'see' what is being discussed in that activity / step. You will see a lot of additional information, provided across the Chapters and the Sections, to help you understand better a topic or a setting or a concept. The entire content of the book, vide various Chapters, has been presented as in SAP IMG (Implementation Guide) for easy comprehension. You will come across with appropriate menu paths and Transactions, to help you to navigate the various activities.

Though this book is on *'Configuring Asset Accounting'* in *SAP S/4HANA Finance*, you will see that an effort has been made to bring in the necessary context and relevance in the form of explanation on SAP HANA, SAP S/4HANA and SAP S/4HANA Finance without straightaway jumping to asset accounting.

The **Chapter 1** discusses on SAP HANA, bringing out the evolution of SAP application from SAP R/1, to SAP ERP, to the current form of SAP HANA 2.0. It helps you to trace the history of SAP HANA with its first introduction in 2008. It makes you understand the HANA architecture and gives you a brief view of the options that are available for its deployment.

In **Chapter 2**, you are provided with an overview of SAP S/4HANA. You will understand why SAP S/4HANA is termed as the digital core or nerve center of modern business. You will learn about the key benefits, the capabilities and the deployment options. You will also understand the SAP's release and maintenance strategy with regard to SAP S/4HANA.

We shall be discussing SAP S/4HANA Finance in **Chapter 3**. You will learn about the overview, the primary capabilities and the key benefits of going in for SAP S/4HANA Finance. You will understand how SAP S/4HANA Finance has been designed to overcome the pain points, that were there in the traditional ERPs, in various application area of SAP FI.

As mentioned already, this book follows a case-study approach with a story-board technique, that provides you with the required business background for a given configuration activity. The **Chapter 4** discusses the case-study (*Project Dolphin*) in its entirety, setting up the tone for further discussions in the remaining Chapters.

From Chapter 5, we discuss SAP Asset Accounting (FI-AA), in detail. The **Chapter 5** deals with the overview of asset accounting in SAP, including the new Asset Accounting.

The **Chapter 6** discusses the organizational structures in FI-AA. As a part of discussions, we shall be outlining the country-specific settings relating to asset accounting in SAP. We shall be discussing the chart of depreciation and on how to create the depreciation areas from copying a reference chart of depreciation.

In **Chapter 7**, you shall be learning how to structure fixed assets in SAP FI-AA. You shall understand some of the special forms of assets that are supported by SAP in FI-AA. You shall also learn about the asset classes in detail, including the asset determination, screen layout rules, numbering, defining an asset class and so on.

The **Chapter 8**, deals with how FI-AA is integrated with other application components including SAP MM, SAP PP, SAP PM etc., with a detailed coverage of integration of FI-AA with SAP G/L Accounting.

We shall be discussing the various aspects of general valuation of fixed assets in **Chapter 9**. We shall discuss, in detail, about the depreciation areas for general valuation, amount specifications, fiscal year specifications, currencies and group assets.

The concept of depreciation and the types of depreciation are covered in **Chapter 10**. This Chapter, also discusses the valuation methods, depreciation key, calculation methods, depreciation methods, scrap value and Depreciation Calculation Program.

You shall learn about special valuations in **Chapter 11**. As of a part of the discussions, you shall learn special reserves, transferred reserves, revaluation of fixed assets, interest and preparations for consolidation.

In **Chapter 12**, we discuss about asset master data. We discuss the data areas in a master record, the screen layout for master records and the asset views.

We cover the various asset transactions in **Chapter 13**. We shall be discussing the configuration required for asset transactions like acquisitions, retirements, transfers including intercompany asset transfer, capitalization of assets under construction etc.

The information system of FI-AA is discussed, in detail, in **Chapter 14**. You shall be learning about the standard asset reports, sort versions, simulation variants, SAP Queries, and asset history sheet. You shall also be learning the key figures and key figure groups required for some of the Fiori apps in FI-AA.

We bring you the details on asset data transfer in *Chapter 15*. Here, we discuss the transfer date and other parameters required for legacy asset data transfer. Besides manual data transfer, we also bring you the details on how to undertake legacy data transfer using Microsoft® Excel.

The *Chapter 16* is devoted for discussing the preparations for going live. You shall learn, here, about authorization management, consistency check, resetting company code, production startup activities and tools that will enable the preparations for going live.

The last Chapter, *Chapter 17*, discusses about the overview for experts. As a part of this, you will understand how to check the various configuration results, from a single IMG node instead of looking at multiple places in the IMG.

In all, you can use this book as a desktop-reference for configuring most of the functions in FI-AA in SAP. As the Chapters have been progressively elaborated, with the help of a case-study, you will certainly find this as informative and easy to comprehend. The screenshots, in each of the Chapters, will help you understand the settings better and will enable for a better learning.

Hope you will enjoy learning SAP FI-AA, through this book!

Contents at a Glance

Contents

1 SAP HANA

SAP, the world's leading *enterprise resource planning* (ERP) application, has been through several changes in its design and functionalities since its launch in 1972: from SAP R/1 to SAP R/2, SAP R/3, SAP HANA, SAP S/4HANA and very recently SAP HANA 2.0. In this chapter, we will take you through the evolution of SAP application first, before getting to the details of SAP HANA. While dealing with SAP HANA, we will help you to understand the inception, the evolution (design and deployment), the architecture, the benefits & advantages, the various editions etc. At the end, we will also discuss SAP S/4 HANA 2.0.

Let us start with the evolution of the SAP application.

1.1 Evolution of SAP

Started by a group of five former employees of IBM, it was called *Systemanalyse und Programmentwicklung* in German, which translates into 'System Analysis and Program Development', popularly known as "SAP". The SAP R/1 was the initial release (1973) and was more of a financial accounting application, with the 'R' standing for 'real-time' data processing. The first technological improvement happened in 1979 leading to the release of SAP R/2 with the packaging of mainframe software application that processed and integrated all the functions of a business enterprise in real-time. In 1993, SAP brought out the client-server version of the software, SAP R/3, enabling businesses to run their operations more efficiently. Until 2001, there were several releases (like 4.0B, 4.0C, 4.5B etc.) to SAP R/3, with SAP R/3 4.6C being the final one released in 2001. SAP called the 4.70 release of the application as SAP R/3 Enterprise Release in 2003, SAP ECC 5.0 ERP (also called as mySAP ERP) in 2004 and SAP ECC 6.0 ERP in 2005. SAP then released the SAP Business Suite 7 (also known as SAP ERP 6) in 2009.

SAP came out with SAP HANA in 2010, offering the in-memory processing platform enabling customers to analyze data in seconds, which would otherwise take days or even weeks. The SAP HANA combines a robust database with services, enabling real-time business by bringing together the transactions and analytics into one, on an in-memory platform. You can run SAP HANA either 'on premise' or 'in the cloud'.

Let us now move on to understand more about SAP HANA in the next section.

1.2   SAP HANA

Historically, the transactional data and analytical data were stored separately in two different databases. Often, data needs to be moved from operational systems to data warehouses and retrieved later for data analysis resulting in considerable delay in the availability of processed data. To address this issue, SAP developed SAP HANA which is an in-memory, column-oriented, *relational database management system* (RDBMS) with its primary function (as a database server) of storing/retrieving data as requested by the applications and performing analytics as an application server.

Let us understand the evolution of SAP HANA, in the next Section.

1.3   History of SAP HANA

SAP, along with Hasso Plattner Institute and Stanford University, demonstrated in 2008, an application architecture for real-time analytics & aggregation, and called the same as 'HANA' (Hasso's New Architecture). For some time, before the name HANA became popular, the database associated with this architecture was known as 'new database', and the software was called as 'SAP High-Performance Analytic Appliance'.

The Table 1.1 provides you with the chronology of SAP HANA since its inception in 2008:

Year	Details
2008	SAP demonstrated the SAP HANA architecture
2010	1st product of SAP HANA
2011	SAP HANA support of SAP NetWeaver Business Warehouse
2012	(1) SAP HANA Cloud Platform as 'Platform as a Service' (2) SAP HANA One (with smaller memory)
2013	(1) SAP HANA Enterprise Cloud (a managed private cloud offering) (2) SAP Business Suite on SAP HANA (to run SAP ERP on SAP HANA platform
2015	SAP S/4HANA (a simplified business suite, combining the functionalities of ERP, CRM, SRM and others, into a single HANA system)
2016	SAP HANA 2.0 (enhanced database management & application management, besides including two new cloud services: Text Analysis & Earth Observation Analysis)
2018	SAP C/4HANA (integrated offering to modernize the sales-only focus of legacy CRM)

Table 1:1 History of SAP HANA

With this, let us understand the architecture of SAP HANA, in brief, next.

1.4   Architecture

The SAP HANA system, in a classical application context, consists of multiple components, including the index server, the name server and the preprocessor server (Figure 1.1).

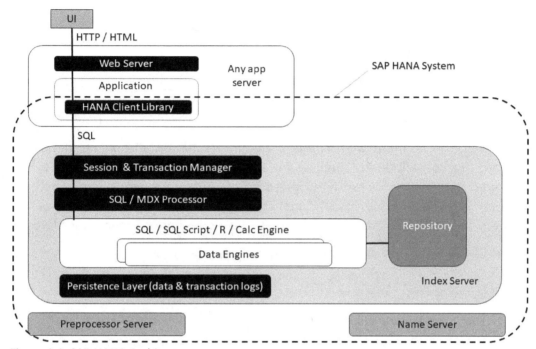

Figure 1.1: SAP HANA Architecture

1.   Index Server

The *'index server'* is the main SAP HANA database management component that contains the actual data stores and the engines for data processing. It processes (using SQL/MDX processor) incoming SQL or MDX statements in the context of authenticated sessions and transactions. Besides the data engines that handle all the SQL/MDX queries, the index server also contains a *'persistence layer'* responsible for durability and atomicity of transactions. It ensures that the SAP HANA system is restored back to the most recently saved state when there is restart, because of a system failure, with the transactions that are either completely executed or completely undone. It also contains the *'session & transaction manager'* that manages the transactions, besides keeping track of all running and closed transactions.

2.   Preprocessor Server

The index server uses the *'preprocessor server'* for analysing text data and extracting the information on which the text search capabilities are based.

3.   *Name Server*

The *'name server'* contains the system landscape information of the HANA system. In a distributed system, the name server knows where the components are running and which data is located on which server. It helps to minimize the time required for re-indexing.

The SAP HANA database has its own scripting language named *SQLScript*, which embeds data-intensive application logic into the database. The classical applications tend to offload only very limited functionality into the database using SQL. This results in extensive copying of data from and to the database, and in programs that slowly iterate over huge data loops and are hard to optimize and parallelize. SQLScript is based on side-effect free functions that operate on tables using SQL queries, and is therefore parallelizable over multiple processors.

Besides SQLScript, SAP HANA supports a framework for installation of specialized and optimized functional libraries, including SAP HANA *Business Function Library* (BFL) and SAP HANA *Predictive Analytics Library* (PAL), that are tightly integrated with different data engines of the index server. Both SQL and SQLScript are implemented using a common infrastructure of built-in data engine functions accessing meta definitions and SQLScript procedures.

With this let us look at the key benefits of going in for SAP HANA.

1.5   Key Benefits

The SAP HANA will be help you to:

- Accelerate response & analysis with in-memory processing, eliminating latency.
- Acquire & integrate data from various sources to boost visibility, besides increasing scalability and lowering complexity.
- Enable stakeholders work smarter, drawing insight from complex data sets and ongoing transactions without compromising data privacy.
- Usher in next wave of change with innovative new applications, supporting geospatial and streaming data.
- Maintain security and business continuity to keep business secure, minimize downtime, and support compliance with security standards.

The three major benefits that will accrue from SAP HANA are:

1.   *Reduced Complexity*

SAP HANA will let you reduce & simplify IT landscape with just ONE platform, combining both transactional & analytical applications. It will bring in 'live data analysis' through its in-memory computing supporting business in real-time, reducing data redundancy, duplication, time lag, multiple hardware etc. The SAP HANA's revolutionary *in-memory database* will deliver required performance to run analytics without slowing down transactions, as it combines memory optimization with unified data.

2. *Flexible Deployment*
    You can be as flexible as you want with SAP HANA deployment, and select the best option:

    - If you want maximum control, then, you should opt for 'on-premise' deployment. Select either (a) *'on-premise: appliance'* option of a pre-configured solution of hardware & software for quick 'go-live' or (b) *'on-premise: tailored data center integration'* option to leverage existing IT infrastructure & reduce cost.
    - To get the deployment faster, opt for 'cloud' deployment (public or private cloud). You may either (a) bring in your own license to run SAP HANA on the cloud platform of your choice via SAP HANA Infrastructure Services, or (b) go for a fully managed SAP HANA instances on the cloud (private or public).
    - A 'hybrid' option combining best of 'on-premise' and 'in-cloud' deployments.

3. *Better Business Outcomes*
    SAP HANA platform can help in creating significant value for your business, through real-time analytical insights. It can deliver applications and services by (a) simplifying operations using a single copy of enterprise data and a secured data platform, (b) processing transactions and analytics data using data virtualisation, integration or replication, and (c) leveraging advanced data processing engines.

Let us now discuss the details of various editions of SAP HANA

1.6   SAP HANA Editions

You will come across several editions (=options) with regard to the licensing and memory, while deploying SAP HANA.

In the case of 'on-premise', you have four editions:

- *SAP HANA Standard Edition*: a database for innovative use cases with the flexibility to go for advanced features as and when needed.
- *SAP HANA Express Edition*: free streamlined application package with up to 32GB of memory, with the provision for additional memory on payment of a licence fee
- *SAP HANA Runtime Edition*: a restricted platform designed exclusively to run SAP applications with limited use of advanced features
- *SAP HANA Enterprise Edition*: unrestricted platform for supporting innovation efforts and the use of SAP applications in modern hybrid environments

If you want to deploy your system 'in the cloud', then, you can try any of the following editions:

- *SAP HANA as a Service (Public Cloud):* this provides you with the on-demand access to the SAP HANA business platform with the latest capabilities for configuring an SAP HANA instance online and expanding the memory size seamlessly without interruption.
- *SAP HANA Enterprise Cloud (Private Cloud):* use this edition to deploy and manage an SAP HANA instance on an enterprise cloud managed by SAP, with the option to bring in your own on-premise licence or purchase subscription based licences.

With this, let us next understand the latest in SAP HANA namely SAP HANA 2.0.

1.7   SAP HANA 2.0

SAP released SAP HANA 2.0, in 2018. It was made up a mix of new and continuous innovations in the areas of data/database management, analytical and application fronts:

- The database enhancements bring in advanced data/privacy protection with additional algorithms, for better and configurable retention policies to enable improved audit functionalities. Some of the major enhancements include:
    o   An increased system availability for business-critical applications.
    o   A 'follow-the-sun' option with optimized latency for 'write' transactions. This can be achieved by rotating the primary system across the globe.
    o   A fast-restart functionality using TMPFS (temporary file storage) at the OS Level that will reduce the restart times to a greater extent.
    o   A new Native Storage Extension (NSE) that can enable denoting tables, columns or partitions as warm data.

> **i** The 'warm data' is loaded to an in-memory buffer cache as and when required for query processing.

- The data management enhancement includes high-availability *Hadoop* clusters and a general framework for *Smart Data Access*. The *Smart Data Integration* (SDI) now allows to group multiple agents, besides providing for real-time support for Mainframe DB2 and integration into *Web IDE*. SAP HANA 2.0 provides geocoding support for India addresses and FIAS compliant address assignments in Russia, to enhance data quality. For better data modeling, the *Enterprise Architecture Designer* (EAD) now supports SAP *Big Data Services, Hadoop Hive* 2.0 data lakes and HANA versioned tables. The *Calculation View* modeling (via Web IDE) now enables integrating data sources more easily than before.
- On the analytical front, the enhancements help increasing the execution performance and productivity for data analysis, by providing additional API's for *Python* and *R*. There is

also a new *Gradient Boosting Tree* (GBT) algorithm. The new linear referencing methods, hexagonal grid-based aggregation and the labelling tools together with the new APIs, will allow more insight from geocoding. With SAP HANA 2.0, you can do more complex analysis and build scenarios with more flexibility, improved debugging and so on.

- The application development enhancements, in SAP HANA 2.0, include new functions for *SQLScript, SQL, SQLScript Debugger* and *Code Anal*yzer enhancements, besides a vastly improved unit test framework. Now, the Web IDE with its improved editors, Python support, wizards etc, allows several workspaces and single import of synonyms. The *HANA Run Time Tools*, now, with its enhanced SQL console, enables more flexibility through session recovery, and performance improvements.

This completes our discussion on SAP HANA

1.8   Conclusion

You learned about the evolution of SAP, from SAP R/1 to the latest, the SAP HANA. You, then, went on to learn, in detail, about SAP HANA which is an in-memory, column-oriented, relational database management system with its primary function of storing / retrieving data, as requested by the applications and performing analytics as an application server. You, also, learned about SAP HANA's history and architecture, before moving on to learn about its benefits and editions ('on-premise' and 'in-cloud'). While learning about the 'on-premise' editions, you understood that there are four variants namely standard, express, runtime and enterprise editions. In addition, you understood that you could go in either for a public cloud (SAP HANA as a Service) or private cloud (SAP HANA Enterprise Cloud) in the case of 'in-cloud' editions. Finally, you learned about the latest in SAP HANA, the SAP HANA 2.0 and its innovations and improvements.

You will learn about SAP S/4HANA in the next chapter.

2 SAP S/4HANA

Launched in 2015, SAP S/4HANA is the short name for *'SAP Business Suite 4 SAP HANA'*, meaning that it is the fourth version of SAP Business Suite, designed to run only on SAP HANA. It is a simplified business suite, combining the functionalities of ERP, CRM, SRM and others into a single HANA system.

SAP S/4HANA is the nerve center (=the digital core) of your entire business, consolidating internal and external elements into a single, living structure that goes beyond traditional ERP. It connects all of your processes, provides you with live information and insights, and seamlessly integrates your enterprise with the digital world. Combining the core capabilities with the solutions in SAP portfolio for each line of business (LoB), SAP S/4HANA LoB solutions allow you to go beyond traditional transactions and drive digitized operations across all LoBs, based on a single source of information from planning, execution, prediction, simulation to analysis, all in real-time with one system. In short, it enables you to leverage today's digital world, by removing common obstacles associated with legacy ERP applications (like, batch latency, complex and/or multiple landscapes, and manual processes).

We shall discuss, in this chapter, the benefits you will reap by going in for SAP S/4HANA, the key capabilities, the various deployment options, the release strategy, the implementation options and its integration with SAP solutions.

Let us start with the major benefits of going in for SAP S/4HANA.

2.1 Major Benefits

The major benefits include:

- Improved user experience across the entire organisation, including a context-aware, business-savvy digital assistant.
- Automating, through intelligent functionality and learning capabilities, key functions and signalling users when input is required.
- Empowering users to make better and faster decisions by unlocking new business value with the latest innovations

Let us move on to understand the major capabilities of SAP S/4HANA.

2.2   Capabilities

The important capabilities of SAP S/4HANA, as depicted in Figure 2.1, include:

Figure 2.1: SAP S/4HANA Capabilities

- *SAP S/4HANA for Finance*: helps you to understand financial performance in real time, to optimise finance processes (from planning & analysis to period end close, and treasury management) and ensures one source of the truth for finance and operational. We will discuss more about this in Chapter 3.
- *SAP S/4HANA Human Resources*: brings in operational alignment between HR and finance to optimize capabilities and align with the business, enables consolidated access to real-time data to provide insights and measures the business impact of HR and integrates end-to-end processes across financials and HR.
- *SAP S/4HANA for Supply Chain*: helps you to control of your supply chain for increased visibility and agility across the digital supply chain by leveraging machine learning for logistics, manufacturing, and asset management.
- *SAP S/4HANA for Sourcing and Procurement*: using intelligent applications with machine learning, it enables improved supplier management, streamlined purchasing, besides helping in deploying collaborative sourcing and contract

management. Coupled with SAP Ariba and SAP Fieldglass solutions, it enables companies to manage spend across every major category while reducing direct costs.

- *SAP S/4HANA Manufacturing*: enables to integrate and embed intelligence in manufacturing processes with one single source of live information, by providing an optimal coordination of planning and execution processes, covering all aspects of the manufacturing cycle from planning to shop floor.
- *SAP S/4HANA for Sales*: provides you with a complete picture of operations and enables using customer insights to help marketing, sales, and service teams to work more productively besides accelerating opportunities to grow revenue.
- *SAP S/4HANA Marketing*: helps in consolidating customer information into one enriched view, and leverages advanced analytics to gain insights. The high performance discovery and targeting tools enables to generate microsegments and group.
- *SAP S/4HANA Asset Management*: enables to manage the entire asset lifecycle, with real-time visibility into asset performance using powerful analytics. It makes it easier to optimize asset usage, lower risks and manage capital expenditures better.
- *SAP S/4HANA for Research and Development*: enables effectively managing product lifecycles through a fully aligned product portfolio thereby controlling costs.
- *SAP S/4HANA Service*: enables seamless transition between communication channels, without losing context by leveraging on-premise systems of record to resolve customer issues or execute service orders.

In the next Section, let us discuss about the deployment options for SAP S/4HANA.

2.3   Deployment Options

As already discussed in Chapter 1, you can deploy SAP S/4HANA 'on-premise' or 'in-cloud' (public or private) option:

- *On-premise*
  You can use your own infrastructure or an infrastructure-as-a-service (IaaS) provider. You will be able to customise and extend SAP S/4HANA with complete control of your environment when deployed on-premise.
- *In-cloud*
  You can leverage the advantages offered by the public cloud to meet your industry-specific needs or you can opt for custom requirements in a dedicated, private cloud (*SAP HANA Enterprise Cloud*) environment.

By going in for SAP HANA Enterprise Cloud, which is a fully scalable and secure service, you can accelerate the path to cloud readiness and transform into an intelligent enterprise. This private cloud offering from SAP provides you with the production availability spanning across your entire application and infrastructure stack. It comes with a full menu of functional and technical services (including guaranteed service levels and availability of IT stack), with the control you will otherwise expect on deploying the solution on-premise.

Now, we can move on to discuss about release and maintenance strategy for SAP S/4HANA.

2.4   Release and Maintenance Strategy

The release and maintenance strategy includes (i) how and when SAP S/4HANA releases are planned, (ii) how long these releases will be in mainstream maintenance, and (iii) what will happen thereafter. This will allow customers using the on-premise edition to benefit from the short innovation cycles of typical cloud deployments, while at the same time providing for long-term stability and investment protection. The strategy follows the principle of 'one innovation codeline': series of releases coming over time combine to form a continued innovation delivery based on an evolving codeline.

SAP delivers innovation through new releases and feature packages: while the annual new releases (also known as *'key releases'*) contain larger innovations, the feature packages (through FPS or *Feature Pack Stack*) are intended to include additional smaller functional enhancements.

Since its first release in 2015, SAP has been offering improvements and innovations in SAP S/4HANA through periodic releases. Instead of the traditional way of numbering the releases (say, ERP 6.0), the releases of SAP S/4HANA are now versioned according to the year and month with a four-digit number (YYMM) with the first two digits indicating the year (like, 17,18 etc) and the last two indicating the month of release (say,11,10,09 etc). So, for SAP S/4HANA 1909, the 1909 stands for September 2019.

---

i   For SAP S/4HANA on premise edition, SAP is currently delivering one new key release per year (say, 1809) and some successive FPS. Then, comes the next key release (say, 1909), followed by several FPS. While the FPS includes non-disruptive and optional innovations in addition to corrections and legal changes, the *Support Pack Stacks* (SPS) are shipped for a given release, once the N+1 release is made available, until the end of the mainstream maintenance. The first SPS of a new release may contain selected features and is labelled as FPS (Figure 2.2). SPS are compiled periodically and made available in the SAP *Service Marketplace*.

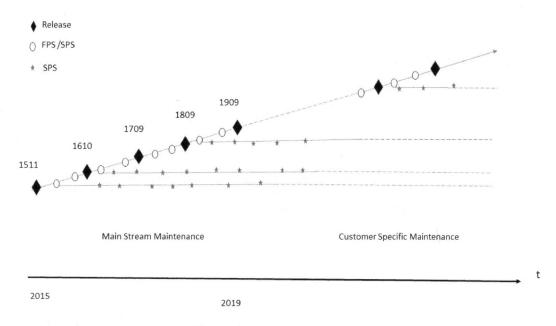

Figure 2.2: Releases, Future Pack Stacks (FPS) and Support Pack Stacks (SPS) in SAP

SAP currently intends to make available:

- One major delivery (release) a year
- Mainstream maintenance (of about five years) for each release
- Ongoing shipment of innovations (releases and feature packs)
- Support packages (SPS) during mainstream maintenance
- Customer-specific maintenance after mainstream maintenance

In SAP S/4HANA, there has been seven on-premise releases and 15 in-cloud release until now. As of September 2019, there were around 2300+ innovations related to SAP S/4HANA, 1000+ user experience innovations, and approximately 500+ innovations in digital transformation.

> **i** While SAP S/4HANA on-premise releases are once per year, SAP S/4HANA in-cloud releases are quarterly.

Let us now understand the release strategy for 2019/2020.

2.4.1   Release Strategy for 2019/2020

The Figure 2.3 displays the release strategy for SAP S/4HANA (on-premise) for year 2019 and beyond.

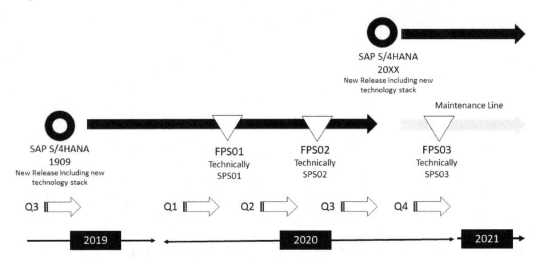

Figure 2.3: SAP S/4HANA Release Strategy for 2019 and beyond

With this, let us see the key innovations in Release 1909

2.4.2   Key Innovations in Release 1909 (SAP FI)

With SAP S/4HANA 1909 release, SAP's innovations are in the 5th wave. It has expanded the ERP core and re-architected the data model enabling customers to benefit from the latest innovations. The list of new capabilities / innovations in SAP S/4HANA 1909 has been extensive: in 2017, the number of SAP S/4HANA innovations was 966, in 2018 it was 2,389, and now, in 2019, it stands at a whopping 3,312. Parallelly, the user experience (UX) innovations have gone from 646 to 1,048, and to now 1,496.

Though the innovations in Release 1909 spans across several application areas like finance, manufacturing, sales & distribution, inventory management etc, we shall restrict our discussion only to finance (SAP /4HANA Finance):

- *The Financial Closing Processes*: Companies typically face a number of bottlenecks in the group close process which delay the time to close the books and report the financial results. SAP has brought in increased process efficiency both on entity and group level, for fast close. The *Group Reporting* in SAP S/4HANA, now, supports intercompany reconciliation and matrix consolidation.

- *Receivables Management*: In this area, the added value of specific cloud applications like *Cloud for Credit Integration, Cloud for Customer Payments* and *Cloud for Digital Payments* not only decrease the cost of the invoice to cash process through the support of self-service scenarios and new payment methods, but also have a risk limiting aspect, ensuring organizations get better forward looking insights.
- *Treasury Management*: SAP has brought in several enhancements in the area of SAP *Treasury and Risk Management*, for example, highlighting the evolution regarding trading platform integration – but also the evolution on the level of treasury reporting and planning.
- *Analytics*: In SAP FI, SAP now ships financial planning with *SAP Analytics Cloud (SAC)*. This helps finance professionals to analyze financial and non-financial information in a transparent way, based on the universal journal and the single source of truth.
- *Universal Allocation*: The new 'Universal Allocation' functionality, along with the universal journal, improves the operational setup and execution of allocations, as well as the transparency and traceability of costs across the organization.
- *Contract and Lease Management*: The new enhancements in the Contract and Lease Management will help users in simplifying lease processing and reporting with help of the integrated SAC.

We shall discuss more about these innovations is SAP S/4HANA Finance in Chapter 3. With this, let us have discuss the implementation options for SAP S/4HANA in the next Section.

2.5 Implementation

You can opt for a new installation of SAP S/4HANA or a system conversion (migration):

- Often referred to as the *'greenfield implementation'*, a new installation of SAP S/4HANA (on-premise or in-cloud) needs to run on the SAP HANA database. You can enhance this very simple landscape with the *SAP Cloud solutions* and *SAP Business Suite* products. to suit your specific business needs.
- You can also integrate SAP S/4HANA into an existing *SAP Business Suite* (ECC) landscape by replacing the SAP ERP with SAP S/4HANA. When performing this *conversion* in your system landscape, you need to do some adaptations; for example, you need to convert some of your existing business processes to the simplified SAP S/4HANA processes. You also need to be aware that some of the existing processes are no longer supported in SAP S/4HANA, some have changed, and there are new processes. Accordingly, you need to convert your existing processes to the SAP S/4HANA processes.

> ℹ️ To move from SAP ECC to SAP S/4HANA, earlier, you had to follow an extended path to migrate. However, with system conversion option, now, it is possible to move directly from ECC 6.0 to SAP S/4HANA (say, 1909) on HANA 2 database, without going through the intermediary steps, irrespective of whether you plan to be in-cloud or on-premise (Figure 2.4)

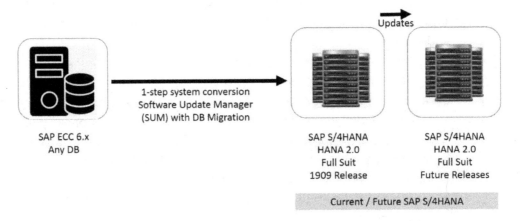

Figure 2.4: System Conversion to SAP S/4HANA

Let us discuss, next, the integration aspects of SAP S/4HANA with the other SAP solutions.

2.6   Integration with SAP Solutions

By integrating various SAP solutions with SAP S/4HANA, you can leverage those SAP solutions for making your business enterprise an efficient one. Let us see some of the solutions that you can integrate with SAP S/4HANA:

- *SAP SuccessFactors Employee Central*
  SAP S/4HANA will be the backend system on premise, when you use *SAP SuccessFactors Employee Central* as your system of records for HR master data. Here, SAP offers a 'full cloud' deployment and integration with predefined integration content. Supporting initial and delta data loads, the integration is web-service based and can be a scheduled middleware job.

- *SAP Fieldglass*
  SAP S/4HANA supports end-to-end business process integration for contingent labour and invoice-to-pay. This integration enables electronic transfer of master data (like, cost objects and organizational data) from SAP S/4HANA to *SAP Fieldglass* automatically.

- *SAP Ariba Network*
  You can leverage the purchase order and invoice automation scenario that offers business process integration between SAP S/4HANA (deployed on-premise), and the *SAP Ariba Network* cloud-based solution.

- *SAP Hybris Cloud for Customer*
  The integration of SAP Hybris Cloud with SAP S/4HANA enables you to transfer all master and transactional data, required for the opportunity-to-order processes. You can extract data like accounts, contacts, materials, prices etc. from SAP S/4HANA and transfer the same to SAP Hybris Cloud for Customer so that it is available for opportunity-to-order processes.

- *SAP Financial Services Network*
  You can connect your SAP S/4HANA system to *the SAP Financial Services Network* via *SAP HANA Cloud Integration* (HCI), enabling integrating A/P and A/R data for payment processes. The data such as payment collections is extracted from the SAP S/4HANA Financials system and transferred via the SAP Financials Service Network, which then connects you to your relationship banks so that the data is available for financial transaction interaction processes.

This completes our discussion on SAP S/4HANA.

2.7   Conclusion

You have, in this chapter, learned that SAP S/4HANA is the digital core of the modern business enterprise, which consolidates internal and external elements into a single structure connecting all the processes, and providing you with live information and insights. You learned about the major benefits and its capabilities. You also learned about the deployment options (on-premise or in-cloud) of SAP S/4HANA with the associated advantages in each case, the release and maintenance strategy for SAP S/4HANA, the innovations that are brought into the release 1909, and the implementation considerations as to whether to go in for a greenfield project or system conversion. You also found out how you can integrate SAP S/4HANA with some of the key SAP solutions like SAP SuccessFactors Employee Central, SAP Ariba Network, SAP Hybris, SAP Fieldglass etc.

Let us now mow on to learn about SAP S/4HANA Finance in the next chapter.

3 SAP S/4HANA Finance

The finance & accounting processes and the erstwhile technical platforms, on which an ERP solution was running in the last couple of decades, were not agile enough and were simply not aimed at today's digital world. They were marked by disconnected silos of data processing and reporting that called for manual intervention at every step. The legacy technologies and the different ERP products limited the seamless integration across finance and other enterprise resource modules resulting in integration issues, outdated reports, data entry repetition, closing delays etc that prevented the businesses from taking timely actions.

SAP launched *SAP S/4HANA Finance* (formerly '*SAP Simple Finance*'), in 2015, to reimagine finance for the digital world. This ERP application is a simplified business suite, combining the functionalities of ERP, CRM, SRM and others into a single HANA system, replacing the earlier SAP system. Running on the in-memory platform of SAP HANA, this solution supports financial planning, general accounting, management accounting, accounts payable, accounts receivable, treasury & cash management, risk management, financial close and much more.

In this chapter, you will learn about the overview, capabilities and benefits for SAP S/4HANA Finance. Let us start, first, with the overview of SAP S/4HANA Finance.

3.1 Overview

SAP S/4HANA Finance is a set of comprehensive financial solutions designed to help your business to meet the demands of today's digital economy. It is a part of the finance solution portfolio from SAP, that is built on a modern digital core of in-memory SAP HANA platform. It is the platform for the modern digital enterprise with advanced digital data architecture. This platform enables future innovations, a single source of the truth for both transactions and analytics, and a digital 'core' that integrates workforce, network, customer, and application extensions like as SAP Ariba, Concur, SAP SuccessFactors, and SAP Fieldglass solutions.

SAP S/4HANA Finance solution (a) covers all areas of finance enabling your finance professionals to transform the business / processes to compete in digital economy, (b) helps to remove bottlenecks in integration, and (c) enables an innovation-driven enterprise–wide simpler and more efficient IT operations. It delivers instant insights with real-time analysis across all dimensions of financial data, empowering you with contextual, live information for faster and better decision making.

SAP S/4HANA Finance comes equipped with a simple and intuitive user experience, offering one common, real-time view of financial and operational data for enterprise-wide consistency and reduces reconciliation time and errors. It also comes with the built-in ability to use prediction, simulation, and analysis to evaluate financial implications while optimizing business processes. It can deliver end-to-end business benefits across the five solution areas (=capabilities) within finance (see Section 3.2 for more details) besides improving the overall operations supporting business transformation.

SAP S/4HANA Finance is available for on-premise, in-cloud and hybrid deployments for both new implementation and existing business (conversion). With massive simplification and optimization within SAP S/4HANA, you can deploy SAP S/4HANA Finance with minimal business disruption and eliminate overly complex processes. You can achieve additional value by deploying solutions and templates within the *SAP Activate* methodology, standardizing master data using the *SAP Master Data Governance* application and focusing on the reduction or elimination of legacy custom code.

With this overview of SAP S/4HANA Finance, let us move on to understand its capabilities.

3.2   Capabilities

The primary capabilities of SAP S/4HANA Finance are depicted in Figure 3.1.

Figure 3.1: Primary Capabilities of SAP S/4HANA Finance

Let us understand them in detail:

3.2.1 Accounting and Financial Close

With the traditional ERP finance, you will encounter several pain points like (i) delayed closing activities that do not begin until period-end, (ii) several manual reconciliations / eliminations, required due to the prevalence of multiple ledgers / subledgers, preventing error-free depiction of intra-period business performance, (iii) delays in batch processing and post-closing activities leading delays in the completion of downstream dependent activities, (iv) separate closing and consolidation activities as the ERP and consolidation systems are often distributed, (v) inability to perform real-time inventory valuation as the valuation data resides in multiple aggregated tables, (vi) manual intervention during currency conversion due to limitation in number of local currencies and (vii) delayed reporting and lack of flexibility to respond to regulatory changes.

SAP S/4HANA Finance alleviates the above pain points as it (i) provides a foundation for soft-close with significant reduction in the need for period-end batch processing with the availability of single-source of data, extension ledger and the ability to derive profitability characteristics in real-time, (ii) comes with a single *universal journal* for data entry of G/L, controlling, asset accounting, material management etc, and revenue recognition process within the universal journal, enabling continuous and real-time reconciliation, (iii) enables more efficient consolidation process through the universal journal with its embedded real-time consolidation, (iv) removes redundancies and aggregates, with all inventory valuation data existing in material ledger, enabling faster actual costing (due to optimized code of SAP HANA), (v) provides for expanded currency support with real-time currency conversion, for all currency types, together with the freely definable currency functionality, (vi) enables live reporting with its predefined reports and configurable reporting tools leveraging G/L, subledgers etc, and (vii) streamlines reporting through a statutory reporting framework.

3.2.2 Finance Operations

Traditionally, the business processes (clearing, bad debt identification, credit risk management, invoice processing, vendor management etc) in various FI components like accounts receivable (A/R), accounts payable (A/P) etc, are often manual, disjointed across multiple solutions, reactive and consume significant time and effort. Also, there are difficulties in (i) setting up a single interconnected process to address some of these pain points, (ii) integrating 3rd party data for an end-to-end back-office processing in shared services, (iii) managing expense related processes that are often handled off-line across different systems making it nearly impossible to forecast, monitor or control expenses in real-time, and (v) managing the real-estate business processes that are disparate across multiple solutions, forcing the enterprises to spend unnecessary lease payments and the associated difficulties in adhering to IFRS 16 standards.

SAP S/4HANA Finance helps in addressing the bottlenecks in finance operations by (i) integrating with external data providers and other data sources to simplify and improve operations besides providing an intuitive user experience (UX) through *SAP Fiori*, (ii) streamlining payment processes through the *SAP Biller Direct*, (iii) integrating multiple A/P systems for a consolidated view of multiple invoices, suppliers, and vendors, (iv) a centralized liquidity planning leveraging SAP *Central Finance* function, (v) integrating with *SAP Ariba* for invoice and discount management, integration of payment capability with supply chain finance for supporting end-to-end fulfilment, (vi) providing *Shared Services Framework* that improves operational excellence by standardizing best practices across various business departments, including procurement (*SAP Ariba* solutions), HR (*SAP SuccessFactors*), and travel expenses (*Concur*), (vii) bringing together expense information (from multiple systems) for making more informed and real-time decisions through *SAP Real Spend* solution, (Viii) increased compliance reporting for managing real estate with *SAP Real Estate Management*, and (ix) using *SAP Lease Administration* for simplified equipment lease accounting.

3.2.3 *Planning and Predictive Analysis*

Prior to SAP S/4HANA Finance, there have been (i) separate and disconnected tools and processes for planning, manual and static budget allocations, (ii) alternate hierarchies and planning master data maintained outside of ERP, (iii) difficulties to model / simulate business innovation, costs, and structural changes to assess financial impacts, and (iv) difficulties in drill-down of financial metrics as data were stored in multiple / disparate systems.

In SAP S/4HANA Finance, you will notice that (i) the planning processes and functions are integrated into transactional system, allowing for closed-loop planning and execution, (ii) there is a single consolidated view of all planning and forecasting information with simplified user experience through *SAP Business Objects Planning and Consolidation* application that enables planning at any level, (iii) the real-time 'what-if' analysis and simulations help to model & test the impact of changes to profitability before committing to plans, with managerial views derived from income statement, obviating manual reconciliation, (iv) the central finance deployment enables faster integration during restructuring, merger and acquisitions, and (v) the real-time access to financial data (with the ability to drill down to line-item levels), merger of FI and CO for a single source of truth (with *universal journal*).

3.2.4 *Treasury and Financial Risk Management*

The ERP on a traditional database is characterised by its (i) limited capabilities to integrate data from multiple treasury systems and external bank interfaces, (ii) manual and offline cash forecasting processes that often resulted in inaccurate and/or delayed planning and forecasting with limited or no analytical capability, (iii) difficulty to centrally manage exposure and mitigate risk with forecasting and controlling foreign exchange (FX), commodity price fluctuation, and contractual information requiring separate add-on solutions, and (iv) basic & manual bank account management capabilities.

SAP S/4HANA Finance comes with integrated liquidity management, including cash flow analysis and embedded liquidity planning. The *SAP Cash Management* enables complete lifecycle management of liquidity. It uses prediction, simulation, and analysis functionality to support an informed and automated forecasting process. Its 'one exposure' functionality enables central storage of all actual / forecast operational transactions. It also comes with additional enhancements in FX risk management and supports hedge accounting as per IFRS 9. It enables simplified yet automated bank reconciliations & workflows, and improved integration with *SAP Bank Communication Management* and *SAP In-House Cash* applications.

3.2.5 Financial Governance and Compliance

Traditionally, the data samples needed to be manually extracted, from multiple systems and analysed to detect a potential fraud. The fragmented compliance processes, across the organization, resulted in lack of transparency and accountability. There has been no link between 'governance, risk and compliance' (GRC) activities and business strategy. The basic audit management capabilities have been through separate offline solutions that are difficult to scale with business expansion. It has been difficult for managing compliance across international trades, as the basic functionalities are from separate offline solutions.

SAP S/4HANA Finance with its cloud / LoB extension enhancements like *SAP Fraud Management* analytic application enables full lifecycle of fraud management from detection, investigation, quantification, and remediation with the ability to monitor performance and optimize the investigation process. The streamlined automated controls, aligning risk to business value drivers, regulations, and policies through the use of the *SAP Process Control* and *SAP Risk Management* applications, in combination with the *SAP Audit Management*, helps in building an effective 3-tier defence framework.

Let us, next, look at the benefits that will accrue to businesses, from SAP S/4HANA Finance.

3.3 Benefits

The major benefits of SAP S/4HANA Finance include:

1. *Single Source of Truth*: with massive process and technology simplification, and with a system that removes data replications, reconciliations, and redundancies, you are always with a 'single source of truth' that enables faster and real-time financial decisions, to keep up with the competition and technology.
2. *Flexible Business Processes*: you can redesign and optimise processes to focus on exceptions and critical tasks, and easily change processes as your business evolves.

3. Best Practices: you can leverage and benefit from cross-company self-learning data, with various roles access to embedded statistics, reporting, and benchmarking.

In quantifying terms, SAP S/4HANA Finance may help in, among others, 5–10% reduction in bank fees, 5–10% reduction in business, operations analysis and reporting costs outside of finance, 5–10% reduction in days sales outstanding, 5–25% reduction in A/R write-offs, 10–40% improvement in invoice processing productivity, 15–20% reduction in single, high-value fraud categories (such as travel expense fraud), 20–40% reduction in audit cost, 20–40% reduction in G/L and financial closing costs, 20–40% reduction in treasury and cash management cost etc.

This completes our discussion on SAP S/4HANA Finance.

3.4   Conclusion

You understood SAP S/4HANA Finance in detail in this chapter.

First, you learned about the overview of SAP S/4HANA Finance as to how it is different from the erstwhile and traditional ERP applications with its digital SAP HANA core, its new and improved set of comprehensive financial solutions designed to help business to meet the demands of today's digital economy, and its improved but intuitive user interface and experience.

Second, you learned about the major capabilities of SAP S/4HANA Finance in accounting and financial close, financial operations, planning and predictive analysis, treasury & risk management, and financial governance & compliance. You understood how this new solution helps to overcome the age-old pains like delayed period-ends and closing, inability to perform real-time inventory valuation, manual reconciliations, issues in integrating multiple A/P systems, difficulties to model and simulate business innovation, costs, and structural changes in the organization to assess the financial impacts etc.

Third, you learned about the major benefits that will accrue to businesses from SAP S/4HANA Finance solution, with its single source of truth, flexible business processes and a plethora of best practices that you can lean on to leverage. You further learned that you will be able save substantially as this solution will help in reducing the bank fees, A/R write-offs, audit cost, cash management cost, days required to close the books etc.

With this background of SAP HANA and SAP S/4HANA Finance, let us move on to our discussion on configuring the SAP S/4HANA Finance system for a typical business.

Before discussing the Asset Accounting, in detail, let us look at the case study in the next Chapter, that will be the basis of discussion for the reminder of the book.

4 Case Study

BEST Machinery, also known as BESTM group, is the corporate group having companies operating out of both United States of America (USA) and India, among other countries. The case study is, however, limited to the operations in USA and India. BESTM group has three companies namely, BESTM Agro, BESTM Construction and BESTM Drives. All the three companies are operating out of USA from the same address as that of the corporate group at Glen Ridge, New Jersey:

- ✓ BESTM Agro is the flagship company and is made up of four company codes – two in USA and two in India. This company, through its various legal entities, is in the business of manufacturing, supplying and servicing tractors for agricultural and other uses, agricultural implements, lawn & garden mowers, and equipments required by the forestry industry.
- ✓ BESTM Construction manufactures and services all kinds of trucks and heavy machinery used in the construction industry like dump trucks, track & crawler loaders, excavators, dozers etc. It has two company codes both of which are operating out of USA.
- ✓ BESTM Drives is in the business of making and servicing industrial diesel engines including diesel generators, and drivetrain related equipments like transmissions, axles, gear drives etc. This company is comprising of two USA-based company codes.

BESTM group had been using a variety of software applications, built and bought over a period of years, to meet all their business requirements. Because of a plethora of applications, which were often different between USA and India, the corporate was finding it difficult to integrate the information that hampered their decision making. Calling for a lot of manual interventions and time-consuming reconciliations, they were finding it hard to close their books in time. Also, there were lot of redundancies and duplicity as the applications were not fully integrated. Hence, the corporate group was thinking of to go in for an ERP that would overcome all these shortcomings, and they wanted to bring in the latest in ERP so that they would have an enterprise solution that would not only be state-of-the-art, but also insulate them from becoming obsolete in the near future. Accordingly, the management had taken decision to implement the SAP S/4HANA suite of applications, and it was decided to deploy the application on-premise.

BESTM decided to partner with a leading IT firm to manage the implementation and the transition to SAP S/4HANA. The implementation was code named as 'Project Dolphin'. The project team had several discussions and workshops with the BESTM management at various levels, and what you see in the following pages is the outcome of those discussions / workshops.

The project team will define three *companies* in SAP, as shown in Table 4.1:

Company	Company ID	Country	Currency
BESTM Agro	B1000	USA	USD
BESTM Construction	B2000	USA	USD
BESTM Drives	B3000	USA	USD

Table 4:1 BESTM - Companies

BESTM Agro company has the following legal entities (company codes) operating out of USA:
1. BESTM Farm Machinery
2. BESTM Garden & Forestry Equipments

BESTM Agro also operates in India through the following company codes:
1. BESTM Farm Machinery
2. BESTM Garden & Forestry Equipments

BESTM Construction company is made up of the following legal units functioning out of USA:
1. BESTM Trucks
2. BESTM Other Construction Equipments

BESTM Drives manages the following legal units:
1. BESTM Drives
2. BESTM Engines

All the *company codes*, except the ones in India, will have USD as their company code currency; the ones in India will have INR as the company code currency. All the company codes will use English as the official language (Table 4.2).

Company Code	Company Code ID	Country	Currency
BESTM Farm Machinery	1110	USA	USD
BESTM Garden & Forestry Equipments	1120	USA	USD
BESTM Farm Machinery	1210	India	INR
BESTM Garden & Forestry Equipments	1220	India	INR
BESTM Trucks	2100	USA	USD
BESTM Other Construction Equipments	2200	USA	USD
BESTM Drives	3100	USA	USD
BESTM Engines	3200	USA	USD

Table 4:2 BESTM - Company Codes, Country and Currency

There will be a total of four *credit control areas*: one each for the companies B2000 (BESTM Construction) and B3000 (BESTM Drives), and two credit control areas for company B1000 (BESTM Agro). These credit control areas will be denoted by a 4-character numeric identifier. The details of credit control area, currency etc will be as shown in Table 4.3

Company	Company Code	Credit Control Area (CCA)	CCA Currency	Default Credit Limit
B1000	1110	1100	USD	10,000
	1120			
	1210	1200	INR	700,000
	1220			
B2000	2100	2000	USD	20,000
	2200			
B3000	3100	3000	USD	30,000
	3200			

Table 4:3 BESTM – Credit Control Areas

Since it has been decided to default some of the credit control data while creating the customer master records in each of the company codes, a default credit limit has been mentioned per credit control area as denoted in the table above. BESTM wants the users not to be allowed to change the default credit control area during document posting.

BESTM group requires several *business areas* cutting across company codes (Table 4.4) to report and monitor the operations of different operational areas like agri. tractor business, agri. equipments, after-sales services, garden equipments etc.

Business Area	Business Area Identifier
Agri Tractor Business	ATRA
Agri Equipments	AEQP
After-sales Service	ASER
Garden Equipments	GEQP
Forestry Equipments	FEQP
Construction Machinery	CONM
Drives & Engines	DREN
Military Sales	MILI

Table 4:4 BESTM – Business Areas

BESTM group plans to create their own *functional areas* with easy-to-remember IDs. The project team shall copy the SAP supplied functional areas into the new ones, like BM20 (Production), BM25 (Consulting/Services), BM30 (Sales & Distribution) and so on. BESTM wants the project team to configure the system to derive the functional areas automatically.

BESTM requires the following four FM (Financial Management) areas:

- BF11: FM area for USA-based company codes of BESTM Agro
- BF12: FM area for India-based company codes of BESTM Agro
- BF21: FM area for USA-based company codes of BESTM
- BF31: FM area for USA-based company codes of BESTM Drives

BESTM requires the following business segments to be defined for segment reporting. BESTM wants to have a 10-character alpha-numeric ID segments, with the first three indicating the company code (say, B11/B12/B13 for company B1000, B21/B22 for company 2000 and so on), and the last seven characters, a meaningful abbreviation of the segment description.

- B11FMTRACT   Farm Tractors
- B12HARCOMB   Harvester Combines
- B12FMIMPLE   Farm Implements
- B12FORESTY   Forestry Equipments
- B13LANTRAC   Lawn Tractors
- B13LANMOWR   Lawn Mowers
- B13GRDNUTL   Garden Utility Vehicles
- B13GOLFSPR   Golf and Sports Equipments
- B21LODRDOZ   Loaders and Dozers
- B22EXCAVAT   Excavators and other Construction Equipments
- B31DRVTRAN   Drivetrain Components
- B32GENERAT   Generators
- B33INDSENGN Industrial Diesel Engines
- B33MARENGN   Marine Engines

BESTM group has decided to have three controlling areas, BESTM Agro (B1000), BESTM Construction (B2000) and BESTM Drives (B3000) with USD as CO area currency. They will need to be denoted as B100, B200 and B300 respectively.

BESTM group has indicated that they need profit centers, defined in such a way, to represent the actual internal management. Accordingly, it has been decided to have the following profit centers / profit center groups under each of the controlling areas (Table 4.5):

Controlling Area	Profit Center Group	Profit Center
B100	Tractors	Farm Tractors
		Lawn Tractors
		Speciality Tractors
	Farm Equipments	Cultivators & Planters
		Harvesters
		Seeding / Fertilizing Equipments
		Sprayers & Liquid Systems

	Garden Equipments	Lawn Movers
		Garden Utility Vehicles
	Others	Misc. Farm / Garden Equipments
		Forest Machinery
		Others (B100)
B200	Light Machinery	Compact Machines
		Building Equipments
	Heavy Machinery	Heavy Equipments
		Road Machinery
		Mining Equipments
	Others	Miscellaneous Construction Machinery
		Others (B200)
B300	Drives	Gear Drives
		Pump Drives
		Transmissions
	Engines	Industrial Engines
		Commercial Marine Engines
		Pleasure Marine Engines
	Generators	Stationary Generators
		Portable Generators
	Others	Military Solutions
		Others (B300)

Table 4:5 BESTM – Profit Centers / Profit Center Groups

Looking at the SAP-supplied transaction types in the system, the Dolphin Project team has decided not to add any new transaction type for consolidation for BESTM. They have also decided not to add any new coding fields in the system. This has been finalised after a thorough study of the SAP defined standard coding fields.

The project team has decided to use a single field status variant (FSV), B100, in all the company codes of BESTM. They have further recommended that (a) 'Business Area' and 'Functional Area' fields to be set as 'required' for data entry, and (b) 'Payment Reference' field as 'optional entry' field.

The team has recommended to use different ledgers to meet the different statutory requirements of the company codes: (1) BESTM group of companies will use the SAP supplied standard ledger 0L as their leading ledger and that will meet the International Accounting Standards (IAS), (2) US-based company codes will use a non-leading ledger (BU) to meet the local accounting requirements (US GAAP) and (3) India-based company codes will use another leading ledger (BI) to meet India's legal reporting (Ind-AS). BESTM management is of the opinion that the project team combines the leading ledger (0L) and the non-leading ledger (BU) into a ledger group called B1 as the accounting principles of IAS (0L) and US GAAP (BU) are the same as there will almost be identical postings to both of these accounting principles.

BESTM wants to leverage the 'extension edger' functionality of SAP S/4HANA. Accordingly, the project team has proposed to define four extension ledgers: one for general purpose, the other for simulation, the third for prediction & commitment and the fourth for valuation purposes accounting for valuation differences. In all the cases, BESTM wants manual postings.

BESTM does not want to create new fiscal year variants (FYVs), but shall use the SAP supplied ones. Accordingly, FYV K4 will be used for all the US-based company codes and V3 will be used by India-based company codes. To simplify opening and closing of posting periods in the system without much complications, it has been decided to define separate posting period variant (PPV) per company code.

There will be two new charts of accounts defined in the system, BEUS for US-based company codes and BEIN for India-based company codes. The respective Financial Statement Version (FSV) will also be created in the same name as that of the chart of accounts. For all the US-based company codes, both the operative and country chart of accounts will be the same: BEUS. In the case of India-based company codes, the operative chart of accounts will be BEUS and the country chart of accounts will be BEIN. A suitable document entry screen variant that facilitates country-specific processing of withholding tax needs to be used in all the US-based company codes.

If there is a difference in currency translation due to exchange rate fluctuations during transaction posting, then, a maximum of 10% has to be allowed as the permitted deviation. However, this will not be applicable to the tax postings as all the tax items have to be translated using the exchange rate from the document header. All the US-based company codes will use a single variant as the workflow variant. It has been decided to allow negative postings, thereby avoiding inflated trial balance.

BESTM does not want the system to propose fiscal year during document change or document display functions as it expects all the company codes to work with year-independent document numbers. However, the current date can be defaulted to as the value date for entering the line items in a document.

BESTM does not want to define any new posting keys in the system. However, BESTM has requested to configure the posting keys in such a way that (a) 'Invoice Reference' to be made mandatory for all payment transactions, (b) 'Payment Reference' is optional for document reversals and (c) a valid reason to be mandatory for all payment difference postings.

The BESTM management has recommended to make use of the standard settings in SAP for tax calculation and posting, for both India and USA. As regards USA, the team has planned to take care of the jurisdiction requirement of taxation, by interfacing with the external tax system, 'Vertex'. The project team will properly structure the tax jurisdiction code identification in the SAP system to make it fully compatible with Vertex. The project team, accordingly, indicated that the tax on sales and purchases, for all the US-based company codes, is to be calculated at the line item level.

The BESTM management has requested the project team to complete the required configurations settings for extended withholding tax (EWT) in the system. They have requested the project team to make use of the standard (a) withholding tax keys, (b) reasons for exemptions and (c) recipient types in the system for EWT.

The project team has been instructed by the BESTM management to configure only one retained earnings account for each of the company codes. Accordingly, the G/L account 33000000 has been designated as the retained earnings account (in the chart of accounts area) of the operative chart of accounts BEUS.

BESTM wants to make use of document splitting functionality for all the company codes, both in US and India. The configuration will make use of SAP's default and standard document splitting method 0000000012; no new method will be defined. Also, no new item categories, document types, business transactions, and business transaction types will be defined as the project feels that the standard offerings from SAP will be enough to meet all the document splitting requirements of BESTM company codes. The 'Business Area', 'Profit Center' and the 'Segment' will be used as the document splitting characteristics, with a zero-balance setting.

The BESTM Corporate wants to take care of cross-company code transactions as the company code 1110 will be the central purchasing organization for all the company codes in US. Besides, the company code 1120 will make sales of their products through company code 1110 which will act as the merchandiser. A similar scenario was envisaged for India-based company codes, as well, with regards to the central purchasing by the company code 1210.

The project team suggested using a single set of accounts, to take care of automatic posting of the exchange rate differences realized in clearing open items: for loss it will be 72010000, and for the gains it will be 72510000. For valuation adjustments, the loss will be posted to 72040000 and the gains to 72540000; B/S adjustments will go to the G/L account 11001099.

BESTM management has requested to configure the country-specific settings for USA and India, for asset accounting: The low value asset (LVA) cut-off limit should be $5,000 for USA and INR 5,000 for India. Also, it should be configured that the system capitalizes the assets under construction (AuC) without considering the down payments. Besides, it should be ensured that the system posts the gain / loss posting when an asset is retired.

BESTM wants to have two charts of depreciations, one for US and the other for India. As with chart of accounts, these new charts of depreciation will also be named as BEUS and BEIN respectively, for US and India.

The project management team has recommended to create easily identifiable new account determination keys to map to the various types of fixed assets for BESTM group of companies. It has been advised to create two account determinations for LVAs: one for collective management and another for individual management. They have also recommended to create new screen layout rules to customize the field status to suit BESTM requirements.

BESTM management has decided to define as many number ranges as that of asset account determination keys, so as to easily identify an asset just by a number. And, all the asset main numbers will be internal but the asset subnumbers will be external, to help in modeling and grouping the assets. BESTM does not want to have cross-company code number assignment for asset master records. Instead, it requires each company code to supply the number range intervals, for numbering their asset master records.

The project team has recommended to BESTM management to have as many asset classes as that of the asset determination keys. However, instead of creating a separate asset class for goodwill, an asset class in the name of 'intangible assets' will have to be created to cover all intangible assets including the goodwill, patent, copyright etc. For AuC, it should be configured for line item settlement. Except the LVA, all other asset classes should be configured to have the subnumber assigned externally. It has also been indicated that there is no need for creating exclusive asset classes for group assets; instead, any of the defined asset classes can be used to create a group asset as well.

The project team has recommended to make use of the control specifications for screen layout and account determination, at the asset class level rather than making the specifications at the chart of depreciation level. It has also been decided to use the SAP's default document type AF for all the depreciation related postings in all the company codes.

BESTM requested the project management team to configure the FSV to ensure that indicator 'Asset retirement' and the field 'Asset number / Subnumber' are set with a field status as 'required entry'. Similar settings need to be carried out for the asset posting keys as well.

BESTM, as it needs asset reporting at the 'Segment' / 'Profit Center' level, has requested to activate segment reporting in FI-AA. The project team has pointed out this activation would also help to carry out the consistency check when users make single / mass asset maintenance of 'Segment' and/or 'Profit Center' details while creating / changing asset master records. This is because, if this activation is not done, then the system will not do the consistency check, for these two fields, when maintaining the asset master.

BESTM management wants to make use of additional account assignment objects like 'Internal Order', 'Investment Order', 'Functional Area', 'Maintenance Order' etc during posting in asset accounting. It was also indicated that if an account assignment object is relevant to B/S, then, no user should be able to change the account assignment object in the asset master record, once the asset has been capitalized. Also, the account assignment object like 'Funds Center', 'Funds Center for Investment', 'Investment Order', 'Functional Area' etc should be prevented from being changed during a posting.

The BESTM management, after a detailed discussion with the implementation team, has decided not to create any new depreciation areas other than the ones that were copied from the country-specific chart of depreciation. It was also decided that all the company codes will use the book depreciation area (01) for updating the quantity information of LVAs. To meet some of the tax requirements in USA, BESTM has requested to specify the appropriate depreciation areas for managing the group assets as well. As in practice, the interest calculated on the capital tied up on fixed assets, needs to be managed in the cost accounting depreciation area, 20 in the case of BESTM.

BESTM has indicated that, when posting values are transferred from the book depreciation area (01) to other areas, all the APC-relevant values should be transferred in a manner that the user will have no option to make any change, later, during posting so as to minimise errors in the transferred values. BESTM has also requested the project team to configure adoption of depreciation terms from one depreciation area to another in such a way that the adopted depreciation terms cannot be changed, manually, later in the asset master.

BESTM management decided to have a uniform economic life policy for the asset classes across company codes, both in US and India. Accordingly, for example, the useful life of vehicles has been set at 10 years, computer hardware at 5 years, computer software at 2 years, furniture & fittings at 5 years, office equipments at 5 years and so on.

BESTM wants to round off, using arithmetic rounding method, the year-end net book value, and also the automatically calculated replacement value of assets. BESTM has indicated that they want to depreciate, all the fixed assets, until the book values become zero. Accordingly, the project team has decided not to use the 'memo value' functionality in the system.

BESTM company codes will use the same FYV that has been defined in SAP FI (G/L) in FI-AA as well. However, the project team has been asked to configure use of half months to take care of mid-month acquisition / depreciation of assets for all the US-based company codes.

Managing depreciation areas in the currency of corporate group, for legal consolidation, is a requirement for all the India-based company codes of BESTM as the local valuation will be in INR but the group consolidation in USD. Accordingly, suitable depreciation areas need to be defined for the chart of depreciation BEIN, which will be used by the India-based company codes1210 and 1220.

BESTM wants to the project team to define a multi-level depreciation method, with three levels for special depreciation. The three levels will correspond to three periods: first 5 years, next 3 years and the last 2 years. The depreciation percentage for these corresponding phases will need to set at 10%, 7% and 3% respectively.

BESTM requested the project management team not to define default values for the company codes and depreciation areas. Also, BESTM does not want to impose the condition that the acquisitions are allowed only in the year in which depreciation started.

BESTM has decided to have a cutoff value key defined for depreciating vehicles with 10 year validity. The scrap value percentage will vary at 5% for the first 5 years, 3% for the next 3 years and 2% for the last 2 years. The scrap value needs to be deducted from the base value and the start of calculation will be from the asset capitalization date.

BESTM has decided to make use of the standard depreciation keys that are pre-defined in the system. However, while handling multiple shift operations, it needs to be configured that the result is increased depreciation / expired useful life. Also, there need not be any stopping of depreciation during asset shutdown. As in line with the standard settings, BESTM wants to calculate the ordinary depreciation before the special depreciation.

In the case of special reserves, BESTM has asked the project team to configure the system, to use the net procedure, so that it posts the allocation amounts and write-off amounts, for the same asset, offsetting against each other instead of the gross method.

The project team has suggested to the BESTM management to use SAP supplied standard transaction types for handling unplanned depreciation, transfer of reserves, asset acquisition, asset revaluations etc.

BESTM, while configuring the depreciation area for revaluation of fixed assets, wants only the APC to be revalued but not the accumulated depreciation that had been debited to the asset in the earlier years. The revaluation of fixed assets for balance sheet purposes, will happen on 31st December, every five years, starting with 31-Dec-2020. The revaluation IDs will be numbered serially and revaluation will be handled in the cost accounting depreciation area.

BESTM, to make physical inventory easier, requires that all the assets be identified with valid 'Inventory number' in their respective asset master records. Accordingly, this field is to be made mandatory for input. Also, to keep track of asset history, they want the 'History indicator' field to be enabled, but not mandatory. Besides, they also insisted that 'Cost center', 'Business area' and 'Maintenance order' fields be made as 'optional' entry fields.

During this discussion, the project team suggested to synchronize all the equipments with SAP Plant Maintenance application.

As regards the screen layout control of depreciation areas is concerned, BESTM has decided to make use of the standard versions supplied by SAP, without changing any of the field status thereon.

For making the selection screen specifications for some of the web transactions including 'My Assets', the project team has indicated that it will use most of the common fields, such as 'Asset', 'Asset Sub Number', 'Asset Class', 'Account Determination', 'Acquisition Year', 'Capitalized On', 'Evaluation Group 1/2/3', 'Asset Super Number', 'Vendor', 'Manufacturer', 'Description', 'Lease Start Date' etc, as the selection fields for the 'Cost Accountant' role. Similar definitions will be created for 'Cost Center Manager' and 'Employee Self-Service'.

While defining the account assignment category of asset purchase orders, BESTM has indicated to make the settings in such a way to have the 'Business Area' and 'Cost Center' as 'optional' entry fields (from their original status of 'suppressed') to have the details captured, wherever possible. In the case of integrated asset accounting, BESTM does not want to use different technical clearing accounts, but wants the system to use the one defined at the chart of accounts level. BESTM wants the project team to configure the system to prevent subsequent adjustments made to APC of an asset arising out of incorrect discount charged in 'net' invoice posting, relating to assets, in FI-A/P and the resulting capitalization. As BESTM uses P&L accounts to post the gain/loss arising out of asset retirements, the project team has been asked not to configure the transaction types to collect gain/loss on an asset itself. Also, BESTM does not want to configure this for asset classes as well.

BESTM does not, in general, need a cross-system depreciation areas to handle intercompany asset transactions, when asset transfer happens among the company codes situated either within US or within India, as all the US-based company codes use the same chart of depreciation BEUS and all the company codes in India use the same chart of depreciation BEIN. In each case, the chart of depreciation is the same and the depreciation areas have the same numbering and meaning. However, BESTM requires the cross-system depreciation area(s), to facilitate intercompany asset transfers between a company in US and another in India, as these company codes use two different charts of accounts (BEUS for US-based company codes and BEIN for India-based company codes). In this case, the depreciation areas, though have the same keys (for some of the areas), their meaning is different across the systems.

For AuC capitalization, the project team will copy the standard profile and create a new one so that settlement is made optional to some of the CO receivers like 'Cost Center', 'Order' etc. This is required to take care of settling debits to these receivers when debits were capitalized to AuC, by mistake. Also, BESTM wants to have the flexibility of settling by 'percentage', 'equivalence numbers' and 'amount'. Besides, it was suggested to have a validation to ensure that the settlement does not exceed 100% in a percentage settlement; above, or below, the system should issue a warning accordingly. Also, BESTM, in AuCs, does not want to ignore the down payments during line item settlement. Instead, they want capitalization of down payments from previous year, and the closing invoice from the current year, together.

BESTM wants to use the standard sort versions without defining anything new, for FI-AA Information System. However, they want to create a new simulation version, to simulate the depreciation in all asset classes, for book depreciation, to understand what happens when the depreciation key is LINS and the useful life is increased by 10% across asset classes. BESTM wants to use the default key figure groups, without going in for any new key figure group definition, for the Fiori apps 'Asset Balances' and 'Asset Transactions'. Also, BESTM will not be renaming any of the value fields meant for the 'asset explorer'. They are good with the short text supplied by SAP.

BESTM will not be requiring any new currency translation methods as they will use the standard ones supplied by SAP as default. BESTM will not be creating any new authorizations; rather, they will be using the standard ones supplied by SAP.

5 Asset Accounting: Overview

Asset Accounting (FI-AA), in SAP, is a subsidiary ledger to SAP G/L Accounting that you can use to manage fixed assets of your business entity. It provides information on various transactions, from acquisition to retirement, of fixed assets. You can use this component to manage different types of assets including 'Assets under Construction' (AuC) and intangible assets. As no country-specific valuation rules are hard-coded in the system, you can use FI-AA internationally, in any country and in any industry. However, you can make this component country-specific and company-specific with the appropriate settings that you make in Customizing.

FI-AA allows you to manage asset values in parallel currencies using different types of valuations, simplifying consolidation preparations for multi-national groups. Using parallel valuation, you can flexibly assign the depreciation areas of FI-AA to the ledgers of SAP G/L Accounting and enable the system posting the parallel values with the actual values in real time; it posts separate documents for each valuation (that is, each accounting principle). With the basic functions covering the entire life cycle of an asset, from the initial purchase / acquisition to retirement, you can use FI-AA to automatically calculate depreciation and interest between two points in time. You can also use the forecasting and simulation functionalities to carry out 'what if' analysis.

FI-AA is tightly integrated with the several applications / functionalities within SAP including material management (SAP MM), plant maintenance (SAP PM), production planning (SAP PP), project systems (SAP PS), investment management (SAP IM) etc that enables direct transfer of data to and from other applications. With these integrations, for example, when an asset is purchased or produced in-house, you can directly post the invoice receipt (IR) or goods receipt (GR), or the withdrawal from the warehouse, to assets in the FI-AA component. Also, it is possible that you can pass on depreciation and interest directly to SAP FI. Though you carry out the technical management of assets, in the form of functional locations / equipment in SAP PM, you can settle the maintenance activities requiring capitalization, to FI-AA.

Besides providing for managing the assets and their values, FI-AA also offers you with the functionality to structure these assets to reflect the organizational structure of your enterprise. This ensures that an asset is clearly and always assigned to an organizational unit at any given point in time.

5.1 New Asset Accounting in S/4HANA

The FI-AA in SAP S/4HANA is also known as 'new Asset Accounting. Actually, it is not really 'new' in the sense that it has been available for a while since SAP ECC EHP6. However, with SAP S/4HANA, it is mandatory to activate that for SAP S/4HANA Finance – whether it is a new implementation or a migration.

Though the core functionalities of 'new Asset Accounting' are the same as that of the 'classic Asset Accounting', there have been several changes and improvements: for example, you will no longer be able to post the asset master data and values together, and post the summary transactions later to SAP FI; instead, similar to A/P and A/R, you can create the master data first and post the value to the asset and also simultaneously to the G/L. This is because, most of the asset tables have since been replaced with the introduction of new Asset Accounting; both asset and financial actuals are now stored in a single table, ACDOCA. The other notable change in new Asset Accounting is that all accounting principles post in real-time without the need for posting them periodically.

As the asset and G/L values are now in the same table (ACDOCA), you do not need to worry about the consistency of data and the reconciliation transactions that were required earlier. Since all ledgers post in real-time, the periodic posting transaction has become redundant. Besides, since the asset postings are now transferred to SAP FI at the asset level and with the availability of more information per asset, it is, now, possible to run asset reports, by asset number, from the SAP G/L. Also, you do not need to wait for the period to close, to see values in the parallel ledgers. Even, the planned depreciation is always up to date.

With the new functionalities in *Depreciation Calculation Program* (DCP), the system, now, updates the planned depreciation every time you post an asset transaction. As a result, the asset explorer and asset reports, now, show you the values that are up-to-date. Because of this, the month-end depreciation runs are faster as the system just need to post the already calculated (planned) values. The system still posts collective documents for depreciation, instead of one document per asset; the DCP posts a separate line item in SAP G/L per asset, facilitating more detail than earlier. Refer Chapter 10.5.2, for more details on DCP.

As regards the Transactions (=Transaction Codes) in new Asset Accounting, the new ones now contain an L suffixed to the erstwhile Transactions to signify that you can post to different ledger groups: for example, the old Transaction ABAA is now ABAAL, Transaction ABUM is now ABUML and so on. However, if you still try any of the old Transactions in S/4HANA, you will automatically be redirected to the new Transaction.

As regards to the tables in new Asset Accounting, even though you will not see the existence most of the old tables (ANEK, ANEP, ANLC, ANLP etc), the programs will still work. This is because, along with the improvements in new Asset Accounting, SAP has introduced the 'compatibility views' which are created from the new tables such as ACDOCA, but linked to the old tables such as ANEP, ANEK etc enabling reading of data from the old tables.

> **i** We shall also refer the new Asset Accounting simply as Asset Accounting (FI-AA) throughout this book.

We shall be discussing the following aspects of FI-AA, in the subsequent Chapters:

- Organizational Structures
- Structuring Fixed Assets in FI-AA
- Integration
- General Valuation
- Depreciation
- Special Valuations

- Master Data
- Transactions
- Information System
- Asset Data Transfer
- Preparations for Going Live
- Overview for Experts

5.2 Conclusion

You learned that you can use SAP Asset Accounting (FI-AA) to manage your business entity's fixed assets internationally, in any country and in any industry. You also learned that FI-AA allows you to manage asset values in parallel currencies using different types of valuations, simplifying consolidation preparations for multi-national groups.

You understood that FI-AA is tightly integrated with the several applications within SAP including material management (SAP MM), plant maintenance (SAP PM), production planning (SAP PP) etc. Though the core functionalities of new Asset Accounting are the same as that of the classic Asset Accounting, you learned that there have been several changes and improvements in the new Asset Accounting.

We shall discuss about asset accounting organizational structures in the next Chapter.

6 Organizational Structures

To represent your organizational structure that is relevant to FI-AA, and to classify your assets according to asset accounting criteria, you have to define the FI-AA organizational objects like chart of depreciation, FI company code, asset class etc. Then, you need to assign all the assets, of the business enterprise, to these organizational objects thus defined:

- FI-AA uses the same company codes as that of SAP G/L Accounting; but, you need to define these company codes further, in FI-AA, with the specifications needed for asset accounting. Unless you do this, you will not be able to use an FI company code in asset accounting.
- If you have, earlier, specified in SAP G/L Accounting configuration that you need business area balance sheets, then, you need to assign the assets (in master data maintenance), to the business areas for adopting the business area automatically from the cost center. With such an assignment, the system makes appropriate account assignments postings – including depreciation and gain / loss postings on asset retirement – to the respective business area.
- If you use segment reporting, you need to enter the profit center and/or segments directly in the asset master record. This unique 'asset-segment assignment' helps in creating asset reports relating to profit centers and segments.
- You can assign a fixed asset to a 'Plant', for a set time frame. And, you can change the assignment to a different plant by changing the asset master record. Though a plant has no asset accounting relevance, you can use that as a sort and selection criterion for the asset reports.
- As in the case of plant, you can also assign a fixed asset to a 'Location' for a set time. Since an 'Address' is attached to a location, you can indirectly assign an asset to an address as well; so, all assets with the same location must have the same address.
- For internal accounting, you need to assign assets to cost centers; you assign (in the asset master) each asset to exactly one cost center. With this, you can post all depreciation and interest for the asset, plan all future depreciation and interest, and statistically post gain or loss from asset sales.

Let us look at the various configuration activities that you need to complete to define the asset accounting organizational structures:

- Check Country-Specific Settings
- Copy Reference Chart of Depreciation/Depreciation Areas
- Assign Chart of Depreciation to Company Code
- Specify Number Assignment Across Company Codes

To start with, let us understand the country-specific settings that are required to fulfil the statutory requirements of a country.

6.1   Check Country-Specific Settings

SAP comes delivered with most of the country-specific settings for FI-AA to meet the legal requirements of a country in which your company code operates. All the country-specific system defaults are company code dependent. As a one-time exercise, the system will assign the settings you make here, to the company code, as soon as you initially assign a chart of depreciation to the company code.

> **i** Note that the default country-specific settings may not be complete in all respects. And, you may need to additionally configure a few settings that does not come as default; for example, the cut-off value for *Low Value Assets* (LVA).

Use the menu path: SAP Customizing Implementation Guide > Financial Accounting > Asset Accounting > Organizational Structures > Check Country-Specific Settings, to check the default country-specific settings, and to add additional settings, if any. You may also use Transaction OA08.

Project Dolphin

BESTM management has requested to configure the country-specific settings for USA and India as indicated below:

The low value asset (LVA) cut-off limit should be $5,000 for USA and INR 5,000 for India. Also, it should be configured that the system capitalizes the assets under construction (AuC) without considering the down payments. Besides, it should be ensured that the system posts the gain / loss posting when an asset is retired.

On the resulting screen, you will see the list of countries for which SAP has provided with the default settings. If the 'Country vers. available' check-box has been selected for any country, then, it indicates that a separate country version is available. Double-click on the selected country row, and check the default settings on the next screen. If required, you can make additional settings (Figure 6.1):

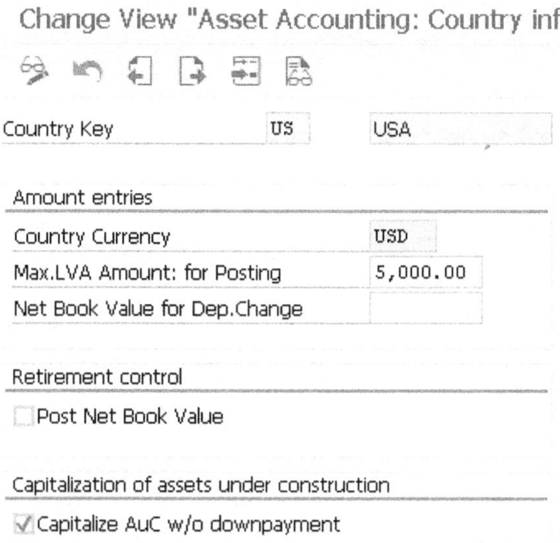

Change View "Asset Accounting: Country information": Details

Country Key   US   USA

Amount entries

Country Currency	USD
Max.LVA Amount: for Posting	5,000.00
Net Book Value for Dep.Change	

Retirement control

☐ Post Net Book Value

Capitalization of assets under construction

☑ Capitalize AuC w/o downpayment

Figure 6.1: Country-Specific Settings for FI-AA: USA

    i.   Under 'Amount entries', you will see that the system has pre-filled the currency for US.

- Enter the amount limit, in the 'Max. LVA Amount: for Posting' field, up to which an asset will be considered as a low value asset (LVA).

> **i** In the case of collectively managed LVAs, the amount is the acquisition amount divided by the quantity of assets.

- If you enter an amount in the 'Net Book Value for Dep. Change' field, then, the system changes over the calculation of depreciation to the changeover key defined in the depreciation key, as soon as the net book value (NBV) is less than this amount. Use an appropriate depreciation key, with an internal calculation key defined with *changeover method* 3 ('Changeover as soon as the net book value is less than the changeover amount'), for this changeover to happen; else, if you use any other changeover methods, the system ignores the amount entered here. This is valid only for depreciation area 01 (master/ book depreciation).

    ii.   Select the 'Post Net Book Value' check-box under 'Retirement control', if you want the system to post the Net Book Value (NBV) at the time of retirement of an asset; the system posts the NBV to the account for clearing of revenue from asset sales or for clearing of revenue from asset sales to affiliated companies. By default, the check-box is not selected as the system posts a gain/loss, for an asset retirement (by sale or scrapping).

> **i** Posting of NBV during asset retirement is not allowed in most of the countries, including USA. Hence, you should not select this, in general. However, you need to select this flag for a country like France, where it is mandatory to post the NBV upon an asset's retirement.

iii. When you select the 'Capitalize AuC w/o down payment' check-box, the system ignores down payments during the line item settlement of AuC, and transfers the total amount of the closing invoice to the capitalized asset using the appropriate transaction type based on the year of the closing invoice.

> **i** When the 'Capitalize AuC w/o down payment' check-box is not selected, and if you capitalize a down payment from a previous year along with the closing invoice from the current year, then, the system transfers the amount of the down payment from the previous year, using a transaction type for old assets data. Then, it transfers the difference between the total amount (of the closing invoice) and the down payment, using a transaction type for new acquisitions.

With this, we are now ready to complete the next configuration activity of creating a new chart of depreciation by copying from a reference chart of depreciation.

6.2   Copy Reference Chart of Depreciation/Depreciation Areas

Using this activity, you will define a new chart of depreciation that you will later assign to each of the company codes in FI-AA. However, before we start this activity to define a chart of depreciation, let us first understand what a chart of depreciation is.

The 'chart of depreciation' is a list of 'depreciation areas' arranged according to business and legal requirements, and it enables you to manage all rules for the depreciation and valuation of assets in a particular country (or economic region). With the chart of depreciation, you can calculate values for assets for different needs, both internal and external: say, book depreciation and cost-accounting depreciation. It is possible that you can flexibly define the keys for the automatic depreciation of assets per chart of depreciation. These keys are based on different elements for calculation of depreciation like calculation methods, period controls etc that are used client-wide. The chart of depreciation also supports special calculations of asset values like investment support through special keys.

i You can manage values for assets, in parallel, in up to 99 depreciation areas in FI-AA.

When you create a new chart of depreciation, by copying from a reference chart, then the system copies all depreciation areas into the new chart. You can, then, delete the depreciation areas that you may not need from the newly defined chart. Alternatively, you can keep all the depreciation areas but activate them later whenever you want. Besides the depreciation areas, the system also copies some of the depreciation area-specific restrictions for the transaction types that were necessary in classic Asset Accounting. As you will not be posting with the restricted transaction types in the new Asset Accounting, you may delete these redundant restrictions for the transaction types defined in table TABWA.

i SAP comes delivered with sample (or reference) charts of depreciation, with predefined depreciation areas, to meet the statutory requirements of countries like USA, UK, Spain, Germany, Austria etc. These reference charts are named as 0US, 0DE, 0GB etc. You can use these charts, as reference, to create your own. Remember, you cannot use the reference chart of depreciation as such, without creating a new one.

Once defined, you will assign a chart of depreciation to each of the company codes to make them available for FI-AA. Let us now look at creating a new chart of depreciation by copying a reference chart in the system:

Project Dolphin

BESTM wants to have two charts of depreciations, one for US and the other for India. As in the case of chart of accounts, these new charts of depreciation will also be named as BEUS and BEIN respectively for US and India charts of depreciation.

Use the menu path: SAP Customizing Implementation Guide > Financial Accounting > Asset Accounting > Organizational Structures > Copy Reference Chart of Depreciation/Depreciation Areas.

i. On the resulting pop-up screen, double-click on the first activity 'Copy Reference Chart of Depreciation'. You may also use Transaction EC08.

ii. On the 'Organizational object: Chart of depreciation' screen, click on 'Copy org.object'. On the resulting pop-up screen, enter 'From Chart of dep' (say, 0US) and 'To Chart of dep' (say, BEUS) and click on 'Continue'. Press 'Continue' on the 'Transport number ranges and addresses' pop-up screen and press 'Yes' for 'Do you really want to transport number ranges?'. The system copies the reference chart of depreciation 0US to the new one, BEUS (Figure 6.2). Do a similar copy for creating a chart of depreciation for India (BEIN) by copying the reference chart, 0IN.

Organizational object Chart of depreciation

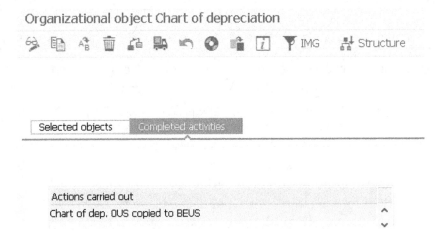

Figure 6.2: Creating New Chart of Depreciation (BEUS)

iii.   The next task is to provide the description for the newly created charts of depreciation. On the initial 'Select Activity' pop-up screen, double-click on the 'Specify Description of Chart of Depreciation' activity, and on the next screen, enter the 'Description' for BEUS and BEIN charts of depreciation (Figure 6.3).

Change View "Chart of depreciation: Specify name": Overview

ChDep	Description	🗑
BEIN	Chart of Depreciation USA (BESTM)	
BEUS	Chart of Depreciation India (BESTM)	

Figure 6.3: Providing Description for Newly Created Chart of Depreciation

iv.   The next activity is to copy / delete the depreciation areas, in the newly created chart of depreciation. From the initial 'Select Activity' pop-up screen, double-click on the 'Copy/Delete Depreciation Areas' activity. On the resulting pop-up, enter the chart of depreciation (BEUS) and proceed. On the next screen, the system brings up all the depreciation areas that have been copied from the reference chart (Figure 6.4). You can directly reach the 'Change View "Define Depreciation Areas": Overview' if you use Transaction OADB. You can rename depreciation areas, copy to create new ones and delete the unwanted areas.

Figure 6.4: List of Depreciation Areas for Chart of Depreciation BEUS

v. You may double click on a particular depreciation area (say, 1) and see / change the depreciation area details on the next screen (Figure 6.5):

a) You can change and/or provide a meaningful long and short text for the depreciation area.

b) Under 'Define Depreciation Areas' data block:

- Select 'Real Depreciation Area' check-box to indicate that this is not a derived depreciation area. When selected, the system updates the values in this area, in the database, each time a posting is made enabling immediate evaluation.

- Select the 'Accounting Principle' and the system automatically brings up the associated 'Target Ledger Group'.

- In 'Alternate Depreciation Area', you may enter the depreciation area from which the system uses the account determination when posting to parallel accounting. If you use ledger approach, specify the depreciation area that posts APC in real time (to the ledger group containing the leading ledger). If you use accounts approach, you should usually leave the field blank.

- Leave the 'Cross-Syst. Dep. Area' field as blank for the time being. We shall define this later (in Chapter 13.4.1.1).

c) For 'Posting in the General Ledger' select the appropriate radio-button: you have four options like 'Are Does not Post', 'Area Posts in Real Time', 'Area Posts Depreciation Only' and 'Area Posts APC Immediately, Depreciation Periodically'. We have selected 'Area Posts in Real Time' for the depreciation area 1 as this is for book depreciation.

d) Under 'Value Maintenance', you need to select the appropriate value for each of the parameters as shown in Figure 6.5. Per parameter, you can select one among the four options: 1 – only positive values or zero allowed, 2 – only negative values or zero allowed, 3 – all values allowed and 4 – no value allowed.

e) You will have to make the appropriate settings under 'Entries for Derived Depreciation Area' if you are configuring a depreciation area that is a derived one.

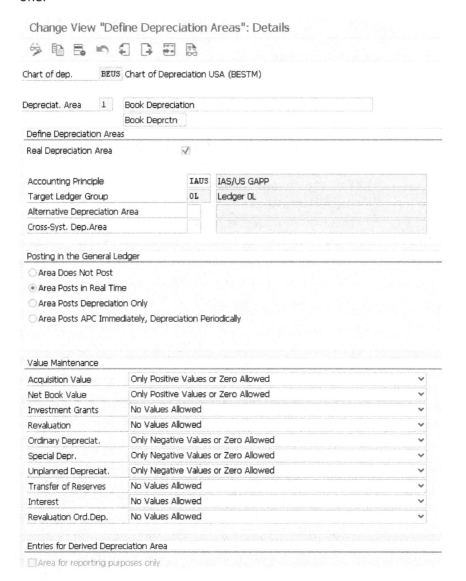

Figure 6.5: Depreciation Area 01 – Details

f) 'Save' the details, and continue with the settings for other depreciation areas.

With this, we are now ready to assign the chart of depreciation to company codes, in the next step.

6.3   Assign Chart of Depreciation to Company Code

By assigning a chart of depreciation to a company code that you have already defined in your FI enterprise structure, you make that company code available for FI-AA.

As in the case of 'chart of accounts and company code relationship', you can have more than one company code using a single chart of depreciation but, you cannot have one company code using more than one chart of depreciation. The essential condition for more than one company code to use a single chart of depreciation is that they should all be (a) operating in the same country / economic zone, or (b) belonging to the same industry even if they are in different countries, or (c) operating with the same set of valuation rules / requirements even if they are in different countries. Normally, you will use the different charts of depreciation if the company codes are in different countries.

The assignment of a company code to a chart of accounts is independent from its assignment to a chart of depreciation. That is, several company codes can use the same chart of accounts, although they have different charts of depreciation (and vice versa).

Use the menu path: SAP Customizing Implementation Guide > Financial Accounting > Asset Accounting > Organizational Structures > Assign Chart of Depreciation to Company Code. You may also use Transaction OAOB.

On the resulting screen, enter the chart of depreciation against each of the company codes: for BESTM, we have assigned the chart of depreciation BEUS for all the US-based company codes (Figure 6.6) and BEIN for all the India-based company codes.

Change View "Maintain company code in Asset Accounting": Overview

CoCd	Company Name	Chrt dep	Description
1110	BESTM Farm Machinery	BEUS	Chart of Depreciation USA (BESTM)
1120	BESTM Garden & Forestry E	BEUS	Chart of Depreciation USA (BESTM)

Figure 6.6: Assignment of Chart of Depreciation to Company Codes

The next task is to specify the company code, for each of the FI-AA company codes, from which the system will use number interval for numbering the asset master records.

6.4   Specify Number Assignment Across Company Codes

For every company code in FI-AA, you can determine from which (other) company code the system should use the number range intervals, for numbering the asset master records. It is possible that you can assign the main asset number across company codes (cross-company code assignment), if required.

 Generally, the numbering of asset master records is carried out per company code.

Project Dolphin

BESTM does not want to have cross-company code number assignment for asset master records. Instead, it requires each company code to supply the number range intervals for numbering their asset master records.

Use the menu path: SAP Customizing Implementation Guide > Financial Accounting > Asset Accounting > Organizational Structures > Specify Number Assignment Across Company Codes. You may also use Transaction AO11.

On the resulting screen (Figure 6.7), you will see that, by default, the system has entered the same company code as the number range supplying company code ('No.CoCd') for each of the FI-AA company codes. You can keep that as such when you do not want cross-company code number assignment. Else, enter the number range supplying company code (say, 9000) against other company codes (say, 9100 and 9200) to make a cross-company code assignment of main asset number: in this case, the system will make use of number ranges from company code 9000 to number the main assets belonging to the company code 9100 and 9200.

Change View "FI-AA: "Assignmt. to company code providing number range"

CoCd	Company Name	No.CoCd
1110	BESTM Farm Machinery	1110
1120	BESTM Garden & Forestry E	1120

Figure 6.7: Number Range Assignment for Company Codes

Though configuring asset classes comes under 'Organization Structures', we will not be discussing that now. To understand asset classes, we first need to look at how to structure fixed assets in FI-AA that we shall discuss in the next Section. Once we understand the fixed assets structuring, we shall discuss about configuring the asset classes.

6.5 Conclusion

You learned that you have to define the FI-AA organizational objects like chart of depreciation, FI company code, asset class etc, to represent your organizational structure that is relevant to FI-AA, and to classify your assets according to asset accounting criteria. You also learned that you need to assign all the assets, of the business enterprise, to these organizational objects thus defined, to establish the relationship.

You understood that though SAP comes delivered with most of the country-specific settings for FI-AA, still you need to check and maintain a couple of settings like the cut-off value for low value assets, which the system will assign to the company code (s), as soon as you initially assign a chart of depreciation to the company code(s).

You learned that the 'chart of depreciation' is a list of 'depreciation areas' arranged according to business and legal requirements, to manage the rules for depreciation and valuation of assets in a particular country. With the chart of depreciation, you learned that you can calculate values for assets for different needs, both internal and external. You also learned that the chart of depreciation supports special calculations of asset values like investment support. You understood that you can use an SAP supplied chart of depreciation as a 'reference' to create your own chart of depreciation.

You learned that you can determine from which (other) company code the system should use the number range intervals, for numbering the asset master records, as it is possible that you can assign the main asset number across company codes (cross-company code assignment), if required.

With this, let us move on to discuss how to structure fixed assets in FI-AA, in the next Chapter.

7 Structuring Fixed Assets in FI-AA

The term 'assets' represents different types of assets, and in a balance sheet (B/S) you normally represent them as (a) *tangible assets*, (b) *intangible assets* and (c) *financial assets*. Every asset type, in SAP, is represented by one or more *asset classes* (we shall define *asset classes*, in detail, later in Section 7.4), with each asset class serving as a kind of sample master record for the assets in that asset class. The asset classes contain certain control indictors. In general, all the asset classes, of an asset type, will use the same account determination and the same screen layout.

With this, let us look at the special forms of assets.

7.1 Special Forms of Assets

Let us understand, in this Section, some of the special forms of assets that are supported by SAP in FI-AA:

- *Assets under Construction (AuC)*: The AuC is a special form of tangible asset that you usually display as a separate B/S item and therefore it needs a separate account determination in the asset class. You can manage AuC as (a) any other asset using an individual master record or (b) collectively (comprising of several assets) on one master record. In most of the countries, ordinary depreciation is not allowed for AuC. You can achieve this by selecting a depreciation key that does not allow ordinary depreciation in the book depreciation area. However, for some AuC, it is possible to perform special tax depreciation: for this, you need to enter the corresponding keys in the asset class, to be used as mandatory default values.

- *Low Value Assets (LVA)*: As against regular fixed assets, you depreciate the LVAs completely in the year of their acquisition. You do not, normally, carry out individual assessment of their values as they individually have little value. Hence, you often manage them, collectively, in a single asset master record. For 'collective management' of LVAs, you need to activate the same by entering a UoM in the asset master record. You need to set the maximum amount for LVAs when defining the depreciation area at company code level while doing the Customizing. You will also specify if you want to manage the LVAs either through 'individual check' (*individual management*) or 'quantity check' (*collective management*) for the verification of the maximum amount for LVAs. In the case of 'individual check', when posting the acquisition, the system compares the entire APC (acquisition and production costs) of the asset with the LVA maximum amount specified earlier. However, in the case of 'collective check', when the system posts the acquisition, the system checks the entire APC of the asset, divided by the total quantity, against the LVA maximum amount.

- *Leased Assets*: The 'leased assets' create special accounting requirements for the lessee. During the term of the lease, the leased assets remain as the property of lessor (or manufacturer). They represent, therefore, a special form of rented asset. Such assets, legally and from a tax perspective, are the responsibility of the lessor, and are not relevant for assessing the value of the asset portfolio of the lessee. However, in certain countries, you are required to capitalize leased assets, depending on the type of financing involved. Depending on the legal terms and the conditions of the lease, the leased assets can be capitalized and depreciated ('capital lease') or they can flow into the P&L as periodic rental expenses ('operating lease'). In FI-AA, besides entering all the essential leasing contract information in the asset master record, you can assign a leasing type (that you have defined in Customizing) in the asset master. The leasing type contains all the information for the acquisition posting.

- *Intangible Assets*: Similar to the tangible assets, you can manage the intangible assets (such as, goodwill, brand recognition, copyrights, patents, trademarks etc) also in the system. SAP does not provide any special system functions for handling the needs of intangible assets. As with other assets, you must assign the account control of the asset class for the intangible assets to the corresponding B/S item. If you want to post down payments, for intangible assets, then, you must specify (in Customizing) in the asset class that posting is allowed with the transaction type group 'down payments'. As you will not normally retire the intangible assets, you cannot post any retirement posting. However, you can specify (in the asset class for intangible assets) that a retirement is simulated when the book value reaches zero. In this way, you can ensure that the intangible assets appear in the retirement column of the *'asset history sheet'* (we shall discuss asset history sheet, in detail, in Chapter 14.7).

- *Technical Assets*: You can manage technical data of an asset only to a limited extent in the asset master record, in FI-AA. However, you can enter a virtually unlimited amount of technical description using the 'long text' function. In addition, it is possible to link any number of original documents (blueprints, bills of material etc) to the asset master record, using the document management system (DMS). If you need to create separate master records for technical assets, you, then, need to deactivate the book depreciation area for these fixed assets so as to prevent any posting. You can, also, enter detailed technical information for the maintenance of equipment in the Plant Maintenance (SAP PM) component: enter this information in the functional location in the equipment master record.

- *Real Estate*: You will not be using FI-AA component for rental contract management of residential buildings, or detailed land register management for real estate. Instead, for these types of activities, you need to use the Flexible Real Estate Management (RE-FX) component of SAP.

With this, we are ready to understand how you can structure the fixed assets in FI-AA.

7.2   Structuring Fixed Assets in FI-AA

You can structure fixed assets, in FI-AA, at three different levels as shown in Figure 7.1:

- Balance sheet structure level
- Classification structure level
- Asset-related structure level

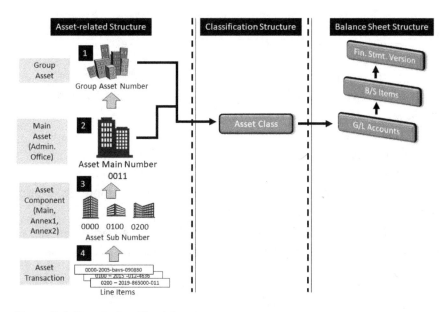

Figure 7.1: Structuring Fixed Assets

At the 'balance sheet structure level', you can structure your fixed assets according to balance sheet criteria. Therefore, you can arrive at a 3-level hierarchy for your assets as shown under:

1) G/L ledger account (level 1)
2) Balance sheet item (level 2)
3) Financial statement version (level 3)

At the 'classification structure level', you can structure fixed assets using 'asset classes' in FI-AA. With the asset classes, you can structure assets according to a country's legal requirements or as per the demands of accounting. With every asset belonging to an asset class, you will use the 'account determination' (in the asset class) to assign an asset to an item in the B/S.

At the 'asset-related structure level', you can set up a maximum of 4-level hierarchy in FI-AA. However, it is not mandatory to have 4-levels. If required, and feasible, you can just have your assets represented by the asset main number, and in this case the asset will be known as a *'simple asset'*. In case you plan to use the 4-level hierarchy then you will structure the assets as detailed below:

- The *'group asset'*, at the top in a 4-level hierarchy, enables grouping a number of assets together for the purpose of uniform evaluation and depreciation. Like any other asset, you will assign a group asset also to an asset class. The concept of group asset is mostly used in USA to meet some tax requirements.

> **i** Note that the asset class of a group asset need not be the same as that of the asset classes of the underlying assets that form the group asset.

- The *'asset main number'*, at the 3rd level, just below the group asset, represents an asset that you will like to evaluate independently, as a single unit. When you do not have group assets in the hierarchy, then, you will assign the asset main number directly to an asset class.
- Below the asset main number, at the 2nd level, you can subdivide your main asset into several component parts, each represented by an *'asset subnumber'*. With this structuring, you can use the subnumbers to depreciate subsequent acquisitions to main asset separately from the original asset.
- At the lowest level, you have the 'line items' that represent the transaction data (such as, acquisitions or retirements), per depreciation area, belonging to the asset master record.

With this, let us move on to discuss how to represent fixed assets in FI-AA.

7.3   Representing Fixed Assets in FI-AA

You normally use the term 'asset' to represent both simple assets as well as complex assets. A *'complex asset'* normally consists of a number of component assets. In a complex asset, you will use a main asset number to represent the asset as a whole (say, CNC lathe1), and use asset subnumbers to represent the various parts / components (say, headstock, CNC lathe bed, chuck, tailstock, tailstock quill, tool turret, control panel etc) of an asset.

In SAP, the system allows a 12-character alpha-numeric number for the main asset and a 4-character numbering for the asset subnumbers. When you create an asset master record, the system automatically creates at least one subnumber, even if there is no sub-asset. The system marks the first master record as the 'asset main number'. When you use internal subnumber assignment, this main number always has an asset subnumber = 0000. You can create any number of additional subnumbers for an asset main number. The system manages the values at the subnumber level, for every individual depreciation area, in the year segments. The system posts the individual transactions directly to the subnumbers, as line items.

- *Simple Asset*: A 'simple asset' is represented by only one asset master record. This master record has the subnumber as 0000. You will post the subsequent acquisitions to this master record. You can meet the most essential business and legal demands with year segments and transaction data. For a simple asset, you cannot separate the accumulated depreciation and book values from closed fiscal years according to their acquisition year. Also, you cannot depreciate the subsequent acquisitions individually.
- *Complex Asset*: A 'complex asset' consists of several sub-assets or component assets. You will denote the whole asset using an asset main number and represent each of the sub-assets using an asset subnumber. This is because, you may want to monitor the sub-assets individually from some accounting point of view: while it may be necessary for uniform depreciation of the entire asset in the book depreciation and tax depreciation areas, you may need to depreciate the sub-assets separately for, say, cost-accounting perspective.

> **i** Use external numbering, as for as possible, for asset subnumbers for meaningful modelling of the specific structure of the asset.

You may want to manage the various asset components of a large asset, in the system, as subnumbers because, (a) the development values of component assets may be different for each of the sub-asset numbers, (b) you may need a different cost accounting assignment for some of the sub-assets, (c) you may want to divide the asset based on certain technical aspects (for example, to link with SAP Plant Maintenance), and/or (d) you may want to represent investment support as negative for the sub-assets.

- *Group Asset*: As already outlined in Section 7.2, a 'group asset' (for example, administrative building) is made up of several assets (for example, administrative office1, administrative offcie2 etc) grouped only for some special purposes in evaluation and reporting. You will represent a group asset using a separate master record.

> **i** Specify, while configuring the IMG node 'Specify Asset Classes for Group Assets' (Transaction OAAX), if a particular asset class is meant strictly for group assets: select the 'Class consists entirely of group assets' check-box (refer Chapter 9.5.2)
>
> Also, while configuring the IMG activity 'Specify Depreciation Areas for Group Assets' (Transaction OAYM), select the 'Grp.asset' check-box, if you want to manage assets at the group asset level, in the respective depreciation areas (refer Chapter 9.5.1)

- *Asset Super Number*: The 'asset super number' offers some advantages of a group asset, without being as complex as that of a group asset. You can use asset super number to assign a number of assets to a single object. You assign assets to an asset super number by entering the common asset super number in the asset master record. You can either create the asset super number as a separate master record, or simply use it as a 'sort' criterion. If you want to manage master data at the asset super number level, you must create a statistical asset master record (without values) for the asset super number.

> **i** You cannot calculate asset values for the assets at the asset super number level.

- *Negative Assets*: Managing assets as 'negative assets' enables you, for example, (a) to collect investment support on negative assets, or (b) to represent investment support as a negative subnumber to the respective main number or (c) to collect credit memos on special assets. For handling a negative asset, you need to specify an asset class that allows assets with negative APC but with positive depreciation; make this specification using an indicator, in the detail screen of the depreciation areas, in the asset class.

With this, we are ready to discuss the asset classes.

7.4   Asset Classes

Valid across company codes of a client, you can use the 'asset classes' to structure your assets according to the legal and accounting requirements of your business enterprise. You can define any number asset classes (like, buildings, vehicles, AuC, machinery, furniture & fittings etc) in the system. The asset class establishes the link (through the account determination key) between asset master records and the G/L accounts in SAP FI (Figure 7.2).

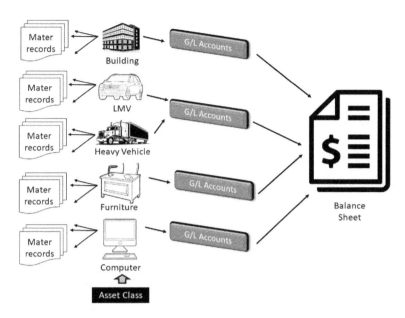

Figure 7.2: Structuring Asset Classes

> **i** Several asset classes can use the same account determination key.

Called as 'sample master record', the asset class, besides providing default values to all the asset master records in that class, also enables and simplifies creation of new asset master records. You can set the screen / tab layout together with the field status characteristics for each of the asset classes. You can also control asset numbering through the asset classes. In almost all the asset reports, you will use asset class as a 'sort' criterion.

By assigning any number of charts of depreciation to each asset class, you can have country-specific depreciation terms for each combination of 'asset class-chart of depreciation'. And, these depreciation terms can become the default values in the given chart of depreciation.

> **i** Even though an asset class with the default values can be used across company codes in a client, it is also possible to specify certain general master data that is dependent on a chart of depreciation, and to use that to provide default data.

An asset class is made up of three sections as shown in Figure 7.3:

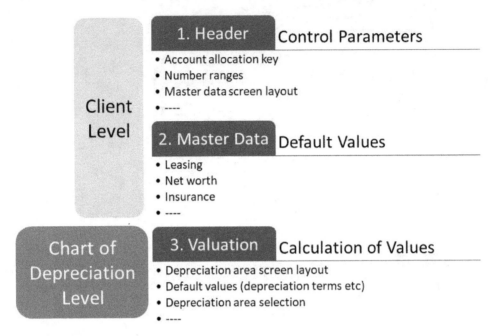

Figure 7.3: Asset Class Sections

1. A 'header section' comprising of control parameters (like account determination key, number & subnumber assignment, special functions etc) for master data maintenance and account determination.
2. A 'master data section' with default values (like, net worth tax, insurance etc) for the administrative data in the asset master record.
3. A 'valuation section' with control parameters (like, depreciation area screen layout, depreciation terms, useful life, index series, control indicator: amount / quantity check for LVA, allowing negative values etc) for valuation and default depreciation terms for each depreciation area.

With this background on asset class, let us look at configuring them (as a part of organizational structuring) in the system. The first activity is to specify the account determination.

7.4.1 Specify Account Determination

Here, you will define the account determination keys and their description for use in FI-AA. Stored in the asset class, the account determination links an asset master record with the FI-G/L accounts to be posted for an accounting transaction using the asset class. You can specify various accounts for each depreciation area to post to.

> **i** The number of account determinations should be at least equal to your asset types that are represented as B/S items.

Project Dolphin

The project management team has recommended to create easily identifiable new account determination keys to map to the various types of fixed assets for BESTM group of companies. It has been advised to create two account determinations for LVAs: one for collective management and another for individual management. They have also recommended to create new screen layout rules to customize the field status to suit BESTM requirements.

Use the menu path: SAP Customizing Implementation Guide > Financial Accounting > Asset Accounting > Organizational Structures > Asset Classes > Specify Account Determination, or Transaction S_ALR_87009195. On the resulting screen, click on 'New Entries' and define the account determination keys ('Acct.determ.') and the description ('Name of Account Determination') as shown in Figure 7.4.

Change View "FI-AA: Account determination": Overview

New Entries

Acct. determ.	Name of Account Determination
B1000	Buildings
B2000	Plant and Machinery
B3000	Vehicles
B4100	Office Equipment
B4200	Furniture and Fixtures
B5100	Computer Hardware
B5200	Computer Software
B6000	Assets under Construction (AuC)
B7000	Low Value Assets (LVA) - Collective Management
B7100	Low Value Assets (LVA) - Individual Management
B8000	Intangible Assets

Figure 7.4: Account Determination Keys

The next task in configuring asset classes, is to specify the screen layout rules.

7.4.2 Create Screen Layout Rules

The screen layout determines the field status in the asset master record. Accordingly, you will use the screen layout to determine if fields are to be of 'required entry' or 'optional entry', or if they are to be 'suppressed'. Here in this activity, you create only the keys and descriptions of the screen layout controls. You will carry out the definition of the field group rules, for the screen layouts, while configuring the IMG node 'Screen Layout' under 'Master Data' (refer Chapter 12.2).

You can enter a *'screen layout rule'* in one of the two places: either in the part of the asset class that is valid for the entire client, or in the part of the asset class that is valid only for the chart of depreciation. Accordingly, the screen layout rule is, then, valid either for all assets in the asset class, or for all assets in the 'asset class/chart of depreciation' combination.

You may use the SAP supplied screen layout rules for the most commonly used asset types, or you may create your own. We have created new screen layout rules to be in line with the different asset types for BESTM.

Use the menu path: SAP Customizing Implementation Guide > Financial Accounting > Asset Accounting > Organizational Structures > Asset Classes > Create Screen Layout Rules or Transaction S_ALR_87009209. On the resulting screen, click on 'New Entries' and create the keys for 'Screen Layout Rule' and also a description ('Name of screen layout rule'). All the screen layout rules for BESTM will start with the letters BE (Figure 7.5).

Change View "Asset Accounting: Screen layout for master record": Overv

Screen Layout Rule	Name of screen layout rule
BE10	Buildings
BE20	Plant and Machine
BE30	Vehicles
BE40	Office Equipments
BE41	Fixtures and fittings
BE50	Computers (Hardware/Software)
BE60	Assets under construction (AuC
BE70	Low value assets (LVA)

Figure 7.5: Screen Layout Rules

The next step is to define the number range interval for the asset classes.

7.4.3   Define Number Range Interval

Define the number ranges, that you will require, per company code, for assigning the main asset numbers. You specify the required number range intervals to cover your entire portfolio of assets. The number assignment of asset subnumbers is controlled by the asset class. You can specify there, in the asset class, whether the assignment of subnumbers is to be internal or external. You do not need to define the number ranges for the assignment of asset subnumbers.

> **i** Always opt for internal numbering for the asset main numbers, and external for asset subnumbers.

Project Dolphin

BESTM management has decided to define as many number ranges as that of asset account determination keys, so as to easily identify an asset just by a number. And, all the asset main numbers will be internal but the asset subnumbers will be external to help in modeling and grouping the assets.

Use the menu path: SAP Customizing Implementation Guide > Financial Accounting > Asset Accounting > Organizational Structures > Asset Classes > Define Number Range Interval. You may also use Transaction AS08. On the resulting screen, enter the 'Company Code' and click on 'Change Intervals'. On the next screen, create the required number ranges (Figure 7.6). And, repeat defining the number ranges for all the company codes of BESTM, both in USA and in India.

Edit Intervals: Asset Number, Object ANLAGENNR, Subobject 1110

N..	From No.	To Number	NR Status	Ext
B1	100000000000	199999999999	0	☐
B2	200000000000	299999999999	0	☐
B3	300000000000	399999999999	0	☐
B4	400000000000	499999999999	0	☐
B5	500000000000	599999999999	0	☐
B6	600000000000	699999999999	0	☐
B7	700000000000	799999999999	0	☐
B8	800000000000	899999999999	0	☐

Figure 7.6: Number Range Intervals for Main Asset (Company Code 1110)

With this, we are now ready to define the asset classes.

7.4.4   Define Asset Classes

From the previous discussion on asset classes at the start of the Section 7.4, we know that defining asset classes is fundamental to SAP FI-AA. We already know that the asset class is the most important way of structuring your fixed assets in the system, as it forms the linkage between your asset masters and the respective G/L accounts.

> **i** Though the number of asset classes you may need depends upon the type of assets in your organization's asset portfolio, you will normally need no more than 50 asset classes at the maximum. Try to have assets with the same depreciation terms in the same asset class.

Project Dolphin

The project team has recommended to BESTM management to have as many asset classes as that of the asset determination keys that have been defined earlier. However, instead of creating a separate asset class for goodwill, an asset class in the name of 'intangible assets' will have to be created to cover all intangible assets including the goodwill, patent, copyright etc. For AuC, it should be configured for line item settlement. Except the LVA, all other asset classes should be configured to have the subnumber assigned externally.

Use the menu path: SAP Customizing Implementation Guide > Financial Accounting > Asset Accounting > Organizational Structures > Asset Classes > Define Asset Classes or Transaction OAOA. On the resulting screen, click on 'New Entries' and define all the required settings for the asset class, say B1000, on the next screen (Figure 7.7):

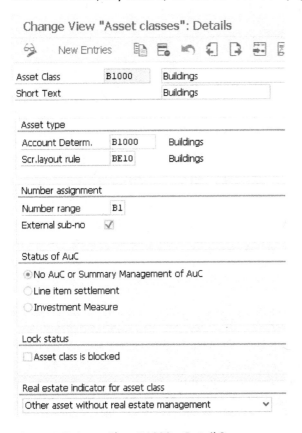

Figure 7.7: Asset Class B1000 – Detail Screen

i. Enter the key for the 'Asset Class', and provide both the description and and 'Short Text'.

ii. Under 'Asset Type', enter the appropriate account determination ('Account Determ.') and also the screen layout rule ('Scr.layout rule') that you have defined earlier.

iii. Enter the appropriate 'Number range', under 'Number assignment', from the number ranges that you have defined earlier. Select the 'External sub-no' check-box if you want all the subnumbers for this asset class are to be externally numbered, as required by BESTM.

iv. Select the first radio-button option 'No AuC or Summary Management of AuC' under 'Status of AuC' as this asset class is not for AuC. However, in the case of an asset class for AuC (say, B6000 in our case), you need to select the appropriate radio button ('Line item settlement' for BESTM).

v. Do not select the check-box 'Asset class is blocked' for now. When selected, this will prevent new assets from being created in this asset class.

vi. Since this is not an asset class for real estate asset, you will select 'Other asset without real estate management' value for the 'Real estate indicator for asset class'. Select 'Real estate – property or buildings' value, if you want to manage the assets of this asset class in SAP-RE as real estate or buildings.

vii. 'Save' when completed, and create all other asset classes as well (Figure 7.8).

Change View "Asset classes": Overview

New Entries

Class	Short Text	Asset Class Description
B1000	Buildings	Buildings
B2000	Plant	Plant & Machinery
B3000	Vehicles	Vehicles
B4100	Office Equipment	Office Equipment
B4200	Furniture	Furniture & Fixtures
B5100	Computer Hardware	Computer Hardware
B5200	Computer Software	Computer Software
B6000	AuC	Assets under Construction (AuC)
B7000	LVA - Collective	Low Value Assets - Collective Management
B7100	LVA - Individua	Low Value Assets -Individual Management
B8000	Intangible Assets	Intangible Assets

Figure 7.8: Asset Classes for BESTM

The last configuration step under asset classes is to specify the chart of depreciation dependent screen layout and account assignment.

7.4.5   Specify Chart-of-Dep.-Dependent Screen Layout/Acct Assignment

In general, the control specifications (the screen layout and the account determination) for the asset class applies throughout the client; that is, it is valid for all the charts of depreciation. Hence, it is sufficient to make control specifications at the asset class level as we have done in the earlier step. However, should you need to control the specifications, per country, using the chart of depreciation, then you need to carry out this configuration step for a given asset class. When done, the system will ignore the general control specifications but will make use of the settings made here.

Project Dolphin

The project team has recommended to make use of the control specifications for screen layout and account determination at the asset class level rather than making the specifications at the chart of depreciation level.

As we want to make use of the control specifications (for the screen layout and account determination) at the asset class level, for all BESTM company codes, we will not be configuring this step here.

However, should you want to do that you may use the menu path: SAP Customizing Implementation Guide > Financial Accounting > Asset Accounting > Organizational Structures > Asset Classes > Specify Chart-of-Dep.-Dependent Screen Layout/Acct Assignment or Transaction ANK1. On the resulting screen, select the appropriate asset class and double-click on 'Chart-of-depreciation-dependent-data' on the left-hand side 'Dialog Structure' and enter the chart of depreciation on the next screen and 'Save'.

This completes our discussion on configuring the asset classes, and thereby configuring the organizational structures. Let us, now, move on to discuss the integration of FI-AA with other SAP application components including SAP FI.

7.5   Conclusion

You learned that you can structure fixed assets, in FI-AA, at three different levels: at balance sheet (B/S) structure level, at classification structure level and at asset-related structure level.

You learned that at the 'balance sheet structure level', you can structure your fixed assets according to B/S criteria, using a 3-level hierarchy with G/L accounts at the first level, B/S items at the second level and financial statement version at the third level. At 'classification structure level', you learned that you can use the 'asset classes' (like buildings, vehicles etc) in structuring the fixed assets. At the 'asset-related structure level', you learned that you can set up a 4-level hierarchy in FI-AA.

You, then, learned about simple assets, group assets, asset main number, asset subnumber etc. You learned that an asset is known as a 'simple asset', when you represent that just by the asset main number alone. You also learned that a 'group asset' enables grouping a number of assets together, for the purpose of uniform evaluation and depreciation. You also learned that a 'complex asset' normally consists of a number of component assets, that you will use a main asset number to represent the asset as a whole and use asset subnumbers to represent the various parts / components. You also learned about 'asset super number' and 'negative assets'.

You learned that you can use the 'asset classes' to structure your assets according to the legal and accounting requirements of your business enterprise. You understood that you can define any number asset classes (like, buildings, vehicles, AuC, machinery, furniture & fittings etc) in the system, and that will be valid across company codes of a client. You also understood that the asset class establishes the link (through the account determination key) between asset master records and the G/L accounts in SAP FI.

With this, let us discuss the integration of asset accounting with various other application components of SAP, including SAP G/L Accounting, in the next Chapter.

8 Integration

It possible that you can make account assignment to FI-AA from other application components of SAP like MM (Materials Management), PM (Plant Maintenance), SAP PP (Production Planning), IM (Investment Management) etc, for data flow from these components into asset accounting. Let us understand some of these integrations, in brief, and the integration with SAP G/L Accounting, in detail, in this Chapter.

Let us start with the FI-AA integration with SAP MM.

8.1 FI-AA Integration with SAP MM

The integration of FI-AA with SAP MM component enables the following:

- When you post to an asset while entering a *purchase requisition* (PR) or an *outline agreement*, the system checks (with reference to the planned delivery date) to ascertain whether the fixed asset actually exists and whether you can post to it. The system carries out the same checks if you post to a fixed asset when entering a purchase order (PO). During the process, the system ensures – for example - that you do not exceed the upper limit for LVAs.

- Also, when you have account assignment to an asset during a material reservation, the system checks whether the asset actually exists. Accordingly, any material withdrawal (with account assignment to an asset) results in capitalization of the purchase or production costs of the material to the fixed asset.

- Depending on the purchase order (PO), you can post the GR for a PO as valuated or non-valuated: if the GR is valuated, then, the system capitalizes the invoiced value of the goods (based on the PO) to the fixed asset; else, the system posts the non-valuated GR to a clearing account. See Chapter 13.1.2 for defining the account assignment category for asset POs.

- Depending upon when invoice receipt (IR) happens vis-à-vis the GR, the system handles the asset capitalization differently: (a) if the IR is before GR, the system capitalizes the invoice amount (without tax & discount) to the asset or (b) if the IR is after GR, then, the system capitalizes the difference between the invoice amount (minus tax & discount) and the posted invoiced value of goods, provided that the GR was valuated. However, in the case of IR after a non-valuated GR, the system capitalizes the total invoice amount (minus tax & cash discount).

> **i** You have to determine, beforehand, if you want the system to deduct the cash discount at IR; you can configure this through an appropriate document type.

With this, let us understand FI-AA integration with SAP PP/PM.

8.2   FI-AA Integration with SAP PP/PM

Since you can enter fixed assets as the 'receivers' for the settlement of *maintenance orders*, you can settle maintenance activities that require capitalization to assets. In this case, the system will propose the asset that is assigned to the given equipment (or functional location) as the settlement receiver. We can now move on to discuss FI-AA's integration with SAP IM.

8.3   FI-AA Integration with SAP IM

You normally need to settle the costs collected on the *investment measure* to different receivers, when you settle capital investment measures. The system carries out most of this process, automatically, using the control parameters and *settlement rules* that you have entered. Accordingly, you can do (a) periodic settlement at the close of the period or (b) full settlement or partial capitalization of the investment measure at its completion:

- During *'periodic settlement'*, the system allocates the actual costs on the order or WBS completely or partially to one or more receivers. Also, it generates automatic offsetting postings that credit the order or WBS element. The original debit postings to the order or WBS element still exist on the receivers after the settlement.
- The system makes a *'full settlement'* when the investment measure is completed. At that time, the system settles the debits that were transferred to the AuC to the completed assets. It is possible that you can make a correction, at this point, and make a final settlement of these debits to the correct cost centers, if debits were incorrectly transferred earlier to the AuC. However, the system allows this only for debits that were posted during the current fiscal year but not for previous fiscal years, since they were already listed under AuC in the B/S for the previous year.

Besides the above, the integration of FI-AA with other FI application components enables you to (a) post asset acquisitions and retirements that are integrated with A/P and A/R, (b) make account assignment of down payments to assets by them in FI, and (c) post depreciation from FI-AA to the appropriate G/L accounts.

Let us now understand the integration of FI-AA with SAP G/L Accounting, in the next section.

8.4   FI-AA Integration with SAP G/L Accounting

Using FI-AA, you can automatically update all relevant accounting transactions that are posted to assets, and all the changes to asset values that are automatically calculated by the system (particularly, depreciation), to SAP G/L Accounting. The system makes these updates in real-time for the leading depreciation areas of an accounting principle; for other depreciation areas (such as depreciation areas for special reserves), the system makes periodic updates.

We shall now discuss the configuration steps that are required to make the integration of FI-AA, with SAP G/L Accounting:

- Define How Depreciation Areas Post to General Ledger
- Assign G/L Accounts
- Define Technical Clearing Account for Integrated Asset Acquisition
- Integrated Transactions: Alternative Document Type for 'Accounting Principle-Specific' Documents
- Specify Posting Key for Asset Posting
- Change the Field Status Variant of the Asset G/L Accounts
- Assign Input Tax Indicator for Non-Taxable Acquisitions
- Specify Financial Statement Version for Asset Reports
- Specify Document Type for Posting of Depreciation
- Specify Intervals and Posting Rules
- Segment Reporting
- Additional Account Assignment Objects

Let us start with the first step of defining how depreciation areas post to the G/L.

8.4.1   Define How Depreciation Areas Post to General Ledger

Here, in this step, you will specify the depreciation areas that post their APC transactions and/or depreciation to the G/L. The system posts the APC transactions of the depreciation areas to the G/L online, automatically. You always have to use periodic processing to post depreciation to the G/L. In the standard settings, the book depreciation area (1) posts the APC transactions and depreciation, in real-time, to the G/L.

Use the menu path: SAP Customizing Implementation Guide > Financial Accounting > Asset Accounting > Integration with General Ledger Accounting > Define How Depreciation Areas Post to General Ledger.

    i.   On the resulting pop-up screen, enter the chart of depreciation to proceed.

   ii.   On the next screen, you will see the list of depreciation areas and how they are posting to the G/L. If you look closely, you will notice that we have already completed this when we maintained the depreciation areas (activity: 'Copy/Delete Depreciation Areas') as a part of the IMG activity 'Copy Reference Chart of Depreciation/Depreciation Areas' vide Chapter 6.2. You can, of course, use this step now to change, if required, the way a depreciation area posts to the G/L.

---

i It is normally sufficient to post APC transactions and depreciation, from one depreciation area automatically to the G/L online. This will always be the book depreciation area (1 or 01). However, you might need additional areas that post automatically to the G/L, (a) when you want to post depreciation that differs from book depreciation to expense accounts (or cost elements) for meeting, say, cost-accounting requirements, or (b) when you need special valuations for the B/S as in the case of *special reserves*, for example, or (c) when you need to meet the special requirements for legal consolidation of your corporate group or (d) when you are using the ledger approach, in SAP G/L Accounting, and you want to specify additional depreciation areas from which APC transactions are posted automatically online to the G/L.

With this, we are now ready to carry out the next step of specifying the B/S accounts, special reserve accounts, and the depreciation accounts for FI-AA.

8.4.2 Assign G/L Accounts

Per account determination and per depreciation area, specify the B/S accounts, depreciation accounts and the special reserve accounts, using the menu path: SAP Customizing Implementation Guide > Financial Accounting > Asset Accounting > Integration with General Ledger Accounting > Assign G/L Accounts. You may also use Transaction AO90:

i.   On the resulting pop-up screen, enter the chart of depreciation (BEUS) and proceed.

ii.   On the next screen, select the chart of accounts row (BEUS), and double-click on 'Account Determination' on the left-hand side 'Dialog Structure' (Figure 8.1).

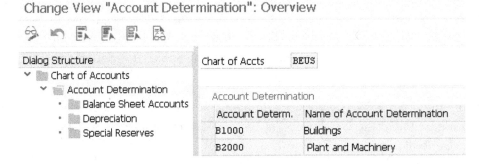

Figure 8.1: Account Determination Screen (Assign G/L Accounts)

iii.   Select a row under 'Account Determination' (say, B1000, Buildings), and double-click on 'Balance Sheet Accounts' on the left-hand side 'Dialog Structure'. The system brings up the next screen listing the depreciation areas. Double-click on a depreciation area, and enter the appropriate G/L accounts for the B/S on the next screen (Figure 8.2).

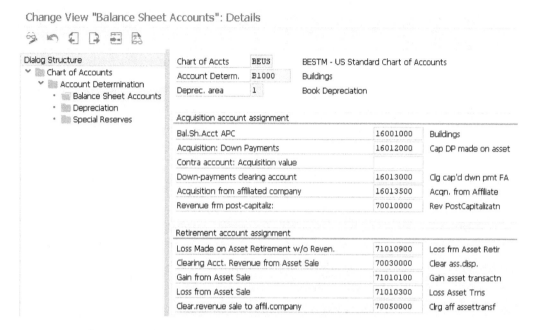

Figure 8.2: B/S Accounts for Account Determination B1000

iv.   Similarly, per depreciation area, maintain the G/L accounts for 'Depreciation' and 'Special Reserves' by double-clicking on the appropriate option, on the left-hand side 'Dialog Structure'.

v.   Repeat the steps for all the other account assignments like B2000, B3000 etc.

> **i** In the case of a *special depreciation area*, if you enter G/L accounts for gains and losses for reserves, the system will not post the revenue from writing off reserves for *special depreciation*. Instead, the system includes this amount in the gain/loss, when there is revenue from write-off of special reserves due to an asset sale. The system, then, balances the loss by a posting to an offsetting account, and posts the sum/difference between the revenue (from the write-off of the special reserve) and the loss to these accounts.

We can now move on to define the technical clearing account for integrated asset acquisition.

8.4.3   Define Technical Clearing Account for Integrated Asset Acquisition

In an *integrated asset acquisition* posting, the system divides the business transaction into an operational part and a valuating part: (a) for the 'operational part' (vendor invoice), the system posts a document valid for all accounting principles against the *technical clearing account*, and (b) for each 'valuating part' (asset posting with capitalization of the asset), the system generates a separate document that is (valid only for the given accounting principle) also posted against the technical clearing account.

---

i By this, the system ensures that the *'technical clearing account'* for integrated asset acquisitions has a zero-balance (for each accounting principle and account assignment object) in the chart of depreciation. To ensure zero balance, the system prevents you from making manual postings to the account.

Note that this technical clearing account, since it has a zero-balance, will not appear in the B/S itself, but in the notes to the financial statement.

Use the menu path: SAP Customizing Implementation Guide > Financial Accounting > Asset Accounting > Integration with General Ledger Accounting > Define Technical Clearing Account for Integrated Asset Acquisition. On the resulting screen, enter the technical clearing account for integrated asset acquisition against the chart of depreciation (Figure 8.3).

Figure 8.3: Technical Clearing Account for Integrated Asset Acquisition

Let us, now, define alternate document types for integrated asset transactions.

8.4.4   Integrated Transactions: Alternative Doc. Type for Acctg-Princpl-Spec. Docs

We have already seen, in the previous Section, that in an integrated asset acquisition posting, the system divides the business transaction into an operational part and a valuating part. For the operative part, the system posts a document that is valid for all accounting principles (ledger-group independent document). And, for each valuating part, the system generates a separate document that is valid only for the given accounting principle (ledger-group-specific documents per accounting principle).

When document splitting is active, then, the system cannot always pass on the document type (of the entry view) to the valuating documents, because in the document type defined, the items have been designated as required, but they exist only in the operational document, and not in the valuating document. So, you need a different document type, to take care of the valuation postings. Also, you may require that the valuating documents be posted with a different document type (than that of the operational documents). Hence, you need to specify alternative document types for accounting-principle-specific documents:

7.4.4.1. Alternative Document Type for Acctg-Principle-Specific Documents

Use the menu path: SAP Customizing Implementation Guide > Financial Accounting > Asset Accounting > Integration with General Ledger Accounting > Integrated Transactions: Alternative Doc. Type for Acctg-Princpl-Spec. Docs > Alternative Document Type for Acctg-Principle-Specific Documents, and specify the general (company code independent) document types for the valuating documents to take care of the different account principles. If necessary, you can further differentiate the valuating documents per company code, which you can achieve through the following activity:

7.4.4.2. Define Separate Document Types by Company Code

Use the menu path: SAP Customizing Implementation Guide > Financial Accounting > Asset Accounting > Integration with General Ledger Accounting > Integrated Transactions: Alternative Doc. Type for Acctg-Princpl-Spec. Docs > Define Separate Document Types by Company Code, and specify the company code dependent document types for the valuating documents to take care of the different account principles.

The next step, is to specify the posting keys for asset accounting.

8.4.5 Specify Posting Key for Asset Posting

You can define the posting keys which the system will use for automatic postings in FI-AA. You may not need to define new keys as you can use the SAP supplied posting keys (Figure 8.4).

Figure 8.4: Posting Keys for Asset Posting

You can see the standard posting keys, for each of the posting procedures, by using the menu path: SAP Customizing Implementation Guide > Financial Accounting > Asset Accounting > Integration with General Ledger Accounting > Specify Posting Key for Asset Posting or Transaction OBYD:

- ANL – Asset Posting (posting keys: 70 debit and 75 credit)
- ANS – G/L Account Posting from Asset Posting (posting keys: 40 debit and 50 credit)

The next step is to define/change the field status variant (FSV) of the asset G/L Accounts.

8.4.6 Change the Field Status Variant of the Asset G/L Accounts

We have already defined the FSV for BESTM company codes, when we configured FI global settings. We defined the FSV, B100, and have assigned the company codes of BESTM to that. Here, in this, activity we shall be viewing/editing the same to make sure that we have the appropriate field status, for enabling asset accounting related postings.

Project Dolphin

BESTM requested the project management team to configure the FSV to ensure that indicator 'Asset retirement' and the field 'Asset number / subnumber' are set to with a field status as 'required entry'. Similar settings need to be carried out for the asset posting keys as well.

Use the menu path: SAP Customizing Implementation Guide > Financial Accounting > Asset Accounting > Integration with General Ledger Accounting > Change the Field Status Variant of the Asset G/L Accounts.

    i.   On the resulting 'Select Activity' pop-up screen, double-click on the 'Define Field Status Variants' activity (Figure 8.5):

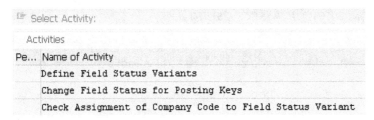

Figure 8.5: 'Select Activity' Pop-Up Screen

- On the next screen (you may also reach this screen directly by using Transaction OBC4), select the appropriate FSV (B100), and double-click on the 'Field status group' on the left-hand side 'Dialog Structure'.
- The system will bring up all the field status groups (FSGs) of FSV B100. Double-click on the FSG YB07 [Asset accts (w/o accumulated depreciatn)].

- On the resulting 'Maintain Field Status Group: Overview' screen, double-click on 'Asset Accounting' under the 'Select Group' block.
- On the next screen, ensure that the 'Asset retirement' indicator and the 'Asset number / subnumber' fields are set to required entry ('Req. Entry'). 'Save' the settings (Figure 8.6).

Maintain Field Status Group: Asset Accounting

← ↳   Field check

General Data

Field status variant B100   Group YB07
Asset accts (w/o accumulated depreciatn)

Asset Accounting

	Suppress	Req. Entry	Opt. entry
Asset retirement	○	⦿	○
Asset number / subnumber	○	⦿	○

Figure 8.6: Field Status for Asset Accounting – FSV B100

ii.   Go back to the initial 'Select Activity' pop-up screen (Figure 8.5), and double-click on the activity 'Change Field Status for Posting Keys'. The system brings up the list of postings keys on the next screen, 'Maintain Accounting Configuration: Posting Keys – List' (you may also reach this screen directly if you use Transaction OB41):

- Double-click on posting key 70 (debit asset), and you will see the posting key's configuration on the next screen.
- Now, click on 'Maintain Field Status' and the system takes you to the 'Maintain Field Status Group: Overview' screen. On this screen, now, double-click on 'Asset Accounting' under the 'Select Group' block.
- On the next screen ensure that the 'Asset retirement' indicator and the 'Asset number / subnumber' fields are set to required entry ('Req. Entry').
- 'Save' the settings (Figure 8.7).
- Go back to the previous screen, 'Maintain Accounting Configuration: Posting Keys – List', and double-click on the posting key 75 (credit asset) and repeat the above steps to set the FSV of the 'Asset retirement' indicator and the 'Asset number / subnumber' fields to required entry.
- 'Save' the details.

Maintain Field Status Group: Asset Accounting

Field check

General Data

Posting keys   ;70 Debit asset

Asset Accounting

	Suppress	Req. Entry	Opt. entry
Asset retirement	○	⦿	○
Asset number / subnumber	○	⦿	○

Figure 8.7: Field Status for Asset Accounting – Posting Key 70

iii.   Again, go back to the initial 'Select Activity' pop-up screen (Figure 8.5), and double click on the 'Check Assignment of Company Code to Field Status Variant' activity. On the resulting 'Change View "Assign Company Code -> Field Status Variant": Overview' screen, you will notice that the FSV B100 has been assigned to the company codes of BESTM (Figure 8.8). If not, assign the FSV to all the asset accounting company codes of BESTM, now.

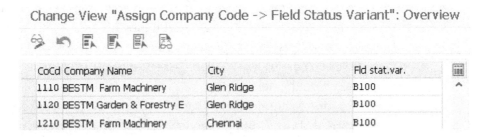

Change View "Assign Company Code -> Field Status Variant": Overview

CoCd	Company Name	City	Fld stat.var.	
1110	BESTM Farm Machinery	Glen Ridge	B100	^
1120	BESTM Garden & Forestry E	Glen Ridge	B100	
1210	BESTM Farm Machinery	Chennai	B100	

Figure 8.8: Assigning Asset Accounting Company Codes to FSV

With this, we can, now, move on to assign the input tax indicator to non-taxable asset acquisition transactions.

8.4.7 Assign Input Tax Indicator for Non-Taxable Acquisitions

Specify an input tax indicator, for non-taxable asset acquisition, per company code so as to enable the system to make use of this indicator when posting acquisitions that are not subject to tax, but posted to accounts that are tax-relevant.

> **i** You will, for example, come across an acquisition transaction from your in-house production wherein the acquisition itself is non-taxable but the transaction should be posted to an account that is tax-relevant.

Use the menu path: SAP Customizing Implementation Guide > Financial Accounting > Asset Accounting > Integration with General Ledger Accounting > Assign Input Tax Indicator for Non-Taxable Acquisitions. You may also use Transaction OBCL.

On the resulting screen, for each of the asset accounting company codes, enter the non-taxable tax code (Figure 8.9) for input tax ('Input Tax Code').

Change View "Allocate Co.Cd. -> Non-Taxable Transactions": Overview

CoCd	Company Name	City	Input ...	Outpu...	Jurisdict. Code
1110	BESTM Farm Machinery	Glen Ridge	IO	00	7700000000
1120	BESTM Garden & Forestry E	Glen Ridge	IO	00	7700000000

Figure 8.9: Assigning Input Tax Code for Non-Taxable Acquisitions

The next step in configuring the FI-AA integration with SAP G/L Accounting, is to specify the financial statement version for asset reports.

8.4.8   Specify Financial Statement Version for Asset Reports

Here, in this step, you need to specify, per depreciation area, which financial statement version the system should use as the default version.

We have already defined the required financial statement versions while configuring the SAP G/L Accounting. We have defined two versions: BEIN as the financial statement version for use by India-based company codes and BEUS for US-based company codes.

Use the menu path: SAP Customizing Implementation Guide > Financial Accounting > Asset Accounting > Integration with General Ledger Accounting > Specify Financial Statement Version for Asset Reports or Transaction OAYN.

On the resulting screen, 'Change View "Company code selection": Overview', select the appropriate company code (say, 1110) and double-click on 'Assign financial statement version' on the left-hand side 'Dialog Structure'. The system brings up all the depreciation areas, for the company code 1110, on the next screen. Enter the appropriate financial statement version ('FS Vers'), say, BEUS (for US-based company codes of BESTM) against each of the depreciation areas, and 'Save' the settings (Figure 8.10).

Figure 8.10: Assigning Financial Statement Version for Asset Reports

Repeat and assign the financial statement version, for all the depreciation areas for all the asset accounting company codes.

With this, we can move on to the next step in the configuration, namely, specifying the document type for depreciation posting.

8.4.9   Specify Document Type for Posting of Depreciation

Here, you need to specify the document type that the system should use for depreciation related postings to the SAP G/L Accounting.

Project Dolphin

The project team has decided to use the SAP's default document type AF for all the depreciation related postings in all the company codes of BESTM, both in India and in US.

Use the menu path: SAP Customizing Implementation Guide > Financial Accounting > Asset Accounting > Integration with General Ledger Accounting > Post Depreciation to General Ledger Accounting > Specify Document Type for Posting of Depreciation or Transaction OAYN.

On entering the Transaction, you will see the 'Select Activity' pop-up screen (Figure 8.11).

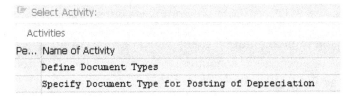

Figure 8.11: 'Select Activity' Pop-Up screen for Defining / Assigning Document Types

We have already configured the required document types, as a part of company code global parameters. However, you can double-click on the 'Define Document Types' activity to ensure that the already defined document type AF is with internal number assignment enabling automatic posting of the depreciation through batch input (Figure 8.12). You may also use this activity, now, to define new document type(s), if required. You may use Transaction OBA7 to reach the 'Change View "Document Types": Overview' screen directly.

Change View "Document Types": Details

⟨icon⟩   New Entries   ⟨icons⟩

Document type   AF   Depreciation Pstngs

Properties

Number range	03	Number range information
Reverse DocumentType		
Authorization Group		

Account types allowed

✓ Assets
☐ Customer
☐ Vendor
☐ Material
✓ G/L Account
☐ Secondary Costs

Control data

☐ Net document type
☐ Cust/vend Check
✓ Negative Postings Permitted
☐ Inter-Company
☐ Enter trading partner

Figure 8.12: Document Type AF - Details

Let us, now, proceed to specify the document type AF, per company code, for posting depreciation: double-click on the 'Specify Document Type for Posting of Depreciation' activity on initial the pop-up screen, and ensure that the document type AF has been specified for all the asset accounting company codes of BESTM (Figure 8.13) on the next screen. You may also reach this screen directly, via Transaction AO71.

Change View "FI-AA: Document Type for Posting Depreciation": Overview

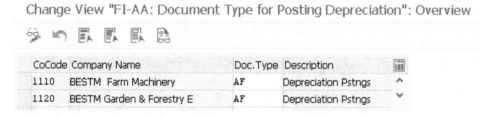

CoCode	Company Name	Doc.Type	Description	
1110	BESTM Farm Machinery	AF	Depreciation Pstngs	⌃
1120	BESTM Garden & Forestry E	AF	Depreciation Pstngs	⌄

Figure 8.13: Specifying Document Type AF for Depreciation Posting

The next task is to specify the intervals and posting rules for depreciation posting.

8.4.10 Specify Intervals and Posting Rules

An asset transaction (depreciation, interest and revaluation) will not immediately lead to an update of the depreciation and value adjustment accounts for the financial statements. The system posts the planned depreciation directly to FI, periodically, whenever you run the depreciation posting run. Besides various depreciation types, interest and revaluation, the system also posts the allocation and write-off of special reserves during this posting run. The system does not create documents for each asset, during the posting of depreciation; instead, it creates only collective documents.

> **i** Though it is difficult to provide a precise information on the performance of depreciation posting run, since it depends on your system configuration, you can safely estimate that the system can perform about 16,000 depreciation calculation, per hour. Even with collective documents, the number of documents the system needs to post in a depreciation run is function of number of G/L accounts to be posted, number of combinations of account assignments and number of account determinations. And, remember that the 'update run' of the depreciation posting run has always to be in the background, for performance reasons.

You can specify the posting cycle (discussed in this Section) and the additional account assignment levels (such as, cost center or order) for the depreciation posting run, per company code and per depreciation area. We shall discuss about specifying account assignment types for account assignment objects, later, in Section 8.4.12.

Here, in this configuration activity, you specify the posting rules for posting the depreciation values to SAP FI component. In doing so, you need to specify the period (posting periodicity or cycle) and the method for posting the depreciation run. Specify these details, per depreciation area, and per company code.

Use the menu path: SAP Customizing Implementation Guide > Financial Accounting > Asset Accounting > Integration with General Ledger Accounting > Post Depreciation to General Ledger Accounting > Specify Intervals and Posting Rules or Transaction OAYR:

i. On the entering the Transaction, the system brings up the list of company codes for making a selection. Select the company code (say, 1110), and double-click on 'Posting rules' on the left-hand side 'Dialog Structure'.

ii. On the resulting screen, double-click on the required depreciation area (say, 1) and enter the settings under the 'Period and method' data block (Figure 8.14):

- Select the appropriate posting radio-button: select 'Monthly posting'. If you select 'Bi-monthly posting', for example, then, the system posts the depreciation in every alternate posting period.

ℹ️ Note that the radio button, 'Bi-monthly posting', 'Quarterly posting' and 'Semi-annual posting' will be disabled if your posting periods in FI is not 12.

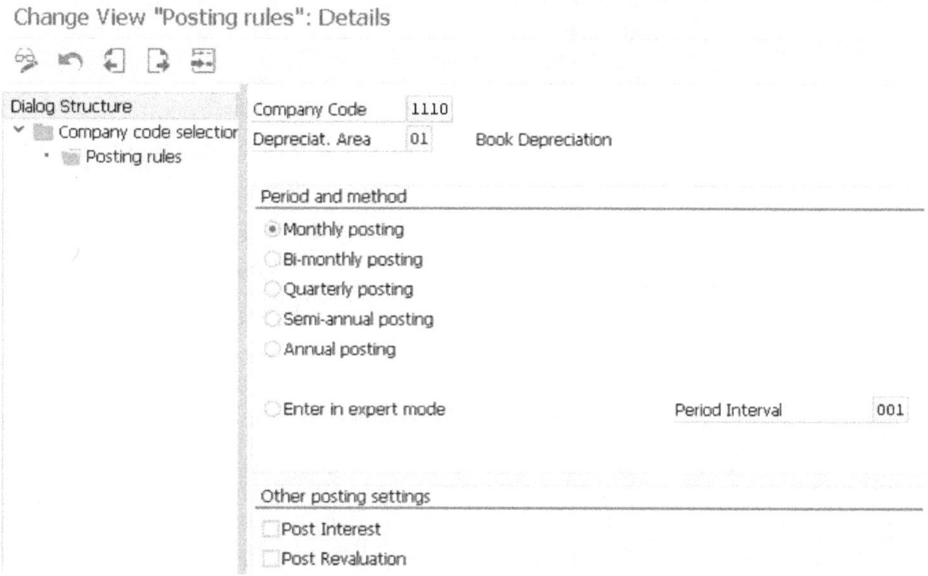

Change View "Posting rules": Details

Dialog Structure
∨ 🗀 Company code selection
   • 🗀 Posting rules

Company Code   1110
Depreciat. Area   01   Book Depreciation

Period and method
◉ Monthly posting
○ Bi-monthly posting
○ Quarterly posting
○ Semi-annual posting
○ Annual posting

○ Enter in expert mode   Period Interval   001

Other posting settings
☐ Post Interest
☐ Post Revaluation

Figure 8.14: Posting Rules for Depreciation Posting

- Depending upon the period you select, the system fills up the 'Period Interval' automatically. For example, when you select 'Monthly posting', then the 'Period Interval' will be 001, for 'Bi-Monthly posting' it will be 002, for 'Quarterly posting' it will be 003, for 'Semi-annual posting' it will be 006 and for 'Annual posting' the value in 'Period Interval' will be 012. The 'Period Interval' denotes the interval between two depreciation posting runs.

ℹ️ You can post the depreciation posting runs, resulting from valuation changes (due to year-end closing and taking place after the fiscal year end), as 'unplanned depreciation' posting runs in the special periods of the given fiscal year version.

- Select 'Enter in expert mode' radio-button, if you want to make your entry for the settings function in an 'expert mode', instead of using the simplified method. When you activate this, you need to enter the 'Period interval' manually.

iii.   Under 'Other posting settings':

- Select 'Post Interest' check-box, if you want the system to post the imputed interest (for cost-accounting), in addition to the depreciation in this depreciation area, during the depreciation posting run. You will select this only for the depreciation areas that handle interest.
- Select 'Post Revaluation' check-box, if you want to post the revaluation of APC and the accumulated ordinary depreciation, of this depreciation area, in SAP G/L during the depreciation posting run, in addition to the depreciation.
- Select 'Below-Zero Acct When Planned Life Ends' check-box, if you want to the system to continue posting of depreciation, for this depreciation area, even after the expiry of the useful life. Here, the system will post this below-zero depreciation to the account specified in the account determination earlier.

iv.   Complete the settings for other depreciation areas of the selected company code (say, 1110) and repeat the steps for defining for all the company codes of FI-AA of BESTM.

The next step is to discuss the settings required to enable segment reporting, as part of configuring the integration of FI-AA with SAP G/L Accounting

8.4.11 Segment Reporting

Here, you need to complete two configuration tasks:

- Activate Segment Reporting
- Fill Master Data for Segment Reporting

Let us start with the first activity of activating segment reporting in FI-AA.

8.4.11.1. Activate Segment Reporting

Use this configuration step to activate segment reporting for FI-AA. When activated, the system includes the 'Profit Center' and 'Segment' fields in the asset master record. As these fields are empty initially, you need to use the IMG activity 'Fill Master Data for Segment Reporting' (discussed in the next Section), to fill the asset master data with the relevant values.

Once you activate segment reporting, when you post/maintain the asset master data, the system checks whether the asset master records have been maintained consistently; that is, it must be possible for the system to derive the profit center and the segment uniquely from the CO account assignments and from the asset master records.

> ℹ️ When you activate 'segment reporting' you can perform reporting at the profit center and segment levels. Note that once activated, you will not able to deactivate this.

Project Dolphin

BESTM, as it needs asset reporting at the segment / profit center level, has requested to activate segment reporting in FI-AA. The project team has pointed out this activation would also help to carry out the consistency check when users make single / mass asset maintenance of segment and/or profit center details while creating / changing asset master records. This is because, if this activation is not done, then the system will not do the consistency check, for these two fields, when maintaining the asset master.

Use the menu path: SAP Customizing Implementation Guide > Financial Accounting > Asset Accounting > Integration with General Ledger Accounting > Segment Reporting > Activate Segment Reporting. On the resulting screen, select the 'Segment Rptng Active' check-box and 'Save' the settings (Figure 8.15).

Change View "Activate Segment Reporting": Details

Activate Segment Reportin
✓ Segment Rptng Active

Figure 8.15: Activating Segment Reporting in FI-AA

With the activation of segment reporting for FI-AA, we can configure the system to fill the required master data for segment reporting.

8.4.11.2. Fill Master Data for Segment Reporting

You can use this configuration activity to fill the 'Profit Center' and 'Segment' fields in existing asset master data.

Use the menu path: SAP Customizing Implementation Guide > Financial Accounting > Asset Accounting > Integration with General Ledger Accounting > Segment Reporting > Fill Master Data for Segment Reporting. You may also use Transaction FAGL_R_AA_ASSET_UPDT.

On the resulting screen, enter the 'Selection Criteria' and 'Further Selections', if required. First, run the program in 'Test Mode'. In a test run, the system lists all fixed assets corresponding to your selection: (a) highlighted in green - the assets to which the system can uniquely assign a profit center and a segment and (b) highlighted in red - the assets to which the system cannot uniquely assign a profit center and a segment.

Now, the system selects all active fixed assets with a CO object in their master data, and checks whether data can be derived consistently. When successful, you can remove the tick in 'Test Mode' check-box and make a production run ('Update Mode'); the system assigns a profit center and a segment to fixed assets wherever a unique assignment can be made; else (where a unique assignment cannot be made), the system issues an error message. Though the online processing of this activity is limited to about 1,000 assets, you can run the program multiple times in 'update' mode.

> **i** Instead of using this configuration activity to fill the 'Profit Center' and 'Segment' fields of the master data, you can also edit the master data using a single / mass change. However, we recommend that you carry out this activity because a consistency check is not carried out when you make single / mass change. Alternatively, you can do the mass maintenance in combination with this configuration.

With this we can, discuss the additional account assignment objects.

8.4.12 Additional Account Assignment Objects

As a part of configuring additional account assignment objects, towards integrating FI-AA with SAP G/L Accounting, you need to complete the following configuration steps:

- Activate Account Assignment Objects
- Specify Account Assignment Types for Account Assignment Objects
- Process Error Table
- Display of Active Account Assignment Objects

Let us start with the first activity of activating account assignment objects

8.4.12.1. Activate Account Assignment Objects

Here, you make the settings for additional account assignment objects like investment order, functional area, maintenance order etc, that you may use during posting in FI-AA. During this configuration, you will (a) activate the account assignment objects that you need, (b) specify whether the account assignment object is relevant to the B/S and (c) specify whether the account assignment object you enter, during posting, has to agree with the account assignment object entered in the asset master record.

Project Dolphin

BESTM management wants to make use of additional account assignment objects like internal order, investment order, functional area, maintenance order etc during posting in asset accounting. It was also indicated that if an account assignment object is relevant to B/S, then, no user should be able to change the account assignment object in the asset master record, once the asset has been capitalized. Also, the account assignment object like funds center, funds center for investment, investment order, functional area etc should be prevented from being changed during a posting.

Use the menu path: SAP Customizing Implementation Guide > Financial Accounting > Asset Accounting > Integration with General Ledger Accounting > Additional Account Assignment Objects > Activate Account Assignment Objects.

On the resulting screen, against the required account assignment objects ('AcctAsgnOb') select the appropriate check-boxes (Figure 8.16):

Change View "Account Assignment Elements for Asset Accounting": O

Account Assignment Elements for Asset Accounting

AcctAsgnOb	Account Assignment Object Name	Active	Bal. Sheet	Agreement
CAUFN	Internal Order	✓	☐	☐
EAUFN	Investment Order	✓	☐	✓
FISTL	Funds Center	✓	✓	✓
FISTL2	Funds Center for Investment	✓	✓	✓
FKBER	Functional Area	✓	✓	✓
FKBER2	Functional Area for Investment	✓	✓	✓
GEBER	Fund	✓	✓	✓
GEBER2	Fund for Investment	✓	✓	✓
GRANT_NBR	Grant	☐	✓	✓
GRANT_NBR2	Grant for Cap. Investment	☐	✓	✓
IAUFN	Maintenance Order	✓	☐	☐

Figure 8.16: Additional Account Assignment Objects for FI-AA

i.   Only when you select the 'Active' check-box, the account assignment object will be made active for you to be able to post to it in FI-AA.

ii. Select 'Bal. Sheet' check-box, if the account assignment object is relevant to B/S. When selected, once the asset has been capitalized, you will be no longer able to change the account assignment object in the asset master record. However, you can make the required changes, by transferring such assets to a new asset master record.

iii. Select 'Agreement' check-box, if you want to prevent the account assignment object from being changed during a posting. This ensures that account assignment is only possible to the account assignment object entered, earlier, in the asset master record.

> **i** Make sure that the account assignment objects, that you want to use, are available for input, by making appropriate field status for posting keys 70 (debit asset) and 75 (credit asset). You can check and maintain the correct field status using Transaction OB41. We have already discussed this in Section 8.4.6.

With this are now ready to move on to the second configuration step under additional account assignment configuration. That is, to specify the account assignment type per account assignment object.

8.4.12.2. Specify Account Assignment Types for Account Assignment Objects

There are two 'account assignment types' (1. APC balance sheet posting and 2. account assignment of depreciation) possible for the additional account assignment objects that you have defined in the previous Section. Now, in this step, you can assign the appropriate account assignment type to these account assignment objects. These assignments depend on company code, depreciation area and transaction type. When you want to assign both the account assignment types to an account assignment object, then you need to make two table entries for that object. However, it is not possible to make two account assignment type entries for some of the objects like investment order (EAUFN), funds center for investment (FISTL2) etc, where you can make only one assignment i.e., APC balance sheet posting.

SAP has provided you with the following default settings:

- A generic (*) entry for company code, valid for all the company codes.
- Two generic (*) entries for depreciation areas, 0 and 1. The settings for depreciation area 0 are valid for all depreciation areas other than 1; the settings for generic depreciation area 1 are valid in all company codes for depreciation area 1 (book depreciation).

You can either make a generic entry or a specific entry for the transaction type. If you use both generic transaction types and 'normal' transaction types in the table, the system gives priority to the non-generic entries before generic entries. The system also gives priority to the non-generic company code over the non-generic transaction type. In all these situations, then the system proceeds as under, until it finds a suitable record as shown in Figure 8.17.

Figure 8.17: How the System Determines the Appropriate Account Assignment

You need to configure the settings, for the account assignment type, in the account assignment object as described below:

First, for the generic company code and the generic transaction type. Then, for the generic company code and non-generic transaction types. Third, for non-generic company codes and the generic transaction type. Finally, for non-generic company codes and non-generic transaction types (Figure 8.18). Activate the account assignments that you need. You do not need to delete the ones that you do not need; just deactivate them, you can activate them, later, if you need.

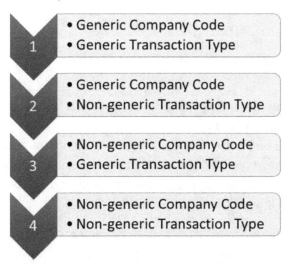

Figure 8.18: Configuration Order for Account Assignment Type

Use the menu path: SAP Customizing Implementation Guide > Financial Accounting > Asset Accounting > Integration with General Ledger Accounting > Additional Account Assignment

Objects > Specify Account Assignment Types for Account Assignment Objects. You may also use Transaction ACSET:

i.   On the resulting screen, you will see the SAP default generic entry for the company codes (Figure 8.19).

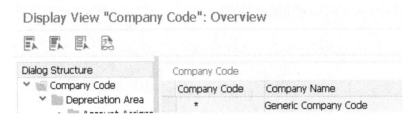

Figure 8.19: Generic Entry for the Company Code

ii.   Select this row generic company code row, and double-click on 'Depreciation Area' on the left-hand side 'Dialog Structure'. You will see the two generic depreciation area entries (00 and 01) on the next screen (Figure 8.20).

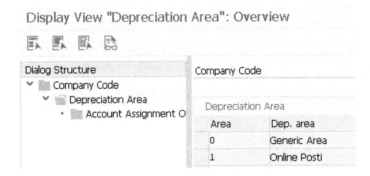

Figure 8.20: Generic Entries for Depreciation Area

iii. Now, select a generic depreciation area (say, 0) and double-click on 'Account Assignment Objects' on the left-hand side 'Dialog Structure'.

iv.   On the next screen, click on 'New Entries'. Per account assignment object ('AcctAsgnOb'), enter the transaction type ('Tra'), select the 'Account Assignment Type' (whether it is 'APC Values Posting' or 'Depreciation Posting') and select the 'AcctAssgnt' check-box if required (Figure 8.21).

You may enter * to allow all transactions in 'Tra' field. In case you want to assign both the account assignment types for an account assignment object, then make two entries for that account assignment object. Use the 'AcctAssgnt' check-box to specify if the account assignment to the given account assignment object is active or inactive. When selected, the system updates the values on the account assignment object. Do not select this, if you do not want an update for this combination of depreciation area, transaction type, and account assignment type for that account assignment object. However, you will be able to select this check-box only for 'Active' account assignment objects (refer Figure 8.16), in the previous Section).

Figure 8.21: Account Assignment Type Specifications

v.   'Save' the settings when completed. Go back, select the generic depreciation area 1 and make the settings, again, as described in (iv) above.

vi.   You can also make these settings to specific company codes (say, 1110), specific / generic depreciation areas and specific/generic transaction types (as outlined earlier in Figure 8.18). In that case, the system will proceed as outlined in Figure 8.17, to find a suitable record for the account assignment object.

With this we are now ready to make the settings for processing the error table.

8.4.12.3.   Process Error Table

You have to configure this step only when you have set the 'Agreement' indicator for the account assignment objects while configuring the IMG node 'Activate Account Assignment Objects'. Since we have selected that indicator for a number of account assignment objects, vide Section 8.4.12.1, let us complete this configuration step. As you are aware, when this indicator is set, then the account assignment object at posting has to be the same as that of the one entered in the asset master record. The settings we make here will not apply to the account assignment objects for which we have not selected this 'Agreement' check-box.

Specify, here, which error message you want the system to output when the account assignment object entered during posting is different from the one entered in the asset master record. We recommend that you select 'Warning' wherever you have selected the 'Agreement' check-box. Then, the system issues this message and makes appropriate account assignment to the account assignment object entered in the asset master record, ignoring what is entered in the posting.

Use the menu path: SAP Customizing Implementation Guide > Financial Accounting > Asset Accounting > Integration with General Ledger Accounting > Additional Account Assignment Objects > Process Error Table. On the resulting screen, select the appropriate 'Error' message per account assignment object in line with the settings that you have made for the 'Agreement' flag for that object (Figure 8.22).

Change View "FI-AA Error Messages for Account Assignment Objects": Ove

FI-AA Error Messages for Account Assignment Objects

AcctAsgnOb	AAObj.Name	Error
CAUFN	Internal Order	No message
EAUFN	Investment Order	Warning
FISTL	Funds Center	Warning

Figure 8.22: Error Message Configuration for Account Assignment Object

With this you can, now, move on to discuss how to display the active account assignment objects in the system.

8.4.12.4. Display of Active Account Assignment Objects

Use the menu path: SAP Customizing Implementation Guide > Financial Accounting > Asset Accounting > Integration with General Ledger Accounting > Additional Account Assignment Objects > Display of Active Account Assignment Objects. You may also use Transaction AACCOBJ, to display the active account assignment objects.

On the resulting screen, maintain the required parameters and run the report. The system will bring up the active account assignments, in SAP List Viewer table (Figure 8.23).

Display of Active Account Assignment Objects

CoCode	Short Name Dep.Area	Account Assignment Object Name	AcctAssignType	TType	Transact. Type Text
1110	Book Deprctn	Functional Area	APC Values Posting	*	Generic Transact.Type
	Book Deprctn		Depreciation Run		Generic Transact.Type
	Book Deprctn	Funds Center	APC Values Posting		Generic Transact.Type
	Book Deprctn		Depreciation Run		Generic Transact.Type
	Book Deprctn	Funds Center for Investment	APC Values Posting		

Figure 8.23: List of Active Account Assignment Objects

This completes our discussion on the configuration settings required for additional account assignment. With this, we have also completed the discussion on configuration settings required for FI-AA integration with SAP G/L Accounting.

8.5 Conclusion

Here, in this Chapter, you learned how FI-AA is integrated with various other SAP applications including SAP MM, SAP PP/PM and SAP IM. You also understood how it is integrated with G/L Accounting, within FI.

You understood that you can automatically update all relevant accounting transactions that are posted to assets, and all the changes to asset values that are automatically calculated by the system (particularly, depreciation), to SAP G/L Accounting. You understood that the system makes these updates in real-time for the leading depreciation areas of an accounting principle; for other depreciation areas (such as depreciation areas for special reserves), the system makes periodic updates.

While discussing the configuration steps that are required to make the integration of FI-AA, with SAP G/L Accounting, you learned that you need to make several settings including defining how depreciation areas post to general ledger, assigning G/L accounts, defining technical clearing account for integrated asset acquisition etc.

With this, let us, now, move on to discuss the settings required for general valuation, in the next Chapter.

9 General Valuation

U sing the basic functions in FI-AA, you can determine the values of all fixed assets - at a given point in time – to meet the statutory and legal requirements of the country and also your own business needs. The valuation provides you not only with the current value of an asset, but also helps in timing your asset replacement, asset retirement etc.

You manage valuation of fixed assets through the various depreciation areas in FI-AA. In this Chapter, we shall make all the configurations that you may need for the valuation of fixed assets. We can group and discuss the configuration activities, as shown under:

- Depreciation Areas
- Amount Specifications (Company Code/Depreciation Area)
- Fiscal Year Specifications
- Currencies
- Group Assets

Let us start with the settings that you need to make for the depreciation areas.

9.1 Depreciation Areas

When you create a chart of depreciation, from a reference chart of depreciation, the system copies the depreciation areas from the reference to the new chart of depreciation. However, you can also create new depreciation areas, by copying an existing depreciation area in your new chart of deprecation. Through various configuration steps, you shall define the characteristics of the depreciation areas in this step.

Let us, first, start with the definition of depreciation areas.

9.1.1 Define Depreciation Areas

We have already created the required depreciation areas, vide Chapter 6.2. Since we have used a country-specific chart of depreciation (0US and 0IN) to create the new chart of depreciation (BEUS and BEIN respectively), we have already defined the various depreciation areas for (a) valuation according to local laws, (b) tax depreciation, (c) cost-accounting, depreciation, (d) special reserves and (e) investment support.

When you need parallel valuation, you can define real depreciation areas and derived depreciation areas. The values in the *'derived depreciation areas'* are calculated from the values of two or more real depreciation areas, using a formula that you define. For a derived depreciation area, the system does not store the derived values permanently, but determines the same, dynamically, during a request. The derived depreciation areas cannot manage any parallel currencies and as such are not allowed to have any parallel currency areas. While denoting a derived depreciation area, ensure that the key of the derived depreciation area (say, 50) is higher than the keys of the depreciation area (say, 01 & 20) from it is derived.

You can use derived depreciation areas for (a) reserve for special depreciation or (b) reporting purposes:

- In the case of 'reserve for special depreciation', you can use the same functions for derived depreciation areas as that of the real depreciation areas. Hence, these derived depreciation areas can be evaluated in the same way, as that of the real depreciation area, and posted to a ledger in the G/L.
- In the case of 'derived depreciation areas for reporting', you cannot post to them.

Project Dolphin

The BESTM management, after a detailed discussion with the implementation team, has decided not to create any new depreciation areas other than the ones that were copied from the country-specific chart of depreciation. It was also decided that all the company codes will use the book depreciation area (1) for updating the quantity information of LVAs.

To create any new depreciation area, or change an existing one, use the menu path: SAP Customizing Implementation Guide > Financial Accounting > Asset Accounting > General Valuation > Depreciation Areas > Define Depreciation Areas.

i.   Set the 'Chart of Depreciation' on entering the Transaction (BEUS). To change chart of depreciation, use IMG activity 'Set Chart of Depreciation' or Transaction OAPL.

ii.   On the resulting 'Select Activity' pop-up screen, double-click on, 'Define Depreciation Areas'. On the next screen (use Transaction OADB to reach this screen directly), you will see the list of depreciation areas that have already been copied. You can copy and create a new depreciation area, or you can change the parameters that you have already defined for a depreciation area.

iii. Go back to the 'Select Activity' pop-up screen, and double-click on 'Specify Area Type'. On the resulting screen (you may also reach this screen directly by using Transaction OADC), per depreciation area, enter the type of depreciation area ('Typ'). You will assign the 'Typ' according to the primary purpose of a depreciation area (Figure 9.1): for example, area 01 (or 1) will be of type 01 - B/S valuation, area 20 will be of type 07 – cost accounting valuation etc. If you use SAP IM, then, the type 07 has a special significance, as you are not allowed to settle differences, due to capitalization as non-operating expense, in this depreciation area. This to ensure that all non-capitalized debits in a capital investment measure are recognized in cost accounting.

Change View ""Actual depreciation areas: area type"": Overview

Chart of dep.   BEUS   Chart of Depreciation USA (BESTM)

Ar.	Name of Depreciation Area	Typ	Description
01	Book Depreciation	01	Valuation for trade bal. sheet
10	Federal Tax ACR / MACRS	10	US: Federal tax ACRS / MACRS
11	Alternative Minimum Tax	12	US: ALTMIN - Alternative minimum tax
12	Adjusted Current Earnings	13	US: ACE - Adjusted Current Earnings
20	Cost Accounting Depreciation	07	Cost-acc. valuation

Figure 9.1: Assigning 'Depreciation Area Type' to Depreciation Areas

With this let us understand how to implement depreciation areas, subsequently.

9.1.1.1.   Subsequent Implementation of a Depreciation Area

Recommended that you define all the required depreciation areas before you 'go-live'. However, you can implement new depreciation areas (for example, to create a new depreciation area for insurable values) in an existing valuation, later, even after the 'go-live'.

Use the menu path: SAP Customizing Implementation Guide > Financial Accounting > Asset Accounting > General Valuation > Depreciation Areas > Subsequent Implementation of a Depreciation Area > Implement Depreciation Area Subsequently or Transaction FAA_AREA_COPY.

The system uses the program RAFAB_COPY_AREA to implement the new depreciation areas and the related settings. This program uses the default implementation of the 'Subsequent Implementation of a Depreciation Area' BAdI (FAA_AA_COPY_AREA). In case you need to have customized influence on source depreciation area, depreciation terms, and the transaction data, then, you need to implement your own BAdI.

With the subsequent implementation of depreciation areas, you can:

- Add a newly created depreciation area (target depreciation area) to the existing asset master records.
- Copy the depreciation terms from the source to the target depreciation area.
- Copy, by default, the balance c/f values and the transaction data of the current fiscal year from the source to the target depreciation area.

> **i** With subsequent implementation of depreciation area(s), note that the system does not copy (a) the depreciation postings of the current fiscal year, and also (b) the data from the previous fiscal years.

Now that we have understood about subsequent implementation of new depreciations areas, let us discuss about the subsequent deletion of depreciation areas.

9.1.1.2.   Subsequent Deletion of a Depreciation Area

SAP allows you to delete the depreciation areas that you do not need, at a later point of time. When you delete the depreciation area, the system deletes the depreciation area marked for deletion from (a) the chart of depreciation and (b) the depreciation data of all affected assets and asset classes, in the system.

When you want to delete a depreciation area subsequently, note that:

- You are not allowed to delete the depreciation area that posts in real time to the leading ledger group.
- You cannot delete an area if it is acting as a reference area for another area.
- You cannot use the area that is to be deleted, in the calculation formula for a derived depreciation area. If you use that area in the calculation formula for a derived area, but still want to delete the area, then, you have to change the calculation formula of the derived depreciation area.
- The area, to be deleted, should not have been defined for automatic posting of APC values to the G/L.
- If the depreciation area, to be deleted, is used for investment support, then, you first need to delete all investment support keys that reference this depreciation area, before deleting the area.

Use the menu path: SAP Customizing Implementation Guide > Financial Accounting > Asset Accounting > General Valuation > Depreciation Areas > Define Depreciation Areas.

i.   On the resulting pop-up screen, select 'Define Depreciation Areas' activity and click on 'Choose'.

ii.   On the next 'Change View "Depreciation Areas": Overview' screen (you can reach here directly by using Transaction OADB), select the depreciation area row that you want to delete and click on 'Delete'.

With this, let us continue with the configuration of depreciation areas. The next step is to define the depreciation area for quantity update.

9.1.2 Define Depreciation Area for Quantity Update

Required for managing LVAs on a collective basis, here, you will specify which depreciation area you want to use for updating quantities. The system updates the quantities in the asset master record only when posting is made to this specified deprecation area. As in the case of SAP's standard settings, you need to use depreciation area 1 (book depreciation) for updating the quantities.

In cases where you subsequently change the depreciation area for quantity update, the system will not update these changes in the respective master records. Accordingly, any asset sub-ledger posting that was done before the area change retains the original quantity information and the same is reflected in the asset master. When you reverse such an earlier document (with the original quantity information), after the change of the depreciation area, then, the system adjusts the quantity regardless of whether postings are made to the depreciation area that is now being used for quantity update.

Use the menu path: SAP Customizing Implementation Guide > Financial Accounting > Asset Accounting > General Valuation > Depreciation Areas > Define Depreciation Area for Quantity Update.

On the resulting screen, select the 'Update Quantity' radio-button against the 'Book Depreciation' area (1) for the chart of depreciation BESTM (Figure 9.2).

Change View "Setting Depreciation Area for Quantity Update": Overview

Chart of dep.   BEUS

Setting Depreciation Area for Quantity Update

Area	Update Quantity	Name of Depreciation Area
1	⦿	Book Depreciation

Figure 9.2: Specifying Depreciation Area for Quantity Update of LVAs

The next task is to make the settings for transferring APC values.

9.1.3 Specify Transfer of APC Values

Use this configuration step to define the transfer rules for posting the values of depreciation areas. These rules enable the system to have certain depreciation areas the identical asset values. This you will achieve, by specifying the reference depreciation area that provides values to another depreciation area. Then, the, system transfers the posting amounts of any transactions that affect APC from this area to the dependent area. You can also decide if the transfer is mandatory or optional: if optional, you will be able to manually enter the posting values, for that depreciation area, during posting.

> **i** When you want to transfer APC values from one depreciation area to another, you need to be aware of the fact that such a transfer is only possible when the 'from' depreciation area and the 'to' depreciation area have the same accounting principle.

Project Dolphin

BESTM has indicated that, when posting values are transferred from the book depreciation area (01) to other areas, all the APC-relevant values should be transferred in a manner that the user will have no option to make any change, later, during posting so as to minimise errors in the transferred values.

Use the menu path: SAP Customizing Implementation Guide > Financial Accounting > Asset Accounting > General Valuation > Depreciation Areas > Specify Transfer of APC Values. You may also use Transaction OABC.

On the resulting screen, specify the reference depreciation area (say, 01) that will provide the values to another depreciation area (say, 10,11 etc) in the field 'ValAd'. Accordingly, the system transfers the posting amounts of any transactions that affect APC from this area (01) to the dependent area (say, 10). If you want to ensure that the system transfers all APC-relevant posting values to the dependent depreciation area(s) from the transferring depreciation area without any change in value, later, during posting, then, you need to select the 'Ident.' check-box for each of these depreciation areas (Figure 9.3).

Change View "Depreciation areas: Rules for value takeover": Overview

Chart of dep.   BEUS   Chart of Depreciation USA (BESTM)

Ar.	Name of Depreciation Area	ValAd	Ident.
01	Book Depreciation	00	☐
10	Federal Tax ACR / MACRS	01	☑
11	Alternative Minimum Tax	01	☑
12	Adjusted Current Earnings	01	☑
20	Cost Accounting Depreciation	01	☑

Figure 9.3: Rules for Transferring APC Values

> **i** When a depreciation area takes over the values from another depreciation area, the taking over depreciation area (say, 12) should have the depreciation key that is higher than that of the area from which the values are being taken over (say, 01). This precisely the reason that you will never be able to transfer values for the book depreciation area (01).

The next step is to define the settings for transferring depreciation terms.

9.1.4 Specify Transfer of Depreciation Terms

You need to specify, here, how the system adopts the depreciation terms, for a depreciation area, from another depreciation area. As in the case of transfer of APC values, here also you can specify if the adoption of values is optional or mandatory. If you specify that the transfer is optional, then you can change the proposed depreciation terms in the dependent areas in the asset master record. Else, if you specify that as a mandatory transfer, then, you cannot maintain any depreciation terms in the asset master record. This is to ensure that depreciation is uniform in certain depreciation areas.

> **i** You will be able to adopt depreciation terms, from one area to another, only when the depreciation areas use the same ledger group. In the case of depreciation areas posting APC values to SAP G/L in real-time, the system will not allow to adopt depreciation terms from another depreciation area. However, the system allows adopting the depreciation terms in case of other depreciation areas that post in real time (as in the case of investment support or revaluation), as long as both areas have the same ledger group.
>
> Unlike derived depreciation area, the depreciation area (say, 11) that adopts depreciation terms from another area (say, 12) can have a smaller key.

Project Dolphin

BESTM has requested the project team to configure adoption of depreciation terms from one depreciation area to another in such a way that the adopted depreciation terms cannot be changed, manually, later in the asset master.

Use the menu path: SAP Customizing Implementation Guide > Financial Accounting > Asset Accounting > General Valuation > Depreciation Areas > Specify Transfer of Depreciation Terms. You may also use Transaction OABD.

    i.   On the resulting screen, per depreciation area, enter the area from where the depreciation terms will be transferred (Figure 9.4).

    ii.   Select 'Identical' check-box, so that the depreciation terms of the selected depreciation area are always identical to that of the referenced area. When selected, the system transfers all changes in the reference depreciation area to the dependent depreciation areas, and it will not possible to change them in the master records, later. When you do not select the 'Identical' check-box, you can change the depreciation terms, in the dependent depreciation areas, in the asset master records.

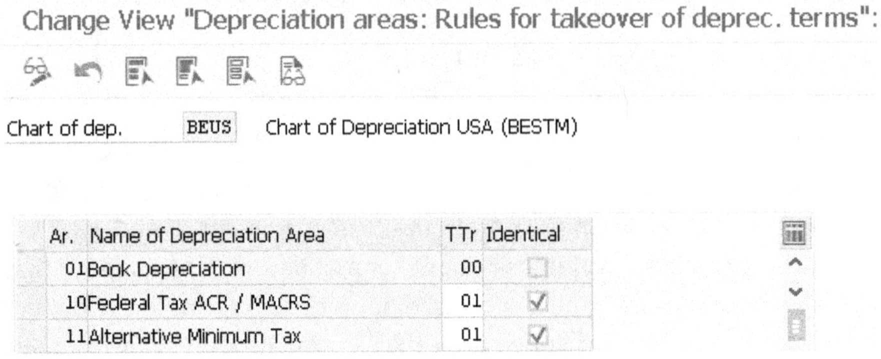

Change View "Depreciation areas: Rules for takeover of deprec. terms":

Chart of dep.   BEUS   Chart of Depreciation USA (BESTM)

Ar.	Name of Depreciation Area	TTr	Identical
01	Book Depreciation	00	☐
10	Federal Tax ACR / MACRS	01	✓
11	Alternative Minimum Tax	01	✓

Figure 9.4: Rules for Adoption of Depreciation Terms

Let us move on to discuss the depreciation area settings in the asset classes.

9.1.5 Determine Depreciation Areas in the Asset Class

Normally, all the assets in an asset class will use the same depreciation terms (depreciation key, useful life, etc). Hence, once maintained at the level of the asset class, you do not need to maintain them in the asset master record as they are offered as the default values from the respective asset classes. Using this configuration activity, you can determine the depreciation terms that are to be used in your asset classes.

---

i If you make changes to the asset class, they only affect the assets that are created after the change. For all the assets that are already existing in the system, and are affected by the changes made at the asset class level, use mass change procedures. As far as the changes made to the depreciation terms, note that the system automatically re-calculates depreciation for the assets affected.

Project Dolphin

BESTM management decided to have a uniform economic life policy for the asset classes across company codes, both in US and India. Accordingly, for example, the useful life of vehicles has been set at 10 years, computer hardware at 5 years, computer software at 2 years, furniture & fittings at 5 years, office equipments at 5 years and so on.

Use the menu path: SAP Customizing Implementation Guide > Financial Accounting > Asset Accounting > General Valuation > Determine Depreciation Areas in the Asset Class. You may also use Transaction OAYZ.

i.   On the resulting screen, select or highlight the appropriate 'Asset Class' (say, B3000 – Vehicles) and double-click on 'Depreciation areas' folder on the left-hand side 'Dialog Structure'. The system takes you to the 'Change View "Depreciation areas": Overview' screen (Figure 9.5).

Figure 9.5: Depreciation Area Settings per Asset Class

ii.   You will notice that the system has copied the standard settings from the reference chart of depreciation. You may change the values, if required by double-clicking on a depreciation area ('Ar.).

iii.   On the resulting screen (Figure 9.6):

- Enter the appropriate 'Screen Layout'. You shall enter 2000 for depreciating the asset at the subnumber level.
- Select 'Negative Val.Allowed' check-box, if you want negative APC and positive depreciation to be allowed for assets like, investment support, AuC (if you need to post a subsequent credit memo after the AuC has been completely settled) etc.
- Select the appropriate value for 'LVA check': select 'No maximum amount check' for all the assets other than LVA. In case of LVAs, you can select 'Value based maximum amount check' when you manage those assets on 'individual management' (that, is each LVA has it is own asset mater record); else, select 'Check maximum amount with quantity' when you manage them 'collectively' in a single asset master record.

Figure 9.6: Depreciation Area Settings in an Asset Class - Detail

> **ℹ** In the case of *'individual maintenance'*, for each acquisition posting, the system checks whether or not the value for the asset exceeds the 'LVA maximum amount' defined for the company code/depreciation area. If yes, the system will not allow the posting.
>
> In the case of *'collective management'*, for every acquisition posting, the system checks whether or not the 'asset value' divided by the 'quantity managed' on the master record exceeds the 'LVA maximum amount' defined for the company code/depreciation area. If yes, the system will not allow you to post.

- You may enter the 'Minimum Life' and 'Maximum Useful Life'. If the life of the asset is in fraction, then enter the fraction (say, 0.5 years) as a period (say, 6) in 'Min. Life Period' / 'Max. Life Period'.
- Select the appropriate depreciation key ('Dep. key'). The 'depreciation key' consisting of (a) the calculation method for the automatic calculation of interest, ordinary and special depreciation, (b) a possible a cutoff value key and (c) various

control parameters, controls the asset valuation in the particular depreciation areas (we shall discuss depreciation key, in detail, in Chapter 10.5.1). The key SLM1, for example, denotes 'Straight Line Method' of depreciation. You will enter the key 0000 for 'no depreciation no interest'.

- Enter the 'Useful Life', in whole number of years, over which the asset needs to be depreciated. If you do not enter the useful life in the asset class, but use depreciation keys that calculate depreciation automatically, the system marks this field is as a 'required entry' field irrespective of other settings in the screen layout control.

> **i** The asset class usually provides a default useful life when you create the asset master record. However, if the system cannot determine useful life for the asset, and if you are using a depreciation method that always operates independently of the useful life, you can enter a very long useful life: say, 100 years!

- If the 'Useful Life' of an asset includes a part of a year in addition to whole years, then, you need to enter the additional time in the form of period in the 'Periods' field, besides entering the whole years in the 'Useful Life' field. You can enter 000 to 365 for 'Periods' field.

> **i** Consider that an asset's useful life is 5.5 years. Now, you need to enter the whole years (5) in the 'Useful Life' field, and 6 in the field 'Periods'; the 6 entered in 'Periods' field represents 6 periods that is nothing but 0.5 years.

- Select 'Area Deact.' check-box, if you want the depreciation area(s) to be inactive in this asset class or asset (although it appears in the chart of depreciation).
- 'Save' the settings and repeat the steps for other depreciation areas for the selected asset class.

iv. Go back to the initial screen and select the other asset classes, and complete the settings, as described above, for all the asset classes and for all the depreciation areas.

The next step is to lock an asset class for asset creation.

9.1.6 Deactivate Asset Class for Chart of Depreciation

It is possible that you can lock asset classes, for entire charts of depreciation, so as prevent someone from using that asset classes inadvertently, in the given chart of depreciation, for creating the fixed assets.

Use the menu path: SAP Customizing Implementation Guide > Financial Accounting > Asset Accounting > General Valuation > Deactivate Asset Class for Chart of Depreciation. You may also use Transaction AM05.

On the resulting screen (Figure 9.7), select the 'Lock' check-box for the required asset classes. When selected, the system prevents creation of new assets in that asset class, specific to the given chart of depreciation. We are not locking any of the asset classes, for BESTM.

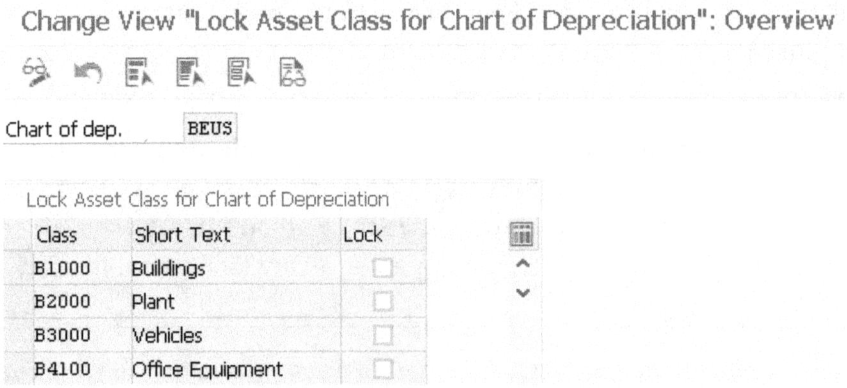

Change View "Lock Asset Class for Chart of Depreciation": Overview

Chart of dep.   BEUS

Lock Asset Class for Chart of Depreciation

Class	Short Text	Lock
B1000	Buildings	☐
B2000	Plant	☐
B3000	Vehicles	☐
B4100	Office Equipment	☐

Figure 9.7: Locking an Asset Class in a Chart of Depreciation

> **i** Even if you lock an asset class in one depreciation, you can still use the same asset class in other charts of depreciation.

This completes our discussion on the configuration settings that you need to make for depreciation areas, as a part of general valuation settings. With this, we are, now, ready to move on to the next topic: configuring the amount specifications.

9.2 Amount Specifications (Company Code/Depreciation Area)

In this Section, let us discuss about some of the settings like, (a) rules for rounding off, (b) memo value and (d) changeover amount, that you need to make, for the calculation of depreciation and/or net book value (NBV) per company code/depreciation area.

Let us start with the specification of maximum amount for LVAs.

9.2.1 Specify Max. Amount for Low-Value Assets + Asset Classes

Use this step, to determine the maximum amount for LVAs (Low-Value Assets) for each company code/depreciation area. Once configured, the system checks this maximum amount limit, during every acquisition posting, provided that you have set the indicator for LVA in the corresponding asset class(es) We have already defined (in Chapter 7.4.4) two asset classes for

LAVs for BESTM: one for collective management (B7000) and the other for individual management (B7100).

Project Dolphin

As configured in the country-specific parameters, for all BESTM company codes in USA, the LVA cut-off amount will be $5,000, and INR 5,000 for India-based company codes. The project team has been asked to configure for both individual and collective management of LVAs using the respective asset classes and account determinations.

Use the menu path: SAP Customizing Implementation Guide > Financial Accounting > Asset Accounting > General Valuation > Amount Specifications (Company Code/Depreciation Area) > Specify Max. Amount for Low-Value Assets + Asset Classes.

    i.   On the resulting pop-up (Figure 9.8), double-click on 'Specify LVA asset classes':

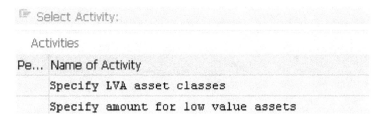

Figure 9.8: Initial Pop-Up Screen for LVA Maintenance Settings

- On the next screen (you may use Transaction OAY2 to reach this screen directly), highlight the appropriate LVA asset class (say, B7000) and double-click on 'Low-val. asset check' on the left-hand side 'Dialog Structure'.
- On the 'Change View "Low-val. asset check": Overview' screen (Figure 9.9), enter the suitable option under 'LVA', for each of the depreciation areas. We have entered the option 2 (Check maximum amount with quantity) as the asset class B7000 is for collective management of LVAs; other options are: 0 – No maximum amount check and 1- value based maximum amount check.

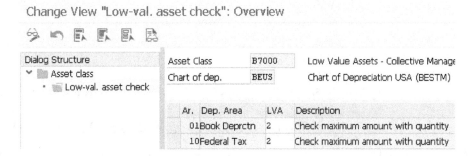

Figure 9.9: LVA Maintenance Settings

- Go back to the initial screen, and now select the other LVA asset class B7100. Repeat the steps, and assign the value 1 in the 'LVA' field for this asset class, as this is for individual management of LVAs.

ii.   Now, go back to the initial pop-up screen, and double-click on 'Specify amount for low value assets':

- On the resulting screen (use Transaction OAYK to reach this screen directly), select the company code (say, 1110) and double-click on 'Amount for low-value assets' on the left-hand side 'Dialog Structure'.

- On the next screen, you will notice that the system has already populated the amounts (Figure 9.10) based on the country-specific settings that we made earlier in Chapter 6.1.

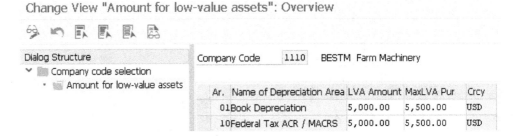

Figure 9.10: Amount Limit for LVAs

- The value in the 'LVA Amount' field, denotes the maximum amount for checking posting to low value assets. When set, this applies to all postings that would cause the acquisition value of the asset not to exceed the specified maximum amount. In the case of collectively managed LVAs, this amount is the acquisition amount divided by the quantity.

- The value in the 'MaxLVA Pur.' Field, specifies the maximum amount for checking purchase orders (PO) for assets. When set, the system applies this maximum limit when you create POs for assets in the SAP MM component. The system prevents the creation of a PO if the acquisition value of the asset exceeds this limit. Again, if you manage LVAs managed collectively, then, this is the acquisition value divided by the quantity.

- Repeat the settings for all the deprecation areas, and for all the company codes, and 'Save' the details.

The next activity is to specify the rounding off rules, per company code / depreciation area.

9.2.2   Specify Rounding of Net Book Value and/or Depreciation

You may define here, the rounding off specifications for (a) year-end net book value (NBV) and (b) for the automatically determined depreciation, per company code and per depreciation area. The system will round off only the decimal places. In the standard system, the NBV is rounded off to the whole currency unit.

Project Dolphin

BESTM wants to round off, using arithmetic rounding method, the year-end net book value, and also the automatically calculated replacement value of assets.

Use the menu path: SAP Customizing Implementation Guide > Financial Accounting > Asset Accounting > General Valuation > Amount Specifications (Company Code/Depreciation Area) > Specify Rounding of Net Book Value and/or Depreciation, or Transaction OAYO:

i. On the resulting screen, select the company code (say,1110) and double-click on 'Rounding specifications' on the left-hand side 'Dialog Structure'.

ii. On the next screen, you will notice that the system has brought up all the depreciation areas defined for the company code. Double-click on the appropriate area, (say, 01) and maintain the settings on the 'Change View: "Rounding specifications: Detail' screen (Figure 9.11):

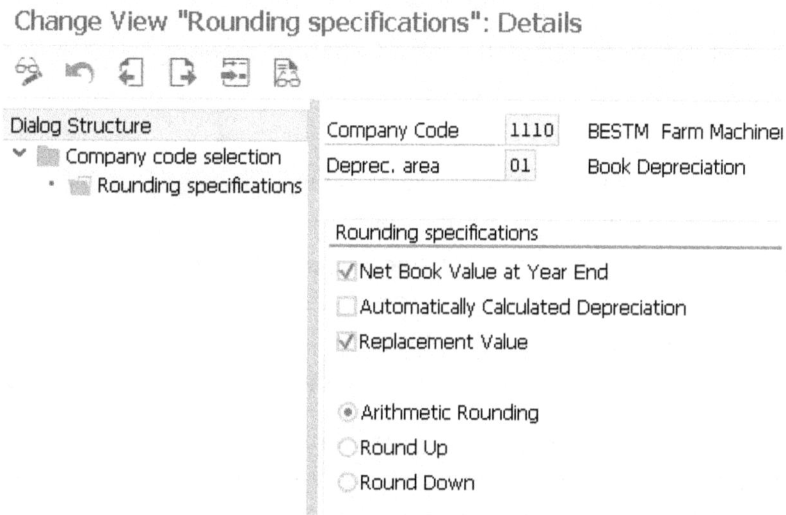

Figure 9.11: Rounding Off Specifications

* Select all the appropriate check-boxes under 'Rounding specifications' block:
  a. Select 'Net Book Value at Year End' check-box, to specify that the net book value of an asset should be rounded off to whole units of currency at the end of the fiscal year.
  b. By selecting 'Automatically Calculated Depreciation' check-box, you specify that the automatically calculated depreciation (ordinary / special depreciation) should be rounded to whole units of currency.

        c. Select the 'Replacement Value' check-box, to specify if you want to round the decimals in the replacement value that you calculate using an index series.

- Select the appropriate rounding off method:
      a. The 'Arithmetic Rounding' specifies that the rounding off should take place according to the rule that tenths up to and including 4 are rounded downward to the next whole number, starting with 5 they are rounded upward to the next whole number. For example, 7.07 or 7.49 is rounded off to 7, and 7.50 or 7.87 is rounded off to 8
      b. With the 'Round Up', you indicate that the system always rounds off to the next highest whole number: for example, 7.07 or 7.47 or 7.88 is rounded off to 8.
      c. The 'Round Down', when selected, indicates that you want to round off to the next lowest whole number: for example, 7.07 or 7.47 or 7.88 is rounded off to 7.

iii.   'Save' and make similar settings for all the depreciation areas of the selected company code and repeat for all the company codes.

The next activity to configure is, specifying the changeover amount.

9.2.3 Specify Changeover Amount

Here, you specify the amount (per depreciation area) at which the system will change the depreciation calculation to the 'changeover key' specified in the depreciation key. The changeover takes place as soon as the net book value (NBV) of the asset goes below the changeover amount. This will work only when you use a depreciation key defined with changeover method 3 ('Changeover when NBV is less than the changeover amount'). In all other changeover methods, the system will not recognize this changeover amount.

Use the menu path: SAP Customizing Implementation Guide > Financial Accounting > Asset Accounting > General Valuation > Amount Specifications (Company Code/Depreciation Area) > Specify Changeover Amount, or Transaction OAYJ.

On the resulting screen, select the appropriate company code, double-click on 'Changeover amount' on the left-hand side 'Dialog Structure' and enter the amount in 'Chnge.NBV' field for all the required depreciation areas.

The last and final configuration step, under amount specifications, is to make the required settings for taking care of memo value.

9.2.4 Specify Memo Value

The 'memo value' function has been provided in FI-AA, by SAP, to allow for managing memo values from a previous system. When you specify a memo value, it is mandatory that all of the affected assets have a book value at least equal to the memo value at all times, even when the planned expected useful life has already been exceeded. It is not normally required to manage memo values. When you do not maintain a memo value, the system always depreciates the assets till the net book value becomes zero.

---

i The *memo value* is the residual book value of an asset that appears in the in your balance sheet. When you maintain a memo value, per depreciation area/company code, for an asset, the system does not depreciate any further when the net book value of the asset becomes equal to the memo value. In general, you do not need to manage memo values in FI-AA, as the system always records the gross values: both the acquisition value and accumulated depreciation of assets. By this, the system ensures that even the fully-depreciated fixed assets appear in all legal reports, even when they have a net book value = 0.

It may, sometimes, be necessary that you want to depreciate assets not to their zero book value, but only up to a specified *scrap value* or *cutoff value*. The system does not depreciate the asset, as soon as this value is reached. You can set up the (time-dependent) scrap value for assets, in two ways: (a) by assigning a *cutoff value key* to the depreciation key used in the depreciation area or (b) by entering an absolute scrap value or a percentage of APC in the asset master data for the depreciation area; when you maintain both an absolute scrap value and a percentage scrap value, the system uses the percentage value. Refer Chapter 10.5.1.4, for understanding how to configure the scrap value / cutoff value.

If you maintain both scrap value and cutoff value key for an asset, at the same time, then, the system accords priority to the scrap value even if the cutoff value (determined from the cutoff value key) is smaller than the scrap value. Accordingly, the system will stop depreciation when the book value of the asset reaches the scrap value.

If all the three values (memo value, scrap value and cutoff value) exist for an asset, then, (a) when the memo value is the smallest amount, it becomes the residual value of the asset, or (b) when the memo value is not the smallest of all the three amounts, then, the system will consider the biggest amount, of all three, and make that as the residual value for the asset.

Project Dolphin

BESTM has indicated that they want to depreciate, all the fixed assets, until the book values become zero. Accordingly, the project team has decided not to use the 'memo value' functionality in the system.

Use the menu path: SAP Customizing Implementation Guide > Financial Accounting > Asset Accounting > General Valuation > Amount Specifications (Company Code/Depreciation Area) > Specify Memo Value.

i.   On the resulting pop-up screen (Figure 9.12), double-click on 'Specify Asset Classes without Memo Value' activity

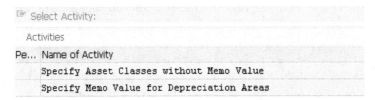

Figure 9.12: Initial Pop-Up Screen for Memo Value Configuration

ii.   On the next screen (you may reach here directly using Transaction OAAW), select the 'Do not take memo value into account' check-box for all the asset classes for which you do not want the memo value functionality. We have selected this check-box for all the asset classes of BESTM (Figure 9.13).

Change View "Asset class: Ignore memo value": Overview

Class	Name of asset class	Do not take memo value into account
B1000	Buildings	☑
B2000	Plant & Machinery	☑
B3000	Vehicles	☑
B4100	Office Equipment	☑
B4200	Furniture & Fixtures	☑

Figure 9.13: Memo Value Configuration for BESTM

iii.   However, should you want to configure memo value, then you do not need to carry out the above step (ii). Instead, you need to double-click on the 'Specify Memo Value for Depreciation Areas' activity on the initial pop-up screen (Figure 9.12), and select the appropriate company code on the next screen (use Transaction OAYI to reach here directly). Then, double-click on 'Memo value' on the left hand-side 'Dialog Structure'. Now, enter the amount in the 'Memo value' field, per depreciation area on the next screen.

With this, we have completed all the configuration steps that are required for configuring the amount specifications. We are, now, ready to discuss the settings required for fiscal year specifications for general valuation in FI-AA.

9.3 Fiscal Year Specifications

FI-AA, generally, uses the same fiscal year variant (FYV) as that of SAP FI (G/L). Accordingly, the depreciation periods of FI-AA correspond to the posting periods in FI, but without considering the special periods. The system, therefore, automatically defaults the FYV of the G/L when you define the FI-AA system settings for a company code. You do not need to make any additional system settings if your depreciation periods and G/L posting periods are identical.

Project Dolphin

BESTM company codes will use the same FYV that has been defined in SAP FI (G/L) in FI-AA as well. However, the project team has been asked to configure use of half months to take care of mid-month acquisition / depreciation of assets for all the US-based company codes.

However, you may come across situations in which the G/L posting periods are not suitable for determining depreciation in FI-AA. In those cases, you need FI-AA-specific fiscal year variants. You can use FI-AA specific FYV (provided you have already defined them in SAP FI G/L Customizing), at company code level or below the company code level:

   i.   *At the company code level* (use menu path: SAP Customizing Implementation Guide > Financial Accounting > Asset Accounting > General Valuation > Fiscal Year Specifications > Fiscal Year Variants > Specify Other Variants on Company Code Level.
   ii. *Below the company code level* and for each of the depreciation areas:
    - You first need to specify in the company code(s) that you will be going in for a differing FYV by using the menu path: SAP Customizing Implementation Guide > Financial Accounting > Asset Accounting > General Valuation > Fiscal Year Specifications > Fiscal Year Variants > Allow Differing Variants for Depreciation Areas with G/L Integration.
    - Later, you need to specify the FYV for each of the depreciation areas by using the menu path: SAP Customizing Implementation Guide > Financial Accounting > Asset Accounting > General Valuation > Fiscal Year Specifications > Fiscal Year Variants > Specify Other Variants on Depreciation Area Level.

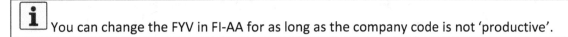 You can change the FYV in FI-AA for as long as the company code is not 'productive'.

With this, let us understand how to configure the system to consider mid-month or mid-quarter acquisition of fixed assets.

9.3.1   Use of Half Months in the Company Code

'Half-periods' or 'half-months' are necessary to represent the 'mid-quarter/month rule'. Used widely in the USA, it helps in determination of depreciation when an acquisition takes place in the first or the second half of a period.

Here, you determine the company codes for which you want to use half periods, so as to calculate depreciation on the basis of half months or half periods. Using this method, you can work with 24 periods in FI-AA, even if the FYV in SAP FI has only 12 normal periods, without resorting to defining a different fiscal year version in FI-AA.

> **i** To use half-periods in asset accounting, ensure that the number of posting periods in the fiscal year variant used correspond to the number of calendar months (12). You cannot use half-periods with non-calendar fiscal months. Once specified, you cannot take back the use of half-periods as the system notes the same internally in the asset master records

Use the menu path: SAP Customizing Implementation Guide > Financial Accounting > Asset Accounting > General Valuation > Fiscal Year Specifications > Use of Half Months in the Company Code. On the resulting screen, enter 15 in 'MidMon' field to specify the middle of month for all the required company codes, and 'Save' the details (Figure 9.14).

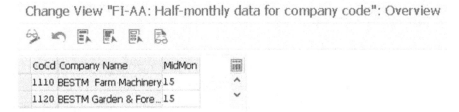

Figure 9.14: Configuring Half Months for US-based Company Codes of BESTM

This completes our discussion on the settings required for fiscal year specification in FI-AA. We shall now discuss the settings required for managing fixed assets in foreign currencies.

9.4   Currencies

You need to make appropriate settings in the system that will allow (a) valuation of fixed assets in FI-AA, in separate depreciation areas with foreign currencies and (b) management of parallel currencies at the G/L level, from the point of asset view point. Essentially, you will define depreciation areas for foreign currencies besides specifying the use of parallel currencies.

Let us start with the depreciation areas for foreign currencies.

9.4.1 Define Depreciation Areas for Foreign Currencies

SAP allows you to manage depreciation areas in various currencies. You can, then, use the values, from these depreciation areas, for group consolidation / analysis. Here, in this activity, you define depreciation areas that manage asset values in a foreign currency, per company code. When in place, during acquisitions, the system makes the foreign currency translation, at the exchange rate prevailing on the posting date. The system calculates the depreciation and proportional value adjustments, for asset retirements, directly in the foreign currency.

When you manage depreciation areas in the currency of the corporate group for legal consolidation, we recommend you to set up separate depreciation areas in the group currency for the historical management of values. This is particularly required, when the valuation of assets at the group level is different from the local valuation.

Project Dolphin

Managing depreciation areas in the currency of corporate group, for legal consolidation, is a requirement for all the India-based company codes of BESTM as the local valuation will be in INR but the group consolidation in USD. Accordingly, suitable depreciation areas need to be defined for the chart of depreciation BEIN which will be used by the India-based company codes1210 and 1220.

Use the menu path: SAP Customizing Implementation Guide > Financial Accounting > Asset Accounting > General Valuation > Currencies > Define Depreciation Areas for Foreign Currencies, or Transaction OAYH.

On the resulting screen, select the appropriate company code (say, 1210) and double-click on 'Depreciation area currency' on the left-hand side 'Dialog Structure'. On the next screen (Figure 9.15), you need to enter the foreign currency (USD) for the required depreciation areas (say, 33).

Figure 9.15: Foreign Currency Specification for Depreciation Area

The next step is to specify the parallel currencies.

9.4.2 Specify the Use of Parallel Currencies

For the legal consolidation of your fixed assets, you need only foreign currency amounts, but not a different basis for valuation (APC/depreciation terms) than the one used in the local currency. That being the case, you can use the functions of SAP FI wherein you can manage all values of a company code in parallel on the same accounts in several currencies. As you can define three local currencies, for each combination of company code and ledger in FI, even the values that are posted within FI-AA, are updated in several currencies along with the local currency in FI.

To ensure that the currency type and currency of the depreciation area are identical to those of the corresponding parallel currency in the company code in question, and that the depreciation area manages depreciation terms and acquisition values that are identical with those of the reference area, use the menu path: SAP Customizing Implementation Guide > Financial Accounting > Asset Accounting > General Valuation > Currencies > Specify the Use of Parallel Currencies. On the resulting screen, select the appropriate 'Currency Type' against the appropriate depreciations area: for example, 30 for area 33. (Figure 9.16).

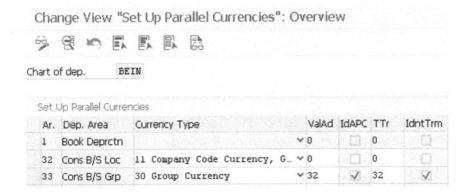

Figure 9.16: Setting up of Parallel Currency for Depreciation Area

This completes our discussion of currency settings required for general valuation. Let us, now, move on to discuss the settings relating to group assets.

9.5 Group Assets

The system, generally, calculates depreciation at the level of individual assets. However, you can calculate depreciation at a higher level (at the level of group asset) to meet certain tax requirements (as in the case of USA). To make the necessary system settings for group assets, you need to specify depreciation area(s) for group assets besides specifying the asset classes for group assets.

Let us start with the specification of depreciation areas for group assets.

9.5.1   Specify Depreciation Areas for Group Assets

If required, you can specify which are the depreciation that you also want to manage at the group asset level. Then, in these depreciation areas, you can make an assignment to a group asset in the respective asset master record. Later, when you post an acquisition to this kind of asset, the system duplicates the line items from this depreciation area on the given group asset.

Project Dolphin

To meet some of the tax requirements in USA, BESTM has requested to specify the appropriate depreciation areas for managing the group assets as well. However, it has been indicated that there is no need for creating exclusive asset classes for group assets, instead any of the defined asset classes can be used to create a group asset as well.

Use the menu path: SAP Customizing Implementation Guide > Financial Accounting > Asset Accounting > General Valuation > Group Assets > Specify Depreciation Areas for Group Assets, or Transaction OAYM:

    i.   On the resulting screen, select the company code, double-click on 'Group assets' on the left-hand side 'Dialog Structure', and select the 'Grp. asset' check-box against the required depreciation areas (Figure 9.17).

    ii.   Repeat the settings for other company codes as well.

We have configured this for all the US-based company codes of BESTM.

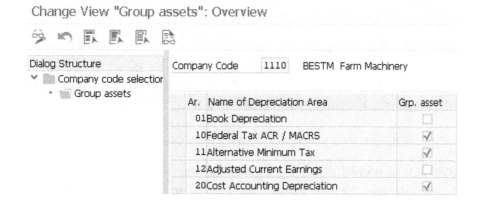

Figure 9.17: Depreciation Areas for Group Assets

The next step is specifying the asset classes, exclusively for group assets.

9.5.2 Specify Asset Classes for Group Assets

Though it is generally possible to use all asset classes for creating group assets, you can set aside particular asset classes for use in conjunction with group assets. These asset classes are then reserved solely for group assets, and are not allowed to be used for normal assets. It is not mandatory to specify asset classes exclusively for group assets.

Use the menu path: SAP Customizing Implementation Guide > Financial Accounting > Asset Accounting > General Valuation > Group Assets > Specify Asset Classes for Group Assets, or Transaction OAAX.

On the resulting screen, to designate an asset class exclusively for group assets, select the 'Class consists entirely of group assets' check-box against those asset classes (Figure 9.18). BESTM does not want any exclusive asset class for group assets.

Change View "Asset class: Indicator for group assets only": Overview

Class	Name of asset class	Class consists entirely of group assets
B1000	Buildings	☐
B2000	Plant & Machinery	☐
B3000	Vehicles	☐
B4100	Office Equipment	☐

Figure 9.18: Specifying Asset Classes Exclusively for Group Assets

This completes our discussion on the settings required for group assets, and this also completes our discussion on the configuration settings for general valuation.

9.6 Conclusion

You learned that, using the basic functions in FI-AA, you can determine the values of all fixed assets to meet the statutory and legal requirements of the country and also your own business needs. You learned that such a valuation provides not only with the current value of an asset, but also helps in timing your asset replacement, asset retirement etc.

You knew that when you create a chart of depreciation, from a reference chart of depreciation, the system copies all the depreciation areas from the reference to the new chart, and that you can also create new depreciation areas, by copying an existing depreciation area in your new chart of deprecation. Though it is recommended that you define all the required depreciation areas before you 'go-live', you learned that you can still implement new depreciation areas, later, in an existing valuation even after going live.

You learned that the values in the 'derived depreciation areas' are calculated from the values of two or more real depreciation areas, using a formula that you define. You also learned that for a derived depreciation area, the system does not store the derived values permanently, but determines the same, dynamically, during a request. You understood that the derived depreciation areas cannot manage any parallel currencies and as such are not allowed to have any parallel currency areas.

Since all the assets in an asset class will use the same depreciation terms (depreciation key, useful life, etc), you learned that you do not need to maintain them in the asset master record, as they are offered as the default values from the respective asset classes. You learned that you can lock asset classes, for entire charts of depreciation, preventing creation of new fixed assets in that asset classes. You learned that, when you specify a memo value, then, all such assets will have a book value at least equal to this memo value, even when the planned expected useful life has already been exceeded.

You understood that FI-AA uses the same FYV as that of SAP FI (G/L), with the depreciation periods (of FI-AA) corresponding to the posting periods in FI, but without the special periods. However, you learned that you can use FI-AA specific FYV, under special circumstances.

Though the system normally calculates depreciation at the level of individual assets, you learned that you can calculate the same at the level of group asset, to meet certain tax requirements. You also learned that, though it is generally possible to use all asset classes for creating group assets, you can set aside specific asset classes exclusively for group assets.

Let us move on to discuss depreciation, in the next Chapter.

10 Depreciation

The term 'depreciation' represents the decrease in value of a fixed asset (other than land), over its economic life, due to its usage including wear and tear. In accounting, this is referred to as the reduction of recorded cost of a fixed asset, in a systematic manner, until the value of that asset becomes zero or a pre-defined scrap value. By depreciating an asset, you are assigning or allocating of the cost of a fixed asset, to an expense account, in the accounting periods encompassing its useful life.

Let us start our discussion with the understanding of depreciation types, in SAP.

10.1 Depreciation Types

SAP supports two depreciation types, (a) automatically calculated depreciation (you can plan this manually as well) and (b) manually planned depreciation (Figure 10.1). The system controls the automatic calculation of depreciation through 'depreciation keys' which you can modify to define your own method of calculation, if required. SAP treats the 'interest' calculation (for cost-accounting purposes) also as a depreciation type, and controls the same by depreciation keys and calculation methods.

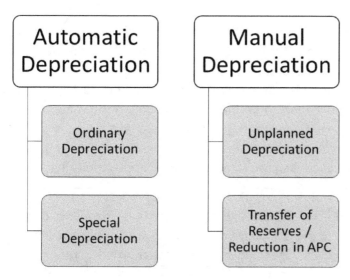

Figure 10.1: Depreciation Types

Let us understand more on the depreciation types:

- *Ordinary Depreciation*: This is the planned deduction for wear and tear during normal use of an asset.
- *Special Depreciation*: This represents the deduction for wear and tear of an asset from a purely tax-based point of view. This allows for a percentage depreciation, normally staggered within a period allowed by the tax authority, without considering the actual wear and tear on the asset.
- *Unplanned Depreciation*: While the ordinary depreciation reflects the deduction for wear and tear during the normal use of the asset, the unplanned depreciation covers the permanent decrease in an asset's value due to certain unusual / unforeseen influence or occurrence like damages to the asset because of fire, flood etc.
- *Transfer of Reserves/Reduction of APC*: By reducing the APC, you can reduce the depreciation base of an asset by a given amount. You cannot post this automatically, using depreciation keys, but only manually.
- *Interest*: It is required, for internal accounting, that you evaluate the fixed capital tied up in an asset, besides the depreciation. You do this by calculating the 'imputed interest' on the capital so tied up and the system treats this also as a depreciation type, and uses the depreciation keys / calculation methods similar to depreciation calculation.

With this, let us see how the system handles manual depreciation.

10.1.1 Manual Depreciation

The system, in general, determines the planned depreciations for the current financial year using the depreciation key entered in the master record. However, the system enables to manually change the planned depreciation for an asset: you can enter the depreciation amount, manually, for all depreciation types; but, usually, you will manually enter only the unplanned depreciation and the transfer of reserves. You will resort to such a manual intervention when (a) there is an unexpected permanent reduction in the value of an asset that needs to be posted as unplanned depreciation, or (b) you need to use the special tax depreciation only partially or (c) you need to schedule the 'unit-of-production' method of depreciation manually instead of scheduling the same using the depreciation keys.

> **i** You can post ordinary depreciation and special depreciation, manually, only if the depreciation key that you entered in the respective depreciation area uses a base method in which no automatic calculation has been specified as the depreciation calculation method.

When you undertake manual depreciation:

- You can use the standard posting transaction of FI-AA, to forecast the manual depreciation. You can also use the special transaction types that enable you to forecast depreciation for specific or all the depreciations areas.
- While posting, the transaction does not initially affect the G/L accounts in SAP FI. The system creates only asset line items, but no FI journal entries. The system updates the G/L accounts and creates the corresponding FI documents only with the periodic depreciation posting run.
- Though the system creates the journal entries, with the depreciation posting run, you can still specify an asset value date so that journal entries thus generated, in the posting period, falls within that value date.

With this, we are now ready to configure the system for various types of depreciation. Let us start with the ordinary depreciation.

10.2 Ordinary Depreciation

We already know that the ordinary depreciation is a form of planned depreciation that you will use to take care of the normal wear and of an asset during its economic life. The first task is to determine the depreciation areas for handling ordinary depreciation in the system.

10.2.1 Determine Depreciation Areas

Here, you determine the depreciation areas in which you want to manage ordinary depreciation. In the detail screen per area, you can also determine which sign (+ or -) the ordinary depreciation is allowed to have in the respective area.

Use the menu path: SAP Customizing Implementation Guide > Financial Accounting > Asset Accounting > Depreciation > Ordinary Depreciation > Determine Depreciation Areas, or Transaction OABN. On the resulting screen (Figure 10.2), select the 'Ord. depr.' check-box against the all the required depreciation areas.

Change View "Specify depreciation areas for ordinary depreciation": Ov

Depr.area	Name of Depreciation Area	Ord. depr.	
01	Book Depreciation	☑	
10	Federal Tax ACR / MACRS	☑	
11	Alternative Minimum Tax	☑	

Figure 10.2: Specifying Areas for Ordinary Depreciation

You may double-click on any of the areas, to see the detailed settings on the next screen (Figure 10.3). For normal depreciation in the book depreciation area (01), you need to select the 'Only negative values and zero allowed' radio-button under the 'Rule for pos./neg. sign for ord. depreciation' data block.

Change View "Specify depreciation areas for ordinary depreciation": De

Chart of dep.   **BEUS**   Chart of Depreciation USA (BESTM)
Depreciat. Area   01   Book Depreciation

Rule for pos./neg. sign for ord. depreciation
○ Ordinary depreciation not desired
○ Only positive values and zero allowed
● Only negative values and zero allowed
○ All values allowed

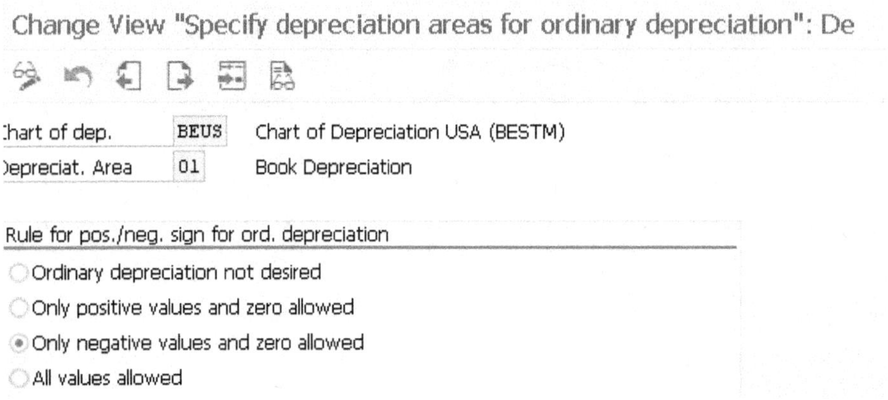

Figure 10.3: Specifying Areas for Ordinary Depreciation – Detailed Settings

The next activity is to assign the G/L accounts for ordinary depreciation

10.2.2 Assign Accounts

Use the menu path: SAP Customizing Implementation Guide > Financial Accounting > Asset Accounting > Depreciation > Ordinary Depreciation > Assign Accounts, or Transaction AO93:

i.   On the resulting screen, select the chart of accounts (BEUS, in our case) and double-click on 'Account Determination' on the left-hand side 'Dialog Structure'.

ii. On the 'Change View "Account Determination"; Overview' screen, select the required account determination (say, B1000 – Buildings), and double-click on 'Ordinary Depreciation' on the left-hand side 'Dialog Structure'.

iii. On the resulting 'Change View "Ordinary Depreciation"; Overview' screen, double-click on the row containing 1 ('Area') – 'Book Depreciation', and enter the appropriate G/L accounts on the next screen in 'Ordinary depreciation account assignment' and 'Account assignment for revaluation on depreciation' data blocks (Figure 10.4), and 'Save' the details.

iv. Complete the G/L account assignment for the rest of the account determinations, for the chart of accounts BEUS, and 'Save' when fully completed.

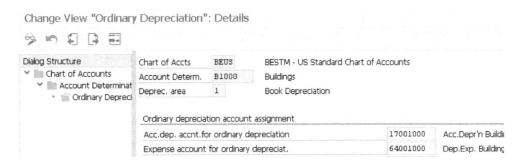

Figure 10.4: G/L Account Assignment – Ordinary Depreciation

With this, we are now ready to configure the settings for special depreciation.

10.3 Special Depreciation

In 'special depreciation', you depreciate an asset from the point of taxation (staggered within the taxation period) without considering the actual wear and tear of the asset. Here, you define the system settings for determining and posting special depreciation. The first task, as in the case of ordinary depreciation, is to determine the depreciation areas for special depreciation.

10.3.1 Determine Depreciation Areas

Using this configuration activity, you will determine the depreciation areas in which you want to manage special depreciation. This specification informs the system that this value type is allowed in that depreciation area so that there is no error message when you enter corresponding depreciation terms in the asset master record.

As in the case of ordinary depreciation areas, use the menu path: SAP Customizing Implementation Guide > Financial Accounting > Asset Accounting > Depreciation > Special Depreciation > Determine Depreciation Areas, or Transaction OABS.

On the resulting screen, select the 'Spec. depr.' check-box against all depreciation areas wherein you want to manage special depreciation. Double-click on a depreciation area, and select the appropriate radio-button ('Only negative values and zero allowed') under the 'Rule for pos./neg. sign for ord. depreciation' data block, on the next screen (Figure 10.5).

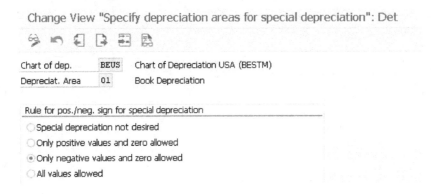

Figure 10.5: Specifying Areas for Special Depreciation – Detailed Settings

The next configuration activity is to define the settings for calculating ordinary depreciation before special depreciation.

10.3.2 Calculate Ordinary Depreciation before Special Depreciation

Though the order in which the system determines different types of depreciation is somewhat flexible, the system always determines the 'transfer of reserves' first, and the 'unplanned depreciation' at the last. However, you can decide the order in which ordinary depreciation and special depreciation should be determined. When you specify, per depreciation area, that the system should determine ordinary depreciation before special depreciation, then, the sequence of depreciation determination will be as shown in Figure 10.6.

Figure 10.6: Depreciation Sequence

i In the standard SAP system, the system calculates the ordinary depreciation before the special depreciation.

When there is a need for reduction in depreciation, then, the system determines the depreciation exactly in the reverse order, starting with 'unplanned depreciation' and finally with the 'transfer of reserves' as shown in Figure 10.7.

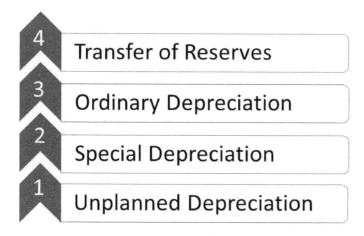

Figure 10.7: Reduction in Depreciation - Sequence

Project Dolphin

As in line with the standard settings, BESTM wants to calculate the ordinary depreciation before the special depreciation.

Use the menu path: SAP Customizing Implementation Guide > Financial Accounting > Asset Accounting > Depreciation > Special Depreciation > Calculate Ordinary Depreciation before Special Depreciation, or Transaction AOBK.

On the resulting screen, select, per depreciation area, the 'O.dep. before sp.dep.' check-box so that the system calculates ordinary depreciation first, before calculating the special depreciation (Figure 10.8).

Change View "Depreciation areas: Calculation sequence for depreciatic

Chart of dep.   BEUS   Chart of Depreciation USA (BESTM)

Ar.	Name of Depreciation Area	O.dep. before sp.dep.
01	Book Depreciation	✓
10	Federal Tax ACR / MACRS	✓
11	Alternative Minimum Tax	✓

Figure 10.8: Specifying Calculation Sequence for Ordinary Depreciation

The last configuration for special depreciation, is to assign the G/L accounts.

10.3.3 Assign Accounts

As in the case of assigning G/L accounts for ordinary depreciation, use the menu path: SAP Customizing Implementation Guide > Financial Accounting > Asset Accounting > Depreciation > Special Depreciation > Assign Accounts, or Transaction AO94, and assign the required G/L accounts for the special depreciation areas. Unlike ordinary depreciation, wherein you have to assign G/L accounts for both 'Ordinary depreciation account assignment' and 'Account assignment for revaluation on depreciation' data block, here, you will assign G/L accounts only for the 'Special depreciation account assignment' data block.

With this, let us move on to discuss the settings required for unplanned depreciation.

10.4 Unplanned Depreciation

As you are already aware, you may need to resort to 'unplanned depreciation' in certain special situations like flooding of the factory or a fire mishap making an asset unusable. You need to use the depreciation key MANU ('Manual depreciation only'), for undertaking unplanned depreciation. Besides (a) determining the depreciation areas for unplanned depreciation, and (b) assigning the appropriate G/L accounts, you also need to (c) define the required transaction types to handle unplanned depreciation.

10.4.1 Determine Depreciation Areas

The determination of depreciation areas to handle unplanned depreciation is similar to what we have already discussed for ordinary depreciation (in Section 10.2.1) and special depreciation (in Section 10.3.1). Use the menu path: SAP Customizing Implementation Guide > Financial Accounting > Asset Accounting > Depreciation > Unplanned Depreciation > Determine Depreciation Areas, or Transaction OABU, and specify the areas for unplanned depreciation by selecting the 'UDep' check-box against the required areas.

10.4.2 Assign Accounts

The other configuration activity of assigning G/L accounts, is also similar to the one that we have already discussed for ordinary and special depreciation in Section 10.2.2 and Section 10.3.3, respectively. Use the menu path: SAP Customizing Implementation Guide > Financial Accounting > Asset Accounting > Depreciation > Unplanned Depreciation > Assign Accounts, or Transaction AO95, and enter the appropriate G/L accounts per account determination for the chart of accounts BEUS.

Now, we can define the transaction types for unplanned depreciation.

10.4.3 Define Transaction Types for Unplanned Depreciation

You will use different 'transaction types' for various postings to manually correct the value of assets, in case of unplanned depreciation, other manually scheduled depreciation (ordinary or special depreciation) and write-ups. SAP provides you with the standard transaction types for all these three purposes, which you can use as such.

Project Dolphin

BESTM does not want to define any new transaction types for unplanned depreciation. Instead, they have indicated that, they want to use the SAP supplied standard ones.

Use the menu path: SAP Customizing Implementation Guide > Financial Accounting > Asset Accounting > Depreciation > Unplanned Depreciation > Define Transaction Types for Unplanned Depreciation, or Transaction AO78.

On the resulting 'Change View "FI-AA: Transaction types": Overview' screen (Figure 10.9) you will see the standard transactions defined by SAP for manual (ordinary & special) depreciation postings, unplanned depreciation postings and for posting write-ups (relating to ordinary, special and unplanned depreciation).

Change View "FI-AA: Transaction types": Overview

New Entries

Transact. type	Transaction Type Name
600	Manual ordinary depreciation on prior-yr acquis.
610	Manual ordinary depreciation on current-yr acquis.
620	Manual spec. dep. on prior-yr acquis per dep. key
630	Manual spec. dep. on curr-yr acquis per dep. key
640	Unplanned depreciation on prior-year acquisitions
650	Unplanned depreciation on current-yr acquisition
6J1	Adjust cut-off value check (Japan)
700	Write-up ordinary and special depreciation
710	Write-up ordinary book and tax depreciation
720	Write-up special tax depreciation
730	Write-up general unplanned depreciation

Figure 10.9: Standard Transaction Types

You will notice that there are three transaction types for handling unplanned depreciation postings:

- 640 - Unplanned depreciation on prior-year acquisitions
- 650 - Unplanned depreciation on current-yr acquisition
- 730 - Write-up general unplanned depreciation

You may double-click on any of the rows in Figure 10.9, to see the detailed settings for the transaction type (Figure 10.10). You will notice that the transaction type (say, 650) has been grouped under the transaction type group 65. Under 'Account assignment', you will see the settings relating to the type of transaction (credit, debit etc). In 'Other features', you will see some more characteristics that can be configured for the transaction type. You will notice that the corresponding 'Consolidation transaction type' is 925 for the transaction type 650.

If you need to create a new transaction type, we recommend you do that by copying an existing entry and making the required changes instead of creating on anew.

Change View "FI-AA: Transaction types": Details

& New Entries   ▤ ▤ ▬ ◀ ▶ ▤

| Trans. Type | 650 | Unplanned depreciation on current-yr acquisition |
| Transaction Type Grp | 65 | Unplanned dep. on curr-yr acquis. |

Account assignment

○ Debit Transaction
◉ Credit Transaction
☐ Capitalize Fixed Asset
☐ Deactivate Fixed Asset
    Document type

Other features

☐ Cannot Be Used Manually   ☐ Set changeover year
☐ Call up individual check   ☐ Trans. Type Obsolete
    Consolidation Transaction Type   925   Increase in deprecia
    Asst Hist Sheet Grp

Figure 10.10: Transaction Type 650 – Details

ℹ️ Now, in FI-AA, it is not required (and also not possible) to restrict the transaction types to depreciation areas. This has become unnecessary because, when you enter a transaction, you can restrict the same to a depreciation area or accounting principle. Besides, in a posting transaction, you can also select the depreciation areas to be posted. This approach vastly reduces the number of transaction types that you need to be define in the system. However, for some reason, if you have restricted certain transaction types to depreciation areas (by making entries in table TABWA or view cluster V_TABWA), the system rejects the same.

This completes our discussion on the settings for unplanned depreciation. Let us move on to discuss the valuation methods in the next Section.

10.5 Valuation Methods

As already indicated, you can modify the depreciation keys in the system to create your own calculation method for asset valuation as the standard methods, in the system, are not hard-coded. Based on a number of flexibly-definable calculation keys, you can easily define your own calculation methods and control parameters, to have your own specific depreciation methods in the system. Of course, you can also use the pre-defined calculation methods and parameters, that come delivered with the standard SAP system, for the most commonly used depreciation methods.

The depreciation calculation, in the system, is based on the 'valuation method' and the 'planned useful life' of the asset that you maintain in the asset master record. Pre-defined in the system, the valuation methods are based on the following variables:

- *Depreciation Key*
  The '*depreciation key*' (also known as 'valuation key') contains all the control data (or control indicators) that the system needs for calculating the planned annual depreciation. Entered in each of the depreciation areas of an asset master record, the depreciation key also contains the 'calculation method'. Refer Section 10.5.1.5 to understand how to define a depreciation key.

  - *Calculation Methods*
    The '*calculation method*' (also known as 'control functions') defined within the depreciation key, is used for the calculation of different types of automatically calculated depreciation (ordinary and special depreciation, and interest). The calculation method is very important for defining the 'depreciation calculation method'. You may refer Section 10.5.1.1, for more details on calculation methods.

    The *depreciation calculation method* is the most important characteristic of the 'base method', as it makes possible to carry out the different types of depreciation calculation in the system. Depending on how you set up the depreciation calculation method, the system determines which further 'control parameters' (or '*control indicators*') that you need to specify in the depreciation key.

    - *Base Method*
      The '*base method*' (of a calculation method) contains general control parameters that the system needs for calculating the depreciation. Refer 'Define Base Methods', for more details.

- Additional Parameters like *'cutoff value' (scrap value)*. You may refer <u>Section 10.5.1.4</u> for more details on scrap value / cutoff value.

Let us understand, in detail, about the depreciation key, next.

10.5.1 Depreciation Key

Defined at the level of the chart of depreciation, the depreciation keys are valid in all company codes. As mentioned earlier, the 'depreciation key' contains the value settings that are necessary for determining depreciation amounts (Figure 10.11).

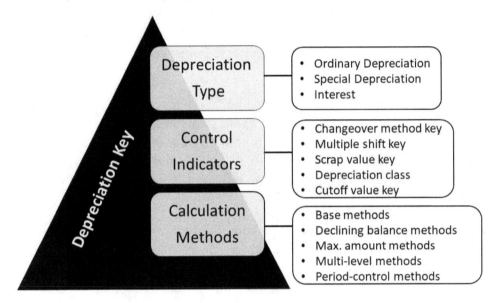

Figure 10.11: Depreciation Key

The depreciation key contains information on the depreciation types, besides a combination of calculation methods and control indicators:

- It has information as to the automatically calculated 'depreciation types' viz., the ordinary depreciation, special depreciation and imputed interest.
- It contains several 'control indicators' as indicated below, besides the ones that are shown in Figure 10.11:
    - No ordinary depreciation with special depreciation
    - No interest if no depreciation is planned
    - Period control according to fiscal years
    - Depreciation to the day
    - Depreciation calculation in shortened fiscal years
    - Number of places for rounding
    - Effect of scrap value on base value for depreciation

- The 'calculation method', in each depreciation key, determines the depreciation amounts.

With this, let us discuss the calculation methods, in detail.

10.5.1.1. Calculation Methods

The system uses 'calculation methods' (also known as, 'control functions') for the calculation of depreciation and (imputed) interest, and they provide the parameters for the 'Depreciation Calculation Program' (DCP); we shall discuss the DCP in detail, in Section 10.5.2. You will assign a calculation method to a depreciation key. Together with the control parameters of the depreciation key, and the cutoff value keys, the calculation method controls the depreciation calculation.

You will maintain the calculation methods separately, independent of the depreciation keys. In this way, you can assign the same calculation method in more than one depreciation key. These individual calculation methods, with the exception of the base method, are dependent on the chart of depreciation: you can represent your country-specific depreciation requirements by means of calculation methods that are chart-of-depreciation-specific. The system offers, for selection, only the methods that apply to your chart of depreciation. If you want a changeover to other calculation methods, during the duration of depreciation, then, you need to define that in the depreciation key.

> **i** You will not be able to alter the standard calculation methods in the SAP system. However, you can modify, any one of them, by copying and making the necessary changes on the copy which need to begin with X, Y or Z.

The following are the various depreciation calculation methods supported in the standard SAP, which can be grouped into two categories:

A. Chart-of-depreciation-independent calculation methods
- Base methods
B. Chart-of-depreciation-dependent calculation methods
- Declining-balance methods
- Maximum amount methods
- Multi-level methods
- Period control methods

> **i** When you are maintaining chart-of-depreciation-dependent calculation methods, you get a display of the existing calculation methods in accordance with the chart of depreciation that has been set.

Let us see each of the calculation methods in detail, and how to maintain the same in the system. Let us start with the base methods.

Define Base Methods

The '*base method*' contains the general control parameters that the system needs for calculating depreciation. Independent of the chart of depreciation, it does not contain any country-specific settings and hence you can use them across charts of depreciation.

For a base method, you have to specify:

i.   The depreciation type (say: ordinary, special or interest)
ii.   The depreciation calculation method (say: 0001-ordinary: sum-of-the-year-digits, 0002-no automatic depreciation, 0021-special: total percentage rate, 0029-interest: explicit percentage etc)
iii. The treatment at the end of the depreciation (for example, continuing depreciation even after the end of the planned life, curb, depreciation below zero etc)

Use the menu path: SAP Customizing Implementation Guide > Financial Accounting > Asset Accounting > Depreciation > Valuation Methods > Depreciation Key > Calculation Methods > Define Base Methods, or Transaction AFMR.

On the resulting 'Change View "Base Method": Overview' screen (Figure 10.12), you will see a listing of default base methods supplied by SAP. Should you ever need a new based method to be defined, you may use the 'New Entries' button or 'Copy in same chart of depreciation' button to create a new one.

Change View "Base Method": Overview

New entries   Usage

Base Method

Base Method	Text
0017	Ordinary: immediate deprec. (after end of life)
0018	Ordinary: Unit-of-production depreciation
0019	Ordinary: Unit-of-production (after end of life)
0020	Ordinary: declining multi-phase (Czech)
0021	Special: total percentage rate

Figure 10.12: Base Methods of Depreciation

To understand the detailed settings of a base method, you may double-click on any of the rows and see the settings on the next screen (Figure 10.13).

Change View "Base Method": Details

New entries

Base Method	0001	Ordinary: sum-of-the-years-digits

Type of Depreciation	Ord.depreciation	⌄
Dep. Method	Sum-of-the-years-digits method of depreciation	⌄
Reduce Use.Life at FY End	☐	

Treatment of end of depreciation

Dep. After Plnd.Life End	No	⌄
Dep.Below NBValue Zero	No	⌄
Curb	No	⌄

Figure 10.13: Base Method of Depreciation: 0001 – Details

With this, let us move on to discuss / maintain declining-balance methods.

Define Declining-Balance Methods

The normal 'declining-balance method' of depreciation (the other variation being 'sum-of-the-years-digits-method') multiplies the straight-line percentage rate resulting from the useful life, by a given factor. Since a relatively short useful life may result in a very large depreciation percentage rate, you can specify a maximum percentage rate as the upper ceiling limit in the declining-balance method. A similar principle applies for a very long useful life. When you enter a minimum percentage rate, the system prevents the percentage rate from sinking below a given level. In this method, you can never make the NBV equal to zero.

Use the menu path: SAP Customizing Implementation Guide > Financial Accounting > Asset Accounting > Depreciation > Valuation Methods > Depreciation Key > Calculation Methods > Define Declining-Balance Methods, or Transaction AFAMD, to view / create declining-rate depreciation methods (Figure 10.14):

- The multiplication factor ('Dec.Factor') is used in determining the depreciation percentage rate for declining-balance depreciation. The system multiplies the depreciation percentage rate resulting from the total useful life by this factor.
- The 'Max.Perc.' is the upper limit for the depreciation percentage rate. If a higher depreciation percentage rate is produced from the useful life, multiplication factor or number of units to be depreciated, then, the system uses the maximum percentage rate specified here.

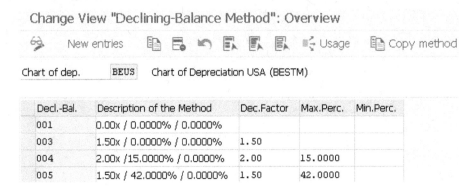

Figure 10.14: Declining-Balance Method of Depreciation

- The 'Min.Perc.' is the lower limit for the depreciation percentage rate. Similar to 'Max.Perc.', if a lower percentage rate is produced from the useful life, multiplication factor, or number of units to be depreciated, then, the system uses the minimum percentage specified here.

With this, let us move on to the maximum amount methods.

Define Maximum Amount Methods

Here, you specify the maximum amount up to which the system should calculate depreciation until a certain calendar date. During the specified time period, the system calculates depreciation only until this amount is reached. If the system arrives at a depreciation that is greater than this maximum amount, then, it reduces the depreciation appropriately so that the overall depreciation is not exceeding the maximum allowed for that time.

You can specify how the maximum amount applies within the time period specified for it. It can either apply to each individual year in the specified time period, or to the accumulated depreciation.

> **i** The *maximum amount method* does not function in the same way as a maximum 'base value' for depreciation. With the maximum base value, the system calculates depreciation based on the limited acquisition value (which may be below the actual acquisition value). But in the 'maximum amount method', it calculates the depreciation without any dependency on the acquisition value.
>
> The 'base value' for depreciation is closely linked to the depreciation calculation method that you select. Since it is not logical to use every depreciation method with every base value, the base value is often already determined by the depreciation method. SAP has already defined several base values in the system including, acquisition Value, acquisition value less unplanned depreciation, half of acquisition value, replacement value, half of replacement

value, current net book value without special depreciation, average net book value, average net book value without special depreciation, current net book value, accumulated ordinary depreciation, accumulated special depreciation, sum of accumulated ordinary and special depreciation and limited base value. You can also define your own custom base value using a customer enhancement (BAdI method FAA_EE_CUSTOMER: Set_BASE_VALUE).

Use the menu path: SAP Customizing Implementation Guide > Financial Accounting > Asset Accounting > Depreciation > Valuation Methods > Depreciation Key > Calculation Methods > Define Maximum Amount Methods, or Transaction AFAMH:

 i.   On the resulting 'Change View "Maximum Amount Method": Overview' screen, click on 'New Entries'.

 ii. On the next screen (Figure 10.15), enter the identifier for the depreciation key for the new maximum amount method in 'Max. Amt.' field, and provide a 'Description of the Method'. Use the 'Annual' check-box to specify if the maximum amount for depreciation should be based on accumulated depreciation or on annual depreciation; when selected it will be on annual depreciation.

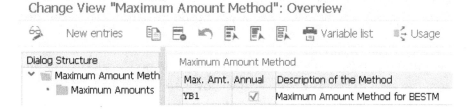

Figure 10.15: New Maximum Amount Method YB1

 iii. Now, select the row YB1 and double-click on 'Maximum Amounts' on the left-hand side 'Dialog Structure' and maintain the settings on the next screen (Figure 10.16):

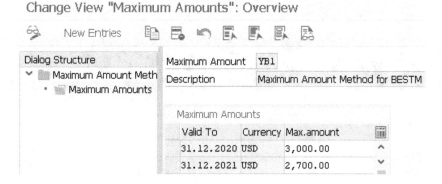

Figure 10.16: Maximum Amount Method YB1: Details

- Enter the 'Valid To' date, the 'Currency' and the 'Max.amount'. The amount in 'Max.amount' field denotes the maximum amount of depreciation allowed up to the calendar date entered in 'Valid To'. If the depreciation amount is below or equal to this maximum, then, the system posts the calculated value; else, if the system-calculated depreciation amount is above the maximum, then the system posts the fixed maximum entered in this field.

With this, let us move on to understand and maintain the next calculation method, the multi-level method.

Define Multi-Level Methods

In the base methods, for example, in 'stated percentage' method you use a total percentage, throughout the life, to depreciate the asset. But, in a multi-level method, you divide the entire life into different periods (phases) using different calculation keys. A level, in this sense, represents the period of validity of a certain percentage rate. This percentage rate is then replaced by the next percentage rate when the period's validity expires. You will determine the validity period, for the individual levels of a key, by specifying the length of time in years and months. You can specify when the defined validity period begins with the: (a) capitalization date, (b) start date for ordinary or tax depreciation, (c) original acquisition date of the AuC, or (d) the changeover year.

The defined time periods, of a key, always have a common start date. This means that the period from the start of one key to its end will overlap with the next period, which has the same start date but a longer validity period. Therefore, you have to enter the validity periods, for the levels, in cumulative form.

When you use 'Total percentage in concessionary period' as the depreciation calculation method, then, you need to enter the depreciation percentage rate in cumulative form. On the other hand, when using the 'Stated percentage method', you do need not enter the percentage rate in cumulative form (see Table 10.1).

Validity (Absolute) Period in Year	Validity (Cumulative) Period in Year	Total Percentage in Concessionary Period Method (%)	Stated Percentage Method (%)
1	1	40	40
1	2	60	20
1	3	80	20
1	4	90	10
1	5	100	10

Table 10:1 Multi-Level Depreciation Method: Periods and Percentages

Use the menu path: SAP Customizing Implementation Guide > Financial Accounting > Asset Accounting > Depreciation > Valuation Methods > Depreciation Key > Calculation Methods > Define Multi-Level Methods, or Transaction AFAMS. You will see a list of default multi-level calculation methods on the resulting screen (Figure 10.17).

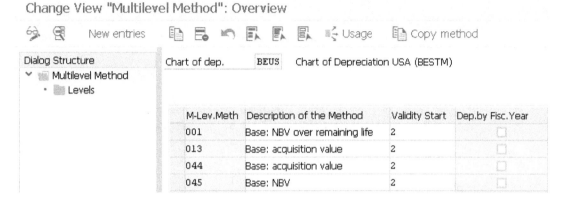

Figure 10.17: Standard Multi-Level Calculation Methods

Project Dolphin

BESTM wants to the project team to define a multi-level depreciation method, with three levels for special depreciation. The three levels will correspond to three periods being first 5 years, next 3 years and the last 2 years. The depreciation percentage for these corresponding phases will need to set at 10%, 7% and 3% respectively.

You may also define your own multi-level methods, if required:

i.   Click on 'New Entries' and enter the key (say, YB1) for the new multi-level method ('M-Lev.Meth'), enter the 'Description of the Method' and select a 'Validity Start'; we have selected 3, as BESTM wanted this to start from the special depreciation. Select the 'Dep.by Fisc. Year' check-box, only when the fiscal year end or period ends are different (Figure 10.18).

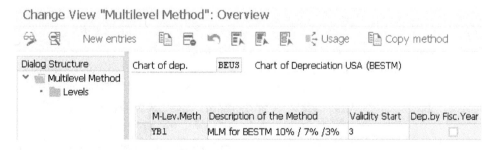

Figure 10.18: New Multilevel Method YB1

ii.   Now, select the YB1 row and double-click on 'Levels' on the left-hand side 'Dialog Structure'. On the next screen (Figure 10.19):

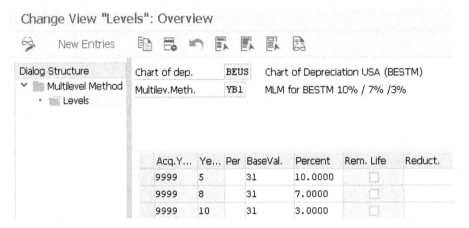

Figure 10.19: New Multilevel Method YB1 - Details

- Entering 9999 in 'Acq. Year' makes the asset's year of acquisition as valid for ever.
- Specify the validity period, for a percentage rate, in calendar 'Years' field. Enter the 'Years' in cumulative form: for example, if 10% is to be applied for the first 5 years, 7% for the next 3 years, and 3% for the last 2 years, then, for level 1 (first row), the 'Years' entry will be 5, level 2 will be 8 and level 3 will be 10.
- You may specify the validity period ('Per'), in calendar months also.
- Select the appropriate base value 'BaseVal.': 31 represents 'cumulative special depreciation'. Besides the base values supplied by SAP, you can also use your own base value (define this user-specific base value using a customer enhancement). Refer the previous Section 'Define Base Methods', for more details on base value.
- Enter the depreciation percentage in 'Percent' field. Only when you use 'Total percentage in concessionary period' depreciation calculation method, then, you need to enter the rates in cumulative form. Else, you need to enter them in absolute values.
- You need to set 'Rem. Life' flag, only if you want the system to determine the periodic depreciation percentage based on the remaining life, as in the case of depreciation keys wherein the base method makes use of 'percentage from the useful life' depreciation calculation method.
- By using the 'Reduct.' Field, you can reduce the base value for the calculation of depreciation by entering a reduction percentage rate. For

example, if you enter 25.0000, then, the system reduces the base value by 25% for that level.

ii.   'Save' the details, when completed.

With this, we are ready, now, to discuss and maintain the last calculation method, namely, period control method.

Maintain Period Control Methods

You can set an appropriate period control in the *'period control method'*, for determining the depreciation start and end date for asset transactions, for the four transaction categories: acquisitions, subsequent acquisitions/post-capitalization, transfer Postings and retirements. By defining a period control method, you can set the depreciation start date for all acquisitions within the same year to the beginning of the year, for example. You can also set the depreciation start date for retirements to the first or last day of each period. Using the asset value date of a transaction (acquisition or retirement), the system determines the start date or end date of depreciation calculation using the period control.

Use the menu path: SAP Customizing Implementation Guide > Financial Accounting > Asset Accounting > Depreciation > Valuation Methods > Depreciation Key > Calculation Methods > Maintain Period Control Methods, or Transaction AFAMP to view the default methods (Figure 10.20). You may click on 'New Entries' to create a new period control method.

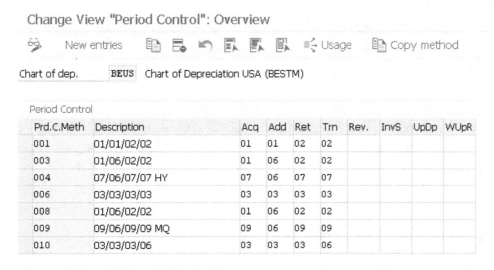

Change View "Period Control": Overview

🐝 New entries 📄 📑 🔄 📊 📊 📊 🔧 Usage 📄 Copy method

Chart of dep.   **BEUS** Chart of Depreciation USA (BESTM)

Period Control

Prd.C.Meth	Description	Acq	Add	Ret	Trn	Rev.	InvS	UpDp	WUpR
001	01/01/02/02	01	01	02	02				
003	01/06/02/02	01	06	02	02				
004	07/06/07/07 HY	07	06	07	07				
006	03/03/03/03	03	03	03	03				
008	01/06/02/02	01	06	02	02				
009	09/06/09/09 MQ	09	06	09	09				
010	03/03/03/06	03	03	03	06				

Figure 10.20: Period Control Methods

Per period control method, you need to select the appropriate start date for the four transaction categories: acquisitions ('Acq'), subsequent acquisitions ('Add') / post-capitalization, transfer Postings ('Trn') and retirements ('Ret'). Consider the period control method 003, where 'asset acquisition' is set for 01 – pro rata at period start date, 'subsequent additions' at 06 – at the start of the year, 'asset retirement' and 'transfer postings' at 02 – pro rata up to mid-period at period start date.

With this, let us understand some of the important depreciation methods, in the next Section.

10.5.1.2. Depreciation Methods

The depreciation keys, with their calculation methods and parameters, enable representing several depreciation methods in the system. Let us understand the most important depreciation methods, and how the system handles them during depreciation calculation.

- *Straight-Line Depreciation over Total Useful Life*: Here, the system depreciates the asset, uniformly, over the specified useful life of the asset, so that at the end of the life the NBV = 0.

  Depreciation = APC / Expected Useful Life

- *Straight-Line from the Book Value over Remaining Useful Life*: Here, the system distributes the NBV of the fixed asset, uniformly, over the remaining life. This method, unlike straight-line depreciation over total useful life, ensures that post-capitalization and subsequent acquisitions do not lead to an extension of expected useful life.

  Depreciation = NBV / Remaining Life

- *Declining-Balance Method of Depreciation*: Here, the system depreciates the asset by a progressively falling rate. A constant percentage rate is calculated, from the expected useful life and a given multiplication factor, which is multiplied with the falling NBV of the asset. Accordingly, the NBV can never reach zero in this method. Therefore, the system changes the method to straight-line or complete the depreciation under certain conditions when (a) declining-balance method of depreciation < straight-line depreciation or (b) NBV < x percent of acquisition value, or (c) NBV < fixed amount, or NBV < straight-line depreciation, or (d) the changeover method is specified in the internal calculation key. Also refer Section 'Define Declining Methods'.

  Depreciation = NBV* Percentage Rate from Useful Life and Factor

> **i** Consider that the asset's APC is 20,000, scrap is estimated at 15% and the useful life is 10 years. Now, the 'Percentage Rate from Useful Life and Factor' is arrived at using the formula = 1 - $\{3000/20000\}^{1/10}$ = 17.28%

- *Declining Multi-Phase Depreciation:* By specifying rate of depreciation and validity period, you can determine a course of depreciation that changes in levels over time (usually decreasing). The validity period can be based, either on the capitalization date or on the depreciation start date. The change between the levels of depreciation does not have to take place at the start or end of a fiscal year. You can also change to another rate of depreciation during the fiscal year. Also refer Section 'Multi-Level Methods'.

Depreciation = APC * Percentage Rate of the Level

> **i** Consider an asset with an APC of 10000, and useful life of 20 years. Assume that the useful life has been divided into 4 phases of 5 years each with the depreciation at 10% for years 1-5, 5% for years 6-10, 3% for years 11-15 and 2% for 16-20.

- *Sum-of-the-Years-Digits Method of Depreciation (Digital)*: Here, the total of the remaining life, of an asset, is mapped in each individual year over the entire useful life. The depreciation percentage rate of a fiscal year is then derived from the respective remaining life, divided by this total. The result of this method leads to depreciation amounts that are reduced by the same amount in each period. As the remaining useful life is no longer defined, after the end of the planned useful life, you can no longer depreciate the asset, using this method once the planned useful life has expired. However, you can changeover to another method once the expected useful life is reached.

Depreciation = APC * Remaining Useful Life (Current Period) / Total of Remaining Useful Life (Over all Periods)

> **i** Consider that the APC of an asset is 10000, and the useful life is 5 years. The sum-of-year-digits = 5+4+3+2+1 = 15. The depreciation of 1st year = 10000*5/15 = 3333, 2nd year = 10000*4/15 = 2667 and so on.

- *Mean Value Method*: You will use this method when you want to have the mean value of two depreciation methods, in a derived depreciation area that links the values of the two depreciation areas. For this, you have to identify the derived depreciation area as a 'mean value area'. Instead of using the arithmetic mean, you can also link the areas proportionally.

Depreciation = (Depreciation in Area 1) / 2 + (Depreciation in Area 2) / 2

- *Depreciation for Multiple-Shift Operation and Shutdown*: When you use an asset in multiple shifts, then you need to calculate additional or increased depreciation. Likewise, when you shut down an asset, you will not calculate any depreciation on that asset. SAP provides you with the 'Shift Factor' field and the 'Asset shutdown' check-box (in 'Time-dependent' tab) in the asset master record (Figure 10.21) for handling these situations.

Depreciation Amount = Fixed Depreciation + (Variable Depreciation * Shift Factor)

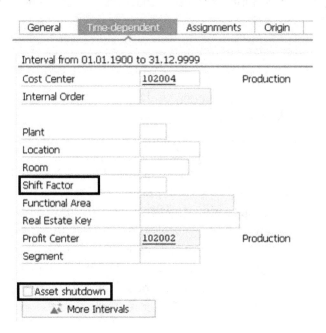

Figure 10.21: Fields for Multiple Shift / Asset Shutdown Specifications

> **i** You can calculate increased depreciation due to multiple-shift operation for all types of depreciation except 'unit-of-production', because the unit-of-production depreciation is by definition 100% variable.

This completes our discussion and maintenance of different calculation / depreciation methods. Let us move on to define the default values.

10.5.1.3. Default Values

You can maintain default values for depreciation keys (a) at the level of company codes and depreciation areas, and (b) at the company code level. Let us, first, understand what are the values you can propose as default values for depreciation areas and company codes

Propose Values for Depreciation Areas and Company Codes
You can enter default values, valid for certain company codes and depreciation areas, so as to configure depreciation keys in such a way that the system uses a different interest key or a special treatment of the end of depreciation, for example, in certain specific company codes

and depreciation areas. Applicable to depreciation areas that manage interest, the system uses this default interest key if there is no interest method entered in the depreciation key.

Use the menu path: SAP Customizing Implementation Guide > Financial Accounting > Asset Accounting > Depreciation > Valuation Methods > Depreciation Key > Default Values > Propose Values for Depreciation Areas and Company Codes, or Transaction AFAM_093B. On the resulting screen, click on 'New Entries', enter the 'Company Code' and depreciation area ('Deprec. area'). You my maintain the default parameters as required.

Project Dolphin

BESTM requested the project management team not to define default values for the company codes and depreciation areas. Also, BESTM does not want to impose the condition that the acquisitions are allowed only in the year in which depreciation started.

The system uses these default values only if you explicitly set 'Default value from company code' in the depreciation key or 'Default value from company code and depreciation area' in the base method of depreciation calculation (Figure 10.22).

Settings in 'Base Method' of Calculation

Treatment of end of depreciation	
Dep. After Plnd.Life End	Default value from company code and depreciation area
Dep.Below NBValue Zero	Default value from company code and depreciation area
Curb	Default value from company code and depreciation area

Settings in Depreciation Key

Acq.Only Allowed in Capitalization Year	Default value from company code
No. of Places	

Figure 10.22: Default Value Settings in Base Method of Calculation / Depreciation Key

You can also make default settings at the company code level so that the system proposes acquisition in capitalization year, for the company codes.

Propose Acquisition Only in Capitalization Year for Company Codes
Here, you set, as a default, for certain company codes that acquisitions in this company code are only allowed in the year in which depreciation started. This setting may be necessary for technical reasons, for example, if you use sum-of-the-years-digits depreciation method. It is

also possible to use this function for organizational purposes. The system uses these default values only if you explicitly set 'Default value from company code' in the depreciation key (Figure 10.22).

Before we move on to define the depreciation keys, let us understand how to handle scrap / cutoff value in the system

10.5.1.4. Scrap Value / Cutoff Value

You may come across situations wherein it may be necessary not to depreciate till the asset's NBV = 0, but only up to a pre-determined value which is known as a 'scrap value' or 'cutoff value'.

You can manage scrap value in two ways:

i. By entering a scrap value in percentage (using the 'cutoff value key') in the depreciation key (Figure 10.23) used in the depreciation area, or

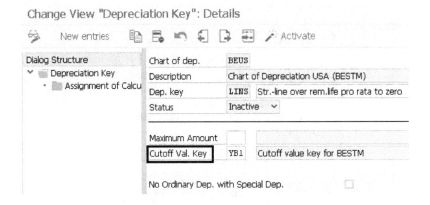

Figure 10.23: Cutoff Value Key in Depreciation Key

ii. By entering an absolute 'scrap value' in the asset master data for the depreciation area (in the detail screen) as shown in Figure 10.24. When you maintain the scrap value in absolute terms, either in the form of percentage and/or amount, in the asset master, note that the system does not depreciate this amount. When you specify both, the system uses the percentage by default.

> **i** SAP recommends that you enter scrap value as a percentage, in the asset master per depreciation area.

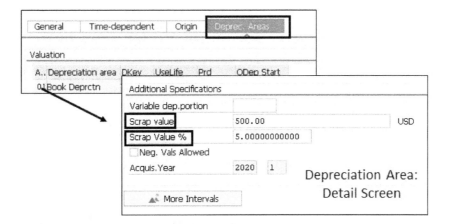

Figure 10.24: Entering Scrap Value in Asset Master

If you have defined a cutoff value key and also have entered the scrap value in the asset master, then, the system ignores the cutoff value percentage of the key, and treats the amount entered in the asset master record as the scrap value (refer Chapter 9.2.4).

Let us understand how to define the cutoff value key.

Define the Cutoff Value Key

Here, you define the 'cutoff value' calculation key for automatically determining scrap values. For each calculation key, you can specify:

- The percentage of the depreciation base that should be used as the cutoff value percentage.
- Whether the cutoff value percentage should be deducted at the start or the end of the calculation of depreciation.
- At what point in time the system should start calculating the validity period.

You can maintain several cutoff percentages for each cutoff value key. You can define the cutoff percentages/levels per acquisition year, and the validity period can be of any length. You have to enter the validity period of the individual percentages or levels of a scrap value key in cumulative form.

Use the menu path: SAP Customizing Implementation Guide > Financial Accounting > Asset Accounting > Depreciation > Valuation Methods > Further Settings > Define the Cutoff Value Key, or Transaction ANHAL. You will see, on the resulting screen, the standard cutoff value keys defined in the system (Figure 10.25).

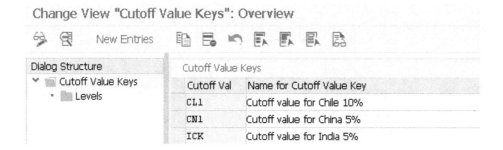

Figure 10.25: Standard Cutoff Value Keys

You may double-click on a row to see the settings for that cutoff value key (Figure 10.26). Depending on the settings, the system deducts the scrap value from the base value of the asset, with the start of date calculation being the asset capitalisation date or start of ordinary depreciation or start of special depreciation or original acquisition date for AuC.

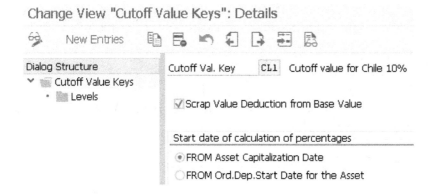

Figure 10.26: Standard Cutoff Value Key CL1 - Details

You can double-click on 'Levels' on the left-hand side 'Dialog Structure' and see the settings associated with the levels (Figure 10.27). What you see is the default entries by SAP; you can customize this to suit your own needs.

Figure 10.27: Standard Cutoff Value Key CL1 - Levels

Project Dolphin

BESTM has decided to have a cutoff value key defined for depreciating vehicles with 10 year validity. The scrap value percentage will vary at 5% for the first 5 years, 3% for the next 3 years and 2% for the last 2 years. The scrap value needs to be deducted from the base value and the start of calculation will be from the asset capitalization date.

You can define your own cutoff values keys, by clicking on 'New Entries' on the initial screen, and maintaining the appropriate validity in cumulative period (years). You can have different cutoff percentages for different levels, with each level defined in cumulative years. Consider BESTM's requirement as an example wherein you want to define a cutoff value key for depreciating assets with a validity period of 10 years, with three different percentages: 5%, 3% and 2%. In this case, you may define a scenario like the one depicted in Figure 10.28.

Figure 10.28: New Cutoff Value Key YB1 – Multiple Levels

With this, we are now ready to discuss how to define the depreciation keys.

10.5.1.5. Maintain Depreciation Key

We have discussed the depreciation key, in detail, in Section 10.5.1. You can use this configuration activity, to maintain the required depreciation keys and assign the appropriate calculation methods to them.

> **i** We recommend using the standard pre-defined depreciation keys (like LINS – Straight line over remaining life pro rata to zero, M150 - MACRS 15, 20 years property, CWG - LVA 100 % Complete write off etc) that are designed to meet country-specific depreciation needs.

Project Dolphin

BESTM has decided to make use of the standard depreciation keys that are pre-defined in the system. However, while handling multiple shift operations, it needs to be configured that the result is increased depreciation / expired useful life. Also, there need not be any stopping of depreciation during asset shutdown.

Use the menu path: SAP Customizing Implementation Guide > Financial Accounting > Asset Accounting > Depreciation > Valuation Methods > Depreciation Key > Maintain Depreciation Key, or Transaction AFAMA. You will see, for the given chart of accounts (BEUS), the system supplied default depreciation keys on the resulting screen (Figure 10.29).

Figure 10.29: Maintaining Depreciation Keys – List of Standard Keys

You may double-click on any of the keys (say, LINS), to see the detailed settings (Figure 10.30).

On the next screen, you will see the 'Status' of the depreciation key. It can have one of three statuses: (a) 'Active': the depreciation key has no errors, and can be used in asset master records, (b) 'Inactive': either the depreciation key or one of its calculation methods has errors, you cannot use the key and (c) 'Migrated': the depreciation key has been migrated from the old table to the new table; the old depreciation key is still valid. Let us look at other fields:

i.   You will use the 'Maximum Amount' field to enter the appropriate maximum amount method's depreciation key for calculating depreciation or imputed interest.

ii.   You may enter the appropriate 'Cutoff Val. Key', if required, for controlling the calculation of the cutoff value for depreciation.

iii. You may maintain the other control parameters, if required, for the various check-boxes like 'No Ordinary Dep. with Special Dep.', 'Dep. to the Day' etc.

iv.   Enter the 'No. of Places', for rounding off the percentage rates internally, to the number of decimal places that you enter here. The standard setting for this field is 0 or blank: the system calculates with 10 decimal places.

Change View "Depreciation Key": Details

New entries   Activate

Dialog Structure		
Depreciation Key	Chart of dep.	BEUS
Assignment of Calcu	Description	Chart of Depreciation USA (BESTM)
	Dep. key	LINS Str.-line over rem.life pro rata to zero
	Status	Active

Maximum Amount

Cutoff Val. Key

No Ordinary Dep. with Special Dep.   ☐
No Interest If No Deprec. Is Planned   ☐
Period control according to fiscal years   ☐
Dep. to the Day   ☐
No reduct. in short year   ☐

Acq.Only Allowed in Capitalization Year   No
No. of Places

Figure 10.30: Maintaining Depreciation Key LINS – Initial Configuration

Now, double-click on 'Assignment of Calculation Methods' on the left-hand side 'Dialog Structure'. Click on 'New Entries' and maintain the settings (Figure 10.31), on the next screen:

i.   Note that the system defaults to 'Ord.depreciation' in 'DepType' field and to 'From the start of depreciation' for the 'Phase' field. You will use 'Phase' to configure the system appropriately, when you divide the duration of depreciation into several phases, during each of which the depreciation key uses different calculation methods for calculating depreciation. You have three options like 'from the start of the depreciation', or 'changeover with planned life' or 'changeover after end of the useful life'.

ii.   Under 'Assignment of Calculation Methods':

• Maintain the appropriate calculation methods in 'Base Methods', 'Decl.-bal. Method'. 'Prd. Cont' and 'Multilev.Method' that we have defined earlier in 'Calculation Methods' (Section 10.5.1.1).

• Enter appropriate classification of ordinary depreciation in the 'Class' field.

- Enter a changeover method, if required in 'Chnge.Method' and also maintain the changeover rate in 'Changeover%Rate' field.
- Select the appropriate value for 'Multiple shift'.

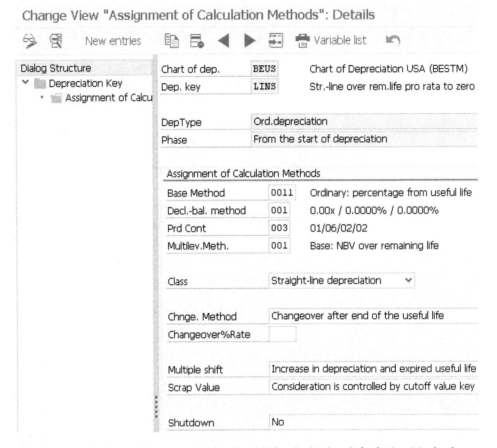

Figure 10.31: Maintaining Depreciation Key LINS – Assigning Calculation Methods

- Enter how the system handles the 'Scrap Value'. Refer to the previous Section 10.5.1.4, for more details on scrap value / cutoff value.
- If you do not want the system to calculate depreciation during asset shutdown, enter 'Yes' in the 'Shutdown' field. We have entered 'No' as we do not want to halt the depreciation during asset shutdown for BESTM. By specifying shutdown periods when maintaining the asset master record, you ensure that depreciation is suspended during the shutdown periods.

iii. 'Save' and repeat the steps to maintain the settings for other depreciation keys.

This completes our discussion on valuation methods, and the settings required to configure the same. Let us now understand the Depreciation Calculation Program (DCP) in the next Section.

10.5.2 Depreciation Calculation Program

The *'Depreciation Calculation Program'* (DCP) is a back-end solution that does not require any special or extra configuration. However, you can the SAP-provided Business Add Ins (BAdI) to modify the calculation of values.

The DCP is made up two components (Figure 10.32):

- An external component, that is application-specific (business-oriented).
- An internal component, (*'Evaluation Engine'*), which controls the calculation logic for depreciation calculations.

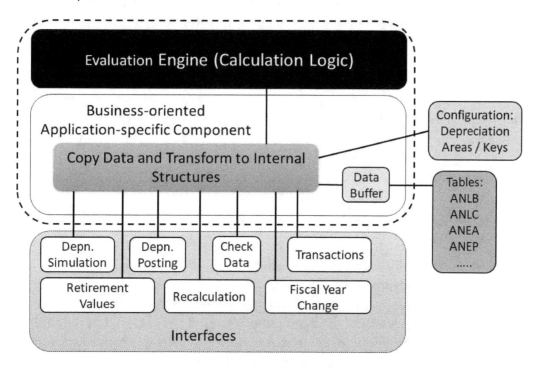

Figure 10.32: Depreciation Calculation Program (DCP)

The *'Business-oriented, Application-specific External Component'* provides an interface to other applications. It transfers asset master data and transaction data to internal work structures, besides grouping the transactions together, based on calculation periods. It reads all configuration settings needed for depreciation calculation, and transfers them to internal work structures. It specifies the depreciation start date and updates the total asset values.

The internal *'Evaluation Engine'* is based on the work structures created by the application-specific part of the program. It calculates replacement values, depreciation, and interest as well as revaluation (both upward and downward), as part of an automatic calculation of inflation. It determines the base value or net value, as well as the shutdown value of the assets besides correcting the values and amounts when derived depreciation areas are used.

The DCP, now, provides the following new and improved functions for calculating depreciation, under the following functionality groups:

A. *Period-Based Calculation*
- The calculation of depreciation is now based on periods, instead of individual transactions, as it was previously. Now, the system groups the transactions for an asset together by the calculation period.
  - The system uses the asset value date and the period control group of the transaction type group to determine the calculation period. The system assigns each transaction to a calculation period.
    - Then, the system creates period intervals from the calculation periods that are determined. Based on these intervals, the system calculates the depreciation.

B. *Time-Dependent Depreciation Terms*

Now, you can make 'time-dependent changes to depreciation terms' (that include useful life, depreciation key, scrap value, scrap value percentage, and variable depreciation portion) in the asset master data. The changes to the depreciation terms become effective on the key date that you specify for the given depreciation area. A mid-year change to depreciation terms, causes the system to set up new calculation period intervals.

C. *Mid-year, Period-Dependent Changeover*

With the new depreciation calculation, you have new options for changeover of the depreciation method. Instead annual changeover, you can, now, specify a mid-year automatic changeover of the depreciation method. The system uses the UMPER field in table ANLB for this function. To make use of this mid-year changeover, you need to use the FAA_DC_CUSTOMER BAdI (method: DEFINE_USE_OF_MAX_PERIODS), and set the CB_USE_MAX_PERIODS parameter to X.

10.6 Conclusion

You learned that 'depreciation' represents the decrease in value of a fixed asset (other than land), over its economic life, due to its usage including wear and tear. You learned that SAP supports two categories of depreciation types: automatically calculated depreciation and manually planned depreciation.

You understood that the standard depreciation types, in SAP, include ordinary depreciation, special depreciation, unplanned depreciation, transfer of reserves and interest. You understood that SAP treats the 'interest' (for cost-accounting purposes) as a depreciation type, and controls the same by depreciation keys and calculation methods.

You learned that though the system determines the planned depreciation, automatically, for the current financial year using the depreciation key, it also enables manually changing the planned depreciation. You also learned that you will take the manual route, generally, for unplanned depreciation and transfer of reserves.

You learned that the 'ordinary depreciation' is a form of planned depreciation that takes care of the normal wear and of an asset, during its economic life. In contrast, you learned that the 'special depreciation' depreciates an asset from the point of taxation, notwithstanding the actual wear and tear. And, you learned that you may need to resort to 'unplanned depreciation' in certain special unforeseen situations. You learned that, in general, the system calculates the ordinary depreciation before the special depreciation.

You understood that the depreciation calculation, in the system, is based on the 'valuation method' and the 'planned useful life' of the asset. You understood that the 'depreciation key' contains all the control data that the system needs for calculating the planned annual depreciation. You further understood that the 'calculation method' (defined within the depreciation key), is used for the actual calculation and is important for defining the 'depreciation calculation method'. You, then, went on to understand the most important depreciation methods, and how the system handles them during depreciation calculation.

You learned that, sometimes, you may not want to depreciate some of your assets to their zero book value, but only up to a specified 'scrap value' / 'cutoff value'. You also learned how the system behaves, when you have both scrap value and cutoff value defined for an asset.

You learned that the 'Depreciation Calculation Program' is a back-end solution containing an application-specific (business-oriented) external component and an internal 'Evaluation Engine', that controls the calculation logic for depreciation calculations.

With this, we can, now, move on to discuss the special valuations, in the next Chapter.

11 Special Valuations

Use 'special valuations' for special value adjustments to assets (like, investment support, special depreciation reserves etc) and for meeting some of the special valuation purposes, like, cost-accounting replacement values, interest, revaluation for the balance sheet etc.

Using special valuations, you can take care of:

- Special Reserves
- Transferred Reserves
- Investment Support
- Revaluation of Fixed Assets
- Interest
- Net Worth Tax
- Preparations for Consolidation
- Leasing Processing

Let us start with the special reserves.

11.1 Special Reserves

You are allowed to use tax valuation approaches, in some of the countries, in the B/S. That being the case, you should make it possible for the person looking at the B/S, to know, that a different approach was used in depreciation calculation. Hence, you carry out both book depreciation and tax depreciation (which exceeds book depreciation) and show the difference as *special reserves* on the liabilities side of the B/S. Showing the difference between book depreciation and tax depreciation, in a derived depreciation area, you can use the values from this derived area to create special depreciation reserves for the B/S.

To configure the system to handle special reserves, you need to complete the following steps:

- Specify Gross or Net Procedure
- Assign Accounts

Let us understand how to specify gross or net procedure.

11.1.1 Specify Gross or Net Procedure

You need to determine, using this configuration step, if you want the system to balance the amounts from the allocation and writing off of special reserves on the same asset in the same posting run against each other (net procedure).

Project Dolphin

In the case of special reserves, BESTM has asked the project team to configure the system, to use the net procedure, so that it posts the allocation amounts and write-off amounts, for the same asset, offsetting against each other instead of the gross method.

Use the menu path: SAP Customizing Implementation Guide > Financial Accounting > Asset Accounting > Special Valuations > Special Reserves > Specify Gross or Net Procedure, or you may use Transaction OAYQ.

On the resulting screen, select the appropriate company code (say, 1110) and double-click on 'Net reserve for special depreciation' on the left-hand side 'Dialog Structure'. On the next screen, against the appropriate depreciation area(s), select the 'Net' check-box indicating that the system will post allocation amounts and write-off amounts, for the same asset, offsetting against each other instead of the 'gross' method (in which the system allocates special depreciation amount to the reserves and writes off the balance of ordinary depreciation of the two depreciation areas).

The next step is to assign the G/L accounts, to handle special reserves.

11.1.2 Assign Accounts

Use this activity, to determine the G/L accounts for write-off or allocation of special reserves.

If you enter gain/loss accounts for a depreciation area, the system does not post any revenue from the write-off of special items for reserve. Instead, the system includes that revenue, resulting from an asset sale, in the calculation of gain/loss itself. The system, then, balances the loss in the book depreciation area against an offsetting posting, and posts the total or the difference (between the write-off of special items for reserve and the book loss) to these accounts.

Use the menu path: SAP Customizing Implementation Guide > Financial Accounting > Asset Accounting > Special Valuations > Special Reserves > Assign Accounts, or Transaction AO99.

On the resulting screen, select the chart of accounts (say, BEUS), and double-click on 'Account Determination' on the left-hand side 'Dialog Structure'. On the next screen (Figure 11.1), select the required 'Account Determination' (say, B2000) and double-click on 'Special Reserves' on the left-hand side 'Dialog Structure' and enter the appropriate G/L accounts, on the next screen, for the required depreciation areas, under 'Special Reserve Balance', 'Allocation to Special Reserves (Expenses)', and 'Write-off Special Reserves after Retirement' data blocks.

Change View "Account Determination": Overview

Dialog Structure
∨ Chart of Accounts
  ∨ Account Determinat
    · Special Reserves

Chart of Accts   BEUS

Account Determination

Account Determ.	Name of Account Determination
B1000	Buildings
B2000	Plant and Machinery
B3000	Vehicles

Figure 11.1: Configuring Account Determination for Special Reserves

We can, now, move on to discuss the settings required for transferred reserves.

11.2 Transferred Reserves

The tax legislation, of many countries, allows you to transfer the entire undisclosed reserves or a part thereof, created by the sale of assets, to replacement acquisitions. The gain on the sale, then, reduces the depreciation base of the newly acquired assets. If you cannot transfer such undisclosed reserves, in the year they are formed because there were no suitable new acquisitions, you can set up a reserve in the year in question to prevent the gain on the sale influencing your profit. You can transfer these reserves, in the next few years, to assets acquired during this time period.

Here, in this Section, you define the configuration settings that are necessary for transfer of reserves (also called as *transfer of reserves, undisclosed reserves, deferred gain, balancing charges*) to newly acquired fixed assets.

The first activity is to determine the depreciation areas for enabling transfer of reserves.

11.2.1 Determine Depreciation Areas

Use the menu path: SAP Customizing Implementation Guide > Financial Accounting > Asset Accounting > Special Valuations > Transferred Reserves > Determine Depreciation Areas, or Transaction OABM. On the resulting screen, select the 'Res.' Check box against the appropriate depreciations area(s). These are all the areas into which you will transfer reserves for fixed assets.

The next activity is to assign the relevant G/L accounts.

11.2.2 Assign Accounts

Use the menu path: SAP Customizing Implementation Guide > Financial Accounting > Asset Accounting > Special Valuations > Transferred Reserves > Assign Accounts, or Transaction AO96. On the resulting screen, for the given chart of accounts, select the 'Account Determination' and double-click on 'Reserves' on the left-hand side 'Dialog Structure'. On the next screen, per depreciation area, enter the relevant G/L account for value adjustment of transfer of reserves, for the contra account etc, under the 'Account assignment for transfer of reserves' data block.

The third and final step is to define the transaction types of transfer of reserves.

11.2.3 Define Transaction Types for Transfer of Reserves

You have to transfer reserves in FI-AA using manual posting. Here, in this activity, you can define transaction types for the transfer of reserves. In fact, you do not need to define any new transaction type, but use the SAP supplied transaction types 680 / 690.

Project Dolphin

The project team has suggested to the BESTM management to use the SAP supplied standard transaction types for handling transfer of reserves in FI-AA.

Use the menu path: SAP Customizing Implementation Guide > Financial Accounting > Asset Accounting > Special Valuations > Transferred Reserves > Define Transaction Types for Transfer of Reserves, or Transaction AO80. On the resulting screen, you shall see SAP's standard transaction types, for transfer of reserves to current / previous year acquisitions (Figure 11.2).

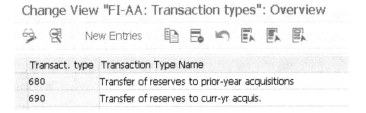

Change View "FI-AA: Transaction types": Overview

Transact. type	Transaction Type Name
680	Transfer of reserves to prior-year acquisitions
690	Transfer of reserves to curr-yr acquis.

Figure 11.2: Transaction Types for Transfer of Reserves

With this, we are, now, ready to discuss revaluation of fixed assets.

11.3 Revaluation of Fixed Assets

It may be required that you need to revalue your fixed assets either to compensate for inflation or to account for the changed replacement values to meet (a) management accounting requirements and/or (b) tax obligations. Using an index series, you can periodically revalue assets' APC and cumulative value adjustments, to arrive at the 'indexed replacement values'. Or, you can carry out revaluation for balance sheet (B/S) once every few years. Let us understand more about these two valuations:

1) *Indexed Replacement Values*
   Using index series, you can automatically account for periodic changes in the value of the assets. When the system posts the depreciation, these changes get reflected in the specific asset (or asset class). The indexed replacement value is influenced by (a) the replacement value of an asset changes due to inflation and/or (b) technical progress resulting in changed price for an appropriate replacement acquisition. Accordingly, you can specify two index series to cover these two situations, for each asset, for determining replacement value in FI-AA. The system, then, determines the replacement value by multiplying the index figures in the two index series.

2) *Revaluation for the Balance Sheet*
   You may need to carry out a single revaluation of the entire fixed asset portfolio, at intervals of every few years. Also known as '*B/S revaluation*', this enables you to comply with the country's tax requirements for a single revaluation of all fixed assets to offset the effects of inflation. The system does not calculate this single revaluation automatically; you need to define and carry that out manually. Of course, you can use collective processing to carry out this revaluation.

   Though you can manage revaluation values in any depreciation area, you must be able to separately identify such changes in value, to meet the country's legal requirements. In this case, you must use a separate depreciation area for each revaluation.

With this, let us look at the configuration settings required for revaluation of fixed assets. The first step is to maintain the accounts for revaluation.

11.3.1 Maintain Accounts for Revaluation

Here, you will specify the G/L accounts for changes to APC or accumulated depreciation due to revaluation, in order to determine the asset replacement value.

Use the menu path: SAP Customizing Implementation Guide > Financial Accounting > Asset Accounting > Special Valuations > Revaluation of Fixed Assets > Maintain Accounts for Revaluation:

i. On the resulting pop-up screen, enter the chart of depreciation (BEUS), and select the chart of accounts (BEUS) on the next screen.

ii. Double-click on 'Account Determination' on the left-hand side 'Dialog Structure' and select an 'Account Determination' (say, B2000).

iii. Now, select the depreciation area ('Area') on the resulting screen and double-click on 'Revaluation of APC' on the left-hand side 'Dialog Structure', and maintain the required G/L account on the next screen.

iv. Similarly, double-click on 'Revaluation of Depreciation' on the left-hand side 'Dialog Structure', and maintain the required G/L account on the next screen, for same account determination.

v. Repeat and maintain the settings for all the required asset determinations.

With this, let us understand the revaluation for B/S in detail.

11.3.2 Revaluation for the Balance Sheet

SAP offers two ways of for carrying out the revaluation for B/S:

1) For a *'one-time revaluation'*, you need to configure the system using the IMG node 'Revaluation for the Balance Sheet' but without carrying out the transaction in the 'Inflation Accounting' node.

   To execute one-time revaluation, use the SAP Easy Access menu path: SAP Menu > Accounting > Financial Accounting > Fixed Assets > Periodic Processing > Revaluation for the Balance Sheet > Post Revaluation and New Valuation, or Transaction AR29N.

2) For *'periodic revaluation'*, you need to configure all the nodes under 'Revaluation for the Balance Sheet' including the IMG node 'Inflation Accounting'.

   To execute periodic revaluation, use the SAP Easy Access menu path: SAP Menu > Accounting > Financial Accounting > Fixed Assets > Periodic Processing > Revaluation for the Balance Sheet > Inflation, or Transaction J1AI.

Let us, now, look at the configuration settings for revaluation for the B/S. The first task is to determine the depreciation areas for this purpose.

11.3.2.1. Determine Depreciation Areas

Use the menu path: SAP Customizing Implementation Guide > Financial Accounting > Asset Accounting > Special Valuations > Revaluation of Fixed Assets > Revaluation for the Balance Sheet > Determine Depreciation Areas, to specify the depreciation areas in which you want to manage revaluation of fixed assets. You may also use Transaction OABW.

Project Dolphin

BESTM, while configuring the depreciation area for revaluation of fixed assets, wants only the APC to be revalued but not the accumulated depreciation that had been debited to the asset in the earlier years.

On the resulting screen (Figure 11.3), select the 'RevlAPC' and/or 'RevlDep' check-boxes against the depreciation area (say, 20 – cost accounting depreciation) wherein you want to manage the revaluation. You will select the 'RevlDep' check-box, if you want the system to use not only the APC, when determining the replacement value, but to also revalue the value adjustments made to the asset, in the past; else, you will select only the "RevlAPC' check-box.

Change View "Asset Accounting: Management of replacement values": Over

Ar.	Name of Depreciation Area	RevlAPC	RevlDep
12	Adjusted Current Earnings	☐	☐
20	Cost Accounting Depreciation	☑	☐

Figure 11.3: Depreciation Area for Revaluation of Assets

The next step is to define the revaluation measures.

11.3.2.2. Define Revaluation Measures

Here, you define the revaluation measures like the key, description, depreciation areas and posting data in the system. Besides the revaluation measures, you also need a special depreciation area for each revaluation. While making the required settings, you need to create the calculation rule for the revaluation using a user exit and include the calculation rule in the function module 'EXIT_RAAUFW01_001'.

Use the report RAAUFW02 ('Post Revaluation and New Valuation'), to carry out the revaluation. The report determines the posted depreciation, writes it back, and posts the required adjustment to the net book value (NBV) for both individual and mass revaluations. You can also use this report to update a nominated evaluation group/user field with a specified characteristic, such as revaluation year, for reporting purposes.

Project Dolphin

The revaluation of fixed assets for balance sheet purposes, will happen on 31st December, every five years, starting with 31-Dec-2020. The revaluation IDs will be numbered serially and the revaluation will be handled in the cost accounting depreciation area.

Use the menu path: SAP Customizing Implementation Guide > Financial Accounting > Asset Accounting > Special Valuations > Revaluation of Fixed Assets > Revaluation for the Balance Sheet > Define Revaluation Measures, or Transaction AUFW:

i.   Enter the chart of depreciation (BEUS) on the resulting pop-up screen, and 'Continue'.

ii.   On the resulting 'Change View "Revaluation Measures": Overview' screen, click on 'New Entries'.

iii.   On the next screen (Figure 11.4), enter the 'Revaluation' ID (say,1) and provide the description. Under 'Date specifications', specify the date on which the system posts the one-time revaluation to fixed assets. The system uses this date as the posting date in FI and as the asset value date in FI-AA.

iv.   Enter the 'Area specifications': enter the 'Base Area' (01) that provides the APC and also the 'Revaluation Area' (20), and 'Save' the settings.

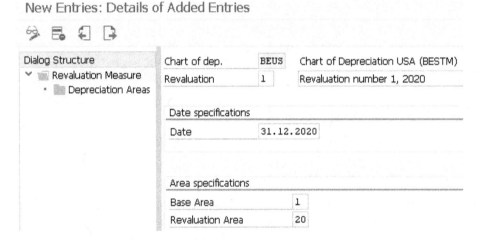

Figure 11.4: Specifying Revaluation Measures

The next and final task in configuring the settings for revaluation for balance sheet is to define the transaction types for asset revaluation.

11.3.2.3. Define Transaction Types for Revaluation

Use the menu path: SAP Customizing Implementation Guide > Financial Accounting > Asset Accounting > Special Valuations > Revaluation of Fixed Assets > Revaluation for the Balance Sheet > Define Transaction Types for Revaluation:

Project Dolphin

BESTM does not want to create any new transaction types for handling asset revaluations in the system. They have decided to use SAP supplied standard transaction types, instead.

i. On the resulting 'Select Activity' pop-up screen, double-click on 'Define Transaction Types for Revaluation'.

ii. On the resulting screen (use Transaction AO84 to reach here, directly), you will see a list of standard transaction types that are available as default (Figure 11.5). You do not need to define anything new, and can use the appropriate standard transaction types.

Change View "FI-AA: Transaction types": Overview

New Entries

Transact. type	Transaction Type Name
800	Post revaluation gross
820	Revaluation of curr-yr acquis. with depreciation
891	Revaluation (downward) prior year
892	Revaluation (upward) current year

Figure 11.5: Standard Transaction Types for Asset Revaluation

iii. Now, go back to the initial 'Select Activity' pop-up screen, and double-click on 'Limit Transaction Types to Depreciation Areas'.

iv. On the resulting 'Change View "Transaction type selection": Overview' screen (you may use Transaction OAXJ to come to this screen directly), select a transaction type (say, 800) and double-click on 'Depreciation area specification' on the left-hand side 'Dialog Structure'.

v. On the next screen, select the depreciation area (say, 20) and 'Save'. Essentially, you use this step to restrict certain transaction types to certain depreciation areas, if required.

This completes our discussion on revaluation of fixed assets. Let us discuss, the settings required for interest, in the next Section.

11.4 Interest

You may need to calculate (imputed) interest on the capital tied up in assets, for cost accounting purposes. In FI-AA, you can calculate this interest, per depreciation area, in addition to ordinary depreciation, special depreciation, unplanned depreciation etc.

The system calculates the interest, as that of automatically calculated depreciation, using the calculation method in a depreciation key. The account assignment is to the G/L accounts that you specify for interest in the respective account determination/depreciation area. In addition, you can make an additional assignment to the cost center of the respective asset, if required.

The calculation of interest to be posted, depends mainly on the base value of the interest key: if the key uses the current net book value (NBV) as the base value, for example, then, the system takes this NBV into account to the exact period during depreciation posting. The system calculates the interest either until book value = 0, or up to the end of expected useful life, or for an unlimited period. And, it then posts interest together with depreciation when you perform a periodic depreciation posting run.

Let us configure the system for calculating interest on the fixed assets. As in the previous Sections, the first step is to determine the depreciation area for managing the interest.

11.4.1 Determine Depreciation Areas

The interest calculation, in general, in most of the countries, is allowed only for cost accounting purposes. Here, in this step, you will make the necessary specification to denote a cost account depreciation area for managing interest.

Project Dolphin

As in practice, the interest calculated on the capital tied up on fixed assets needs to be managed in the cost accounting depreciation area, 20 in the case of BESTM.

Use the menu path: SAP Customizing Implementation Guide > Financial Accounting > Asset Accounting > Special Valuations > Revaluation of Fixed Assets > Interest > Determine Depreciation Areas, or Transaction OABZ.

On the resulting screen, select the 'Int.' check-box against the cost accounting depreciation area (20) for the chart of depreciation, BEUS (Figure 11.6).

Change View "Asset Accounting: Define management of interest": Overvie

Ar.	Name of Depreciation Area	Int.
11	Alternative Minimum Tax	☐
12	Adjusted Current Earnings	☐
20	Cost Accounting Depreciation	☑

Figure 11.6: Depreciation Area for Managing Interest

The next activity is to assign the appropriate G/L accounts to manage interest.

11.4.2 Assign Accounts

Use the menu path: SAP Customizing Implementation Guide > Financial Accounting > Asset Accounting > Special Valuations > Revaluation of Fixed Assets > Interest > Assign Accounts, or Transaction AO98:

i.   Select the chart of depreciation (say, BEUS), on the resulting screen and double-click on 'Account Determination' on the left-hand side 'Dialog Structure'.
ii. Select an 'Account Determination' (say, B3000 – Vehicles) and double-click on 'Interest' on the left-hand side 'Dialog Structure'.
iii. Now, select the depreciation area on the next screen, and enter the G/L accounts in 'Expense account for interest' (say, 71100400) and 'Clearing interest posting' (contra account) fields under 'Interest account assignment' data block on the next screen.
iv. Repeat and maintain the required accounts for all the other account determinations.

The last activity for interest determination, is to define the required depreciation key.

11.4.3 Maintain Depreciation Key

Use menu path: SAP Customizing Implementation Guide > Financial Accounting > Asset Accounting > Special Valuations > Revaluation of Fixed Assets > Interest > Maintain Depreciation Key, or Transaction AFAMA, to configure interest calculation in depreciation key.

Similar to the configuration step ('Maintain Depreciation Key') that we have discussed in Chapter 10.5.1.5, here, for a given depreciation key, select 'Interest' in 'DepType', instead of 'ordinary depreciation' or 'special depreciation'. Also, assign the appropriate calculation method for 'Base Method' (say, 0029) and other calculation methods (Figure 11.7).

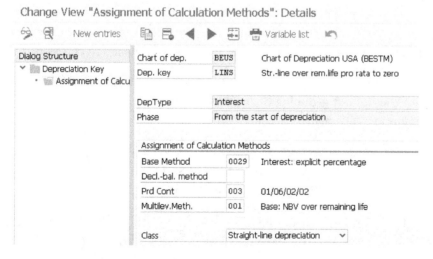

Figure 11.7: Depreciation Key for Interest Calculation - Details

Once defined and activated, the overview screen will show this depreciation key for interest calculation, with the appropriate calculation methods already assigned. (Figure 11.8).

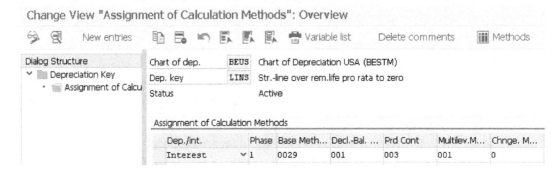

Figure 11.8: Depreciation Key for Interest Calculation – Overview

This completes our discussion on configuring the system for interest calculation. Let us, now, understand the settings required for legal consolidation, from asset accounting side.

11.5 Preparations for Consolidation

The settings you make here in this Section, for preparation for consolidation from asset accounting side, mostly relate to the features of transaction types, besides specifying the depreciation areas for handling legal consolidation.

Let us start with the consolidation transaction types of APC transactions.

11.5.1 Specify Consolidation Transaction Types for APC Transactions

Here, you can group FI-AA transaction types together for legal consolidation. You can make this grouping by assigning a common transaction type to all FI-AA transaction types in a transaction category, for consolidation purposes. This consolidation transaction type is generally the FI-AA transaction type used for the corresponding transaction category.

SAP supplied transaction types will be adequate to meet your business needs. And, you just need to go ahead with the default grouping of the consolidation transaction types; there is, in general, no need to define your own grouping.

Use the menu path: SAP Customizing Implementation Guide > Financial Accounting > Asset Accounting > Special Valuations > Revaluation of Fixed Assets > Preparations for Consolidation > Specify Consolidation Transaction Types for APC Transactions.

On the resulting screen (Figure 11.9), you will notice the standard transaction types that are already categorised into consolidation transaction types ('Cons TType'). For example, the consolidation transaction type 900 denotes 'opening balance', 920 indicates 'increase/ purchase', 930 'decrease /disposal' etc.

Change View "Asset transaction types -> Consolidation": Overview

Trans. Type	Transaction Type Name	Cons TType
1A1	CYr Acq: Accum APC, Acq Not Affect P&L	920
1A2	PYr Acq, Aff.Comp: Accum APC, Acq Not Affect ...	920
1A3	CYr Acq, Aff.Comp: Accum APC, Acq Not Affect ...	920
1W0	PYr Acq: Accum Depr, Acq Not Affect P&L	900
1W1	CYr Acq: Accum Depr, Acq Not Affect P&L	900
1W2	PYr Acq, Aff.Comp: Accum Depr, Acq Not Affect...	900
1W3	CYr Acq, Aff.Comp: Accum Depr, Acq Not Affect...	900
200	Retirement without revenue	930
201	Retirement due to catastrophe, without revenue	930

Figure 11.9: Consolidation Transaction Types for APC Transactions

The next task is to specify the transaction types for proportional value adjustments.

11.5.2 Specify Transaction Types for Proportional Value Adjustments

For consolidation purposes, you need to post the 'APC retirement' and the 'retirement of proportional value adjustments', with different transaction types, for a fixed asset retirement. This is to ensure that these two items remain separable, for the legal consolidation, even though they are posted to the same consolidated item.

Here, in this step, you define, for each retirement transaction type, from which transaction types the system should derive the consolidation transaction type with which the system posts the proportional value adjustments.

Use the menu path: SAP Customizing Implementation Guide > Financial Accounting > Asset Accounting > Special Valuations > Revaluation of Fixed Assets > Preparations for Consolidation > Specify Transaction Types for Proportional Value Adjustments. You may also use Transaction OAYT.

On the resulting screen, select the appropriate transaction type (say, 200 - Retirement without revenue) and double-click on 'Value adjustment procedure' on the left-hand side 'Dialog Structure'. On the next screen, you will see the standard transaction types for proportional value adjustments for each of the transaction like ordinary depreciation, special depreciation etc (Figure 11.10). We strongly recommend that you use the standard settings, instead of defining your own.

Figure 11.10: Transaction Types for Proportional Value Adjustments

The last configuration activity for consolidation preparation is to specify the group depreciation areas.

11.5.3 Specify Group Depreciation Areas

The asset transfers, between affiliated companies, represent either an acquisition or a retirement from the point of view of the participating individual companies. From the point of view of the corporate group, it is a transfer. The business transaction is posted as an acquisition or a retirement, and that should appear as a transfer from a consolidation point of view.

Hence, you can specify the group depreciation areas, so that the system represents transfers between affiliated companies correctly as transfers in reports, using these areas, for the corporate group.

Use the menu path: SAP Customizing Implementation Guide > Financial Accounting > Asset Accounting > Special Valuations > Revaluation of Fixed Assets > Preparations for Consolidation > Specify Group Depreciation Areas. You may also use Transaction OABE.

Select the 'GrossTrnsf' check-box for the appropriate depreciation areas, on the resulting screen. Once done, now, the asset transfers are not represented in these areas as acquisitions or retirements but as transfers, particularly in the asset history sheet. You may refer to Chapter 14.7 for details on asset history sheet.

This completes our discussion on the settings required for legal consolidation from asset accounting side; and this also completes our discussion on special valuation for fixed assets.

11.6 Conclusion

You learned that you will use 'special valuations' for special value adjustments to assets (like, investment support, special depreciation reserves etc) and for meeting some of the special valuation purposes, like, cost-accounting replacement values, interest, revaluation for the balance sheet etc. Using special valuations, you learned that you can take care of special reserves, transferred reserves, investment support, revaluation of fixed assets, interest, net worth tax, preparations for consolidation and leasing processing.

You learned that when you are allowed to use tax valuation approach in the B/S, you can carry out both book depreciation and tax depreciation (which exceeds book depreciation) and show the difference as special reserves on the liabilities side of the B/S.

You learned that, as per tax legislation of many countries, you can transfer the entire undisclosed reserves or a part thereof (created by the sale of assets), to replacement acquisitions. You also learned that if you cannot transfer such undisclosed reserves, in the year they are formed, because there were no suitable new acquisitions, you can set up a reserve in the year in question to prevent the gain on the sale influencing your profit. You, understood, that you can transfer these reserves, in the next few years, to assets acquired during this time period.

You learned that you need to revalue your fixed assets either to compensate for inflation or to account for the changed replacement values to meet (a) management accounting requirements and/or (b) tax obligations. You further learned that, using an index series, you can periodically revalue assets' APC and cumulative value adjustments, to arrive at the indexed replacement values, or, you can carry out revaluation for balance sheet, once every few years.

You learned that you can calculate (imputed) interest on the capital tied up in assets, for cost accounting purposes, per depreciation area, in addition to ordinary depreciation, special depreciation, unplanned depreciation etc. You understood that the system calculates the interest, as that of automatically calculated depreciation, using the calculation method in a depreciation key.

You learned that you can make the required settings in FI-AA, for consolidation preparation from asset accounting side, using the appropriate transaction types, besides specifying the depreciation areas for handling legal consolidation.

Let us, now, move on to discuss the settings required for managing asset master data, in the next Chapter.

12 Master Data

You need to make the necessary system settings for master data maintenance in FI-AA. This will, for example, help you define your own evaluation groups. SAP provides you with several functions, for asset master data maintenance, including control of the screen layout, validation / substitution of entries, mass changes to master record fields etc.

In this Chapter, we shall first discuss the asset master record in detail. We shall, then, discuss the control functions for asset master data using screen layout. We shall, finally, discuss the asset views and their usage in FI-AA.

Before we look at configuring some of these functions, let us, first understand how the asset information is stored in an asset master record.

12.1 Asset Master Record

To enable easy creation, management and evaluation of asset master data, SAP has structured the asset data according to its use and function. Accordingly, an asset master record consists of two areas: (a) general master data and (b) data for calculating asset values (Figure 12.1).

The *'general master data'* contains the information about the fixed asset. This includes general information (description, serial number, account determination, quantity etc), time-dependent assignments (cost center, internal order, plant, location, shift factor, profit center, segment, asset shutdown etc), origin data (vendor, manufacturer, country of origin, original acquisition year etc), entries for net worth tax, information on real estate, information on investment support measures, information on asset origin, insurance data, leasing information (leasing company, agreement number, lease start date, payment cycle etc), and user fields/evaluation groups. Besides, there are long texts, that you can create, for the individual field groups belonging to the general data part of the asset master record.

In the *'data for calculating asset values'*, you can specify depreciation terms in the asset master record, for each depreciation area. When doing so, you can get into the 'detailed display' for each depreciation area wherein you can maintain, for example, the depreciation key, useful life, changeover year, variable depreciation proportion, scrap value etc. If there are depreciation areas proposed from the asset class that you do not need for a specific asset, you can deactivate these depreciation areas at the asset level.

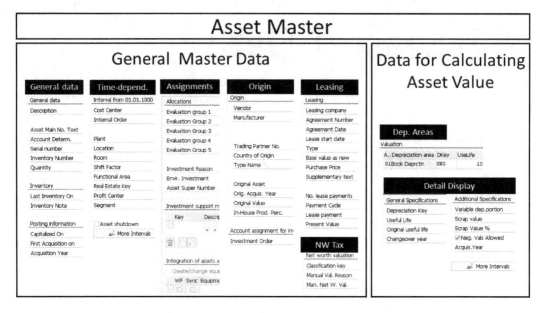

Figure 12.1: Data Sections of an Asset Master

With this, let us see the settings required for screen layout.

12.2 Screen Layout

We have already discussed the screen layout rules in Chapter 7.4.2.

Here, you will define the structure of your asset master records with the help of screen layout rules. In these screen layout rules, you can assign the field status to individual master record fields (for example, if the fields can be changed, or if they are to be suppressed completely etc). Besides, the screen layout also determines whether you can copy the fields as reference fields, for example. You can define screen layout for master records and also for depreciation areas. Also, you can make the settings for individual tabs on a master record screen.

Let us configure the screen lay out for asset master data.

12.2.1 Define Screen Layout for Asset Master Data

The '*screen layout control*' contains the specifications for the field groups in the asset master record. By entering the screen layout control in the asset class, you may structure the master record individually per asset class.

Project Dolphin

BESTM, to make physical inventory easier, requires that all the assets be identified with the valid 'Inventory number' in their respective asset master records. Accordingly, this field is to be made mandatory for data input. Also, to keep track of asset history, they want the 'History indicator' field to be enabled, but not mandatory to input. Besides, they also insisted that the 'Cost center', 'Business area' and 'Maintenance order' fields be made as a 'optional entry' field. During this discussion, the project team suggested to synchronize all the equipments with SAP Plant Maintenance application.

Use the menu path: SAP Customizing Implementation Guide > Financial Accounting > Asset Accounting > Master Data > Screen Layout > Define Screen Layout for Asset Master Data. On entering the transaction, you will see the 'Select Activity' pop-up screen:

i.   First, double-click 'Define Screen Layout for Asset Master Data' on the pop-up or use Transaction S_ALR_87009044. On the resulting 'Change View "Screen layout": Overview' screen (Figure 12.2), you will see several screen layout rules (that we have defined earlier in Chapter 7.4.2) listed.

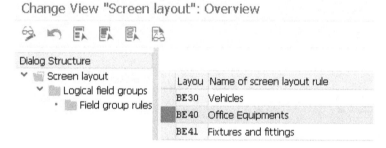

Figure 12.2: Selecting a Layout Rule

ii.   Now, select a rule (say, BE40), and double-click on 'Logical field groups' on the left-hand side 'Dialog Structure' (Figure 12.2). The system will display the logical field groups, on the next screen (Figure 12.3).

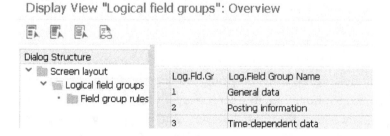

Figure 12.3: Logical Field Groups

iii.   Select the appropriate field group, and double-click on 'Field group rules' on the left-hand side 'Dialog Structure'. Since BESTM has requested to make 'Inventory number' as a mandatory field, and also enable 'History indictor', you need to select the logical field group 1 ('General data') and double-click on 'Field group rules' on the left-hand side 'Dialog Structure'.

iv.   On the resulting screen, you make changes so that the 'Inventory number' field becomes a 'required entry' ('Req.') from optional ('Opt.'). And, change the field status of 'History indicator' from suppressed ('No') status to 'optional entry' ('Opt.'), as shown in Figure 12.4.

Screen Layout   BE40   Office Equipments
Logical Fld Grp   1   General data

FG	Field group name	Req.	Opt.	No	Disp	Class	MnNo.	Sbno.	Copy	Mult
01	Description 1	●	○	○			✓	✓	✓	☐
02	Description 2	○	●	○			✓	✓	✓	☐
03	General long text	○	●	○			✓	✓		
04	Inventory number	● ← ○		○			✓	✓	✓	☐
05	Unit of measure	○	●	○		☐	✓	✓	✓	☐
06	Quantity	○	●	○	○		✓	✓	✓	☐
07	Asset main no. text	○	●	○			✓	✓	✓	☐
09	Account allocation	●				☐				
75	Serial number	○	●	○			✓	✓	☐	☐
79	Longtxt.:C-acc.view	○	●	○			✓	✓		
80	Longtxt.:Tech.view	○	●	○			✓	✓		
82	History indicator	○	● ← ○			☐	✓	✓	✓	☐

Figure 12.4: Field Status Change for Field Group 04 / 82

v.   Similarly, to make the required field status changes to 'Cost center', 'Business area' and 'Maintenance order' fields, use the logical field group 3 ('Time-dependent data'), and change the status from 'suppressed' ('No') status to 'optional entry' ('Opt.').

vi.   To enable synchronization of all the equipment assets with SAP Plant Maintenance application, use the logical field group 13 ('Equipment') and change the status of the 'Synchronize Asset' field to 'required entry'.

If you want to disable a field from maintenance, then you need to select the 'Disp' radio button against the field (Figure 12.4), so that the screen layout rule makes the corresponding field group as display only which you cannot be maintain. When you select 'MnNo.' check-box, then, the screen layout rule defines the asset main number as the maintenance level for the field group. Accordingly, when the system creates a subnumber for the asset, then, the values for this field group in the subnumber are supplied by the asset main number. However, when you select 'Sbno.' check-box, the screen layout rule defines the subnumber as the maintenance level for the corresponding field group. The 'Copy' check-box, when selected, makes the screen layout rule to indicate that when you create a new asset, using another as reference, the system copies the values, automatically from the referenced asset, for this specified field group.

vii.   Now, go back to the initial 'Select Activity' pop-up screen, and double-click on the 'Create Screen Layout Rules for Asset Master Record' activity if you need to define any more screen layout rules. This is the same Transaction S_ALR_87009209, that we maintained in Chapter 7.4.2.

viii.   On the initial 'Select Activity' pop-up screen, you may, finally, double-click on the 'Configurable Entry Screen for Creating Multiple Assets' activity, to activate configurable entry screen for creating multiple assets (12.5).

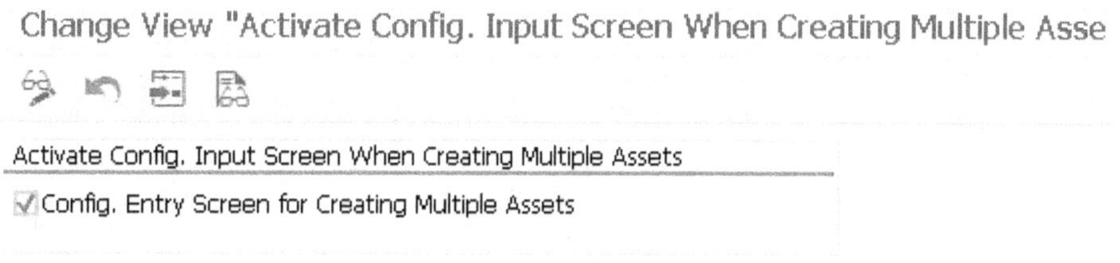

Change View "Activate Config. Input Screen When Creating Multiple Asse

Activate Config. Input Screen When Creating Multiple Assets

☑ Config. Entry Screen for Creating Multiple Assets

Figure 12.5: Activating Configurable Input Screen for Creating Multiple Assets

With this, we can move on to define the screen layout for depreciation areas.

12.2.2 Define Screen Layout for Asset Depreciation Areas

Use this configuration step, to define the screen layout control for the depreciation terms (depreciation key, useful life etc) in the asset master record. Similar to the screen layout control of general master data section of asset master, that we discussed in the previous Section 12.2.1, you can use this to control the features of the depreciation areas in the asset master record. You can make different specifications in each depreciation area.

---

i SAP delivers two standard versions: (a) 1000 - depreciation on main number level and (b) 2000 - depreciation on subnumber level. Recommended that you use these screen layout controls, as such, without making any changes.

Project Dolphin

As regards the screen layout control of depreciation areas is concerned, BESTM has decided to make use of the standard versions supplied by SAP, without changing any of the field status thereon.

Use the menu path: SAP Customizing Implementation Guide > Financial Accounting > Asset Accounting > Master Data > Screen Layout > Define Screen Layout for Asset Depreciation Areas, or Transaction AO21.

On the resulting screen, you will notice the two standard layout versions, 1000 and 2000. You may select any one of them, and double-click on 'Field group rules' on the left-hand side 'Dialog Structure' to view the field status of various field groups (Figure 12.6). We are not making any changes to the standard versions, as BESTM wants to use them as such.

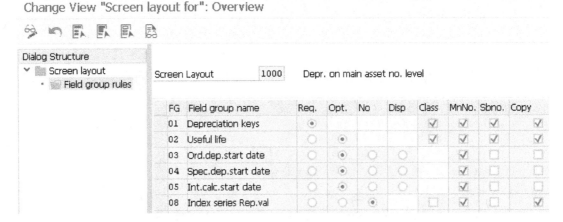

Figure 12.6: Standard Screen Layout 1000 – Depreciation on Main Asset Number Level

With this, we are now ready to define the layout for tabs on a screen of an asset master.

12.2.3 Specify Tab Layout for Asset Master Record

As you are aware, the asset master record is split over several tab pages, due to its large number of possible fields. Here, in this configuration step, you define the layout of these tab pages: specify which tab pages are seen for each asset class (or if needed, by chart of depreciation within the asset class); then, for each tab page, specify which field groups appear in which positions on the tab page.

Use the menu path: SAP Customizing Implementation Guide > Financial Accounting > Asset Accounting > Master Data > Screen Layout > Specify Tab Layout for Asset Master Record:

    i.   On the resulting 'Select Activity' pop-up screen, double-click on 'Define Tab Layout for Asset Master Data'. On the next screen (you can reach this directly through Transaction AOLA), you will see the list of standard layouts (Figure 12.7).

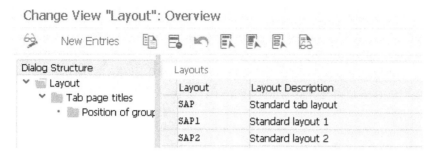

Figure 12.7: Standard Layouts for Tabs

ii.   Select any of the standard layouts (say, SAP), and double-click 'Tab page titles' on the left-hand side 'Dialog Structure', to view list of tabs / tab names (Figure 12.8).

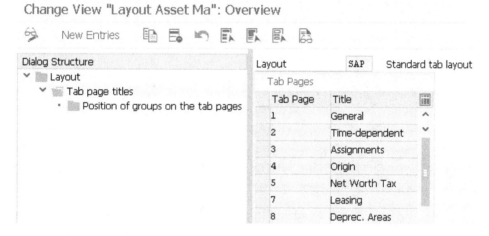

Figure 12.8: Tab Pages of Layout 'SAP'

iii.   Select a 'Tab Page' and double-click 'Position of groups on the tab pages' on the left-hand side 'Dialog Structure', to view field group placement on that tab (Figure 12.9).

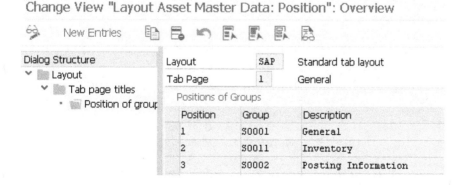

Figure 12.9: Field Group Position on Tab Page 1, for Layout 'SAP'

iv. You may also create a new tab layout, if required, by clicking on 'New Entries' on the screen (Figure 12.7) under step (i) above. Once defined, then, you need to go back to the initial 'Select Activity' pop-up screen, and double-click on the 'Assign Tab Layouts to Asset Classes' activity, to assign the newly defined tab layout to the required asset classes. You may also use Transaction AOLK to accomplish this.

With this, we are ready to process selection criteria, for web transactions.

12.2.4 Process Selection Criteria

Here, using this step, you can make specifications for the 'My assets' and 'Assets on my cost center' web transactions (internet / intranet). Per transaction, you can specify the 'selection criteria' that are available for selecting assets when you call up the Transaction. Besides, you can also specify the standard selection criteria that are presented when you start each of these Transactions.

Project Dolphin

For making the selection screen specifications for some of the web transactions including 'my assets', the project team has indicated that it will use most of the common fields, such as asset, asset sub number, asset class, account determination, acquisition year, capitalized on, evaluation group 1/2/3, asset super number, vendor, manufacturer, description, lease start date etc, as the selection fields for the 'cost accountant' role. Similar definitions will be created for 'cost center manager' and 'employee self-service'.

Use the menu path: SAP Customizing Implementation Guide > Financial Accounting > Asset Accounting > Master Data > Screen Layout > Process Selection Criteria:

Change View "Selectable Selection Criteria": Overview

New Entries

Dialog Structure

- Transactions
  - Selectable Selection

Transactions   Asset accountant

Selectable Selection Criteria

Fld no.	Field Label	Table	Field name
0300	Asset	ANLAV	ANLN1
0301	Sub-number	ANLAV	ANLN2
0302	Asset Class	ANLAV	ANLKL
0311	Account Determination	ANLAV	KTOGR
0314	Acquisition Year	ANLAV	ZUJHR
0317	Capitalized On	ANLAV	AKTIV
0322	Evaluation group 1	ANLAV	ORD41
0323	Evaluation Group 2	ANLAV	ORD42
0324	Evaluation Group 3	ANLAV	ORD43

Figure 12.10: Defining Selectable Selection Criteria

i.   On the resulting 'Select Activity' pop-up screen, double-click on 'Process Selection Options for List Box'.

ii.   On the next screen (you can also reach this directly through Transaction CUSTSEL_FIAA), you will see the list of Transactions like 'Cost center manager', 'Employee Self-Service' and 'Asset accountant'.

iii. Select a transaction (say, 'Asset accountant'), and double-click on 'Selectable Selection Criteria' on the left-hand side 'Dialog Structure'. On the next screen, use 'New Entries' and build the selection criteria fields for that transaction (Figure 12.10).

This completes our discussion on screen layout, and let us move on to discuss asset views.

12.3 Asset Views

FI-AA makes use of a 'view' concept for the protection of authorizations and also to provide access to some of the data in asset master data to certain employees who have only occasional and/or limited contact with fixed assets. The 'asset view', then, allows such employees only a limited view of asset data and values, whether or not they formally have access to every other master record. With the 'Purchasing asset view', for example, you can grant a person responsible for purchases, access only to the data that is purchase-relevant.

> **i** The 'asset view' determines which fields / depreciation areas can be processed from that particular view. There are 8 pre-defined asset views, as default; use them as such, or adopt them to meet your needs. You cannot add more views or delete the pre-defined ones.

Use the menu path: SAP Customizing Implementation Guide > Financial Accounting > Asset Accounting > Preparations for Going Live > Authorization Management > Process Asset Views. You may also use Transaction ANSCHT. On the resulting screen (Figure 12.11) you will the pre-defined asset views.

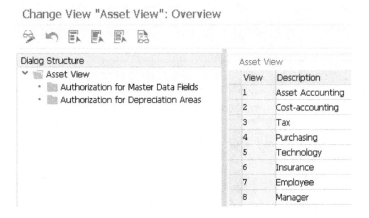

Figure 12.11: Standard Asset Views

You can assign different processing authorizations, for each asset view, to every field group of the asset master record. For that, you need to select a view (say, 1) and double-click on 'Authorization for Master Data Fields' on the left-hand side 'Dialog Structure' (Figure 12.12). On the resulting screen, you may change the processing authorization per field group, as required.

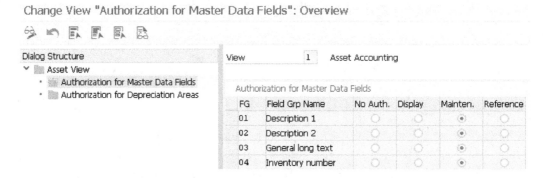

Figure 12.12: Authorization for Master Data Fields, for a given View

You may also manage authorizations as the depreciation area level. For that, you need to select a field group, say 04, and then, double-click on 'Authorization for Depreciation Areas' on the left-hand side 'Dialog Structure' (Figure 12.13). On the resulting screen, you may change the default processing authorization per depreciation area, as you may require.

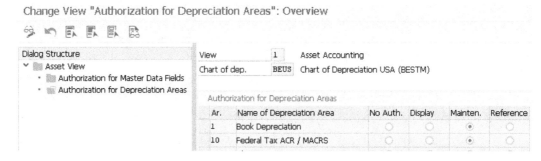

Figure 12.13: Authorization for Master Data Fields, for Depreciation Areas

> **i** Note that creating complete assets is only possible with asset view 1 ('Asset Accounting view'). The users who do not have this view cannot create any assets, in the system.

This completes our discussion on configuring for master data maintenance in FI-AA.

12.4 Conclusion

You learned that SAP has structured the asset data, in FI-AA, according to its use and function, for easy creation, management and evaluation of asset master data. You learned that an asset master record consists of two data areas: (a) general master data and (b) data for calculating asset values. You learned that the 'general master data' contains the information about the fixed asset including general information, time-dependent assignments, data on net worth tax, information on real estate, information on investment support measures, information on asset origin etc. You also learned that the 'data for calculating asset values' contains depreciation terms in the asset master record, per depreciation area. While maintaining the depreciation terms in the asset mater, you learned that you can get into the 'detailed display', for each depreciation area, and maintain, for example, the depreciation key, useful life, changeover year, variable depreciation proportion, scrap value etc.

You learned that you can define the structure of your asset master records with the help of screen layout rules wherein, you can assign the field status to individual master record fields (for example, if the fields can be changed, or if they are to be suppressed completely etc). You learned that you can define screen layout for master records and depreciation areas, besides maintaining the settings for individual tabs on a master record screen.

You learned that FI-AA makes use of a 'view' concept for the protection of authorizations and also to provide access to some of the data in asset master data to certain employees who have only occasional and/or limited contact with fixed assets. Accordingly, you learned that an 'asset view' allows such employees only a limited view of asset data and values, whether or not they formally have access to every other master record. You learned that there are 8 asset views, pre-defined in the system that you can use as such or adopt to meet your own needs. You understood that you can neither add more views nor delete the standard ones.

In the next Chapter, let us discuss the settings required for configuring the most important transactions in FI-AA.

13 Transactions

The 'transactions' component, in FI-AA, enables you to carry out all accounting transactions that occurs during the life of a fixed asset, including acquisitions, retirements, intracompany / intercompany transfers, and capitalizations of AuC.

The asset 'transaction types', in FI-AA, identify individual business transactions, and you need to associate a transaction type, manually or automatically, with each transaction that affects the assets in the system. Besides controlling the account assignment (debit / credit entry, document numbering etc), the transaction type also takes care of posting type (gross or net, for example) and other features. You can assign the business transactions to an 'asset history sheet' using these transaction types.

Each transaction type is assigned exactly to one 'transaction type group'. The transaction type group, determines, among others, which value fields are updated in year segments, whether the transaction refers to the past (for example, write-ups) or to the current fiscal year, whether the total of transactions of a group is positive or negative with reference to a fiscal year, according to which rule the start period for the depreciation calculation is determined, in which G/L accounts posting is to take place, whether the acquisition date of the fixed asset is set on the date of the first transaction of a group, whether proportional accumulated depreciation can be entered for a transaction (for example, during post-capitalization), or is to be determined by the system (for example, with asset retirements) and so on.

> **i** It is not possible to change either the number of transaction type groups or their characteristics, in the standard system. However, unlike transaction type groups, you can add new transaction types in the system to meet your exact business needs: when you create your own transaction types, make sure to enter the letter x, y, or z at any position in the three place transaction type key so that SAP does not over-write them with the future release updates.

On the basis of transaction type groups, you can segregate the asset business transactions into various categories, like:

- Transactions that influence the APC of fixed assets
    - Acquisitions
    - Retirements

- o   Transfer postings
- o   Post-capitalization
- Down payments
- Investment support measures
- Manual depreciation
- Write-ups

Let us start discussing the configuration settings that are required for asset acquisitions.

13.1 Acquisitions

The 'acquisition' is the primary business process in FI-AA relating to the purchase of assets and/or the capitalization of in-house produced goods or services. The system supports three distinct methods of asset acquisition:

1.   *Direct Capitalization*: This refers to asset acquisitions that do not have an AuC phase. Hence, the assets are capitalized and you begin the depreciation immediately on such assets. You can represent acquisitions of this kind using the following three options:
     - Direct account assignment to the final asset and possible statistical updating to an order or work breakdown structure (WBS) element. This includes:
          - ✓ External asset acquisitions
          - ✓ Processing asset acquisitions in Purchasing (FI-AA/MM)
          - ✓ Goods Receipt (GR) and Invoice Receipt (IR) with reference to asset
     - Account assignment to an order or WBS element (with allocation cost element) and settlement to the final asset:
          - ✓ Acquisition from internal activity
     - Account assignment to a clearing account and transferring from this account to the final asset.
2.   *Assets under Construction (AuC):* These are acquisitions to fixed assets that are not permitted to be capitalized and depreciated immediately. You can represent acquisitions of this kind using the following options:
     - Collect the costs using an investment measure (an order or a WBS element) with an AuC linked to it.
     - Collect the costs on an independent AuC in FI-AA.
3.   *Budget Monitoring using Statistical Orders or WBS Elements:* The system offers the option of automatic statistical updating to an order or WBS element of all acquisitions posted to an asset as this may be required for CO purposes that you monitor spending on asset acquisitions for the budget.

A *'subsequent acquisition'* is an addition or enhancement, to an already capitalized asset, in the current fiscal year with the depreciation start date for the enhancement in the current fiscal year. You can post a subsequent acquisition to an already existing asset either to the existing asset master record or to a new subnumber. When you post to an already existing asset master record, the system creates separate line items for each acquisition; however, it cannot display the depreciation from the subsequent acquisition after the end of the current fiscal year separately from the historical original acquisition. If you need to separately display the depreciation, then, you need to use a separate subnumber for the subsequent acquisition.

An *'acquisition resulting from extraordinary revenue'* is an asset acquisition that you post in FI-AA without any reference to a valuated GR or IR. You may need this type of transaction because (a) you have discovered a new fixed asset, requiring capitalization, during a physical inventory and /or (b) you receive an asset as a gift.

With this background in asset acquisition, let us look at the various configuration steps to set up the functionality.

13.1.1 Define Transaction Types for Acquisitions

You can use the standard transaction types, from SAP, without making any changes to them, for asset acquisitions. However, you may want to define your own transaction types (a) if you want to have certain types of acquisitions appear in different asset history sheet items; to meet this, define new acquisition transaction types and assign them to exceptional history sheet groups (in the IMG), (b) that do not lead to the capitalization of the assets posted; for this, you need to uncheck the 'Capitalize Fixed Asset' check-box while defining the new one, or (c) to monitor a budget using statistical orders/projects; here, you need set the flag for statistical updating of an order/project.

Project Dolphin

BESTM does not want to define any new transaction types for asset acquisitions; they are good with the standard ones supplied by SAP. However, while defining the account assignment category of asset purchase orders, BESTM has indicated to make the settings in such a way to have the 'Business Area' and 'Cost Center' as optional entry fields (from their original status of 'suppressed') to have the details captured, wherever possible.

Use the menu path: SAP Customizing Implementation Guide > Financial Accounting > Asset Accounting > Transactions > Acquisitions > Define Transaction Types for Acquisitions. You may also use Transaction AO73.

On the resulting screen, you can view the standard transaction types for various functions in asset acquisition (Figure 13.1). You may use 'New Entries' button, if you need to define a new transaction type.

Change View "FI-AA: Transaction types": Overview

New Entries

Transact. type	Transaction Type Name
100	External asset acquisition
101	Acquisition for a negative asset
102	External asset acquisition – set changeover year
103	Incidental costs, non-deduct. input tax (fol.yrs)
105	Credit memo in invoice year
106	Credit memo in invoice year to affiliated company
107	Gross acquisition of prior year balances (merger)
108	Gross acquisition of curren year balances (merger)
110	In-house acquisition
114	Acquis. - internal settlemt to AuC (positive only)
115	Settlement from CO to assets

Figure 13.1: Standard Transaction Types for Asset Acquisition

The next configuration step is to define the account assignment category for asset purchase orders.

13.1.2 Define Account Assignment Category for Asset Purch. Orders

You can post asset acquisitions during the processing of purchase orders (POs) in SAP MM (see also Chapter 8.1 for FI-AA integration with SAP MM). You can post a PO or a purchase requisition (PR) with account assignment to an asset. In order to make this assignment, however, you should have already created the asset in the system. Then, the system, automatically capitalizes the asset when the GR or IR is posted.

When you create a PO, you need to enter an 'account assignment category' (in the standard system, account assignment category A is pre-defined for valuated GR): entering account assignment category A tells the system that you are entering a PO for a fixed asset. The account assignment category also has specification as to whether the GR should be valuated (as in the case of standard account assignment category A) or not: if the GR is valuated, then, the asset is capitalized at the time of the GR; else, (that is, when it is non-valuated), the asset is capitalized at the time of the IR.

Use the menu path: SAP Customizing Implementation Guide > Financial Accounting > Asset Accounting > Transactions > Acquisitions > Define Account Assignment Category for Asset Purch. Orders. You may also use Transaction OME9.

On the resulting screen, you will see a list of account assignment categories including the standard account assignment category A for asset POs. Double-click on account assignment category A to see the detailed settings, on the next screen (13.2).

Change View "Account Assignment Categories": Details

⚙ New Entries   🗐 🗟 ↶ ⏴ ⏵ ⇥

Acct Assignment Cat.   A Asset

Detailed information

☐ Acct.assg.changeable   Consumption posting   A   Distribution   1
☑ AA Chgable at IR   Account Modification   Partial invoice   2
☐ Derive acct. assgt.   ID: AcctAssgt Scrn   2   Multiple account ass
☐ Del.CstsSep.   Special Stock

☑ Goods receipt   ☐ GR non-valuated   ☑ Invoice receipt
☐ GR Ind. Firm   ☐ GR NonVal. Firm   ☐ IR Ind. Firm

Fields

Field Label	Mand.Ent.	Opt.Entry	Display	Hidden
Asset	◉	○	○	○
Asset Subnumber	○	◉	○	○
Business Area	○	◉	○	○
Business process	○	○	○	◉

Figure 13.2: Standard Account Assignment Category (A) for Asset POs

Make changes, if required:

- Use the 'Acct.assg.changeable' check-box to determine if the account assignment of an item with the specified account assignment category can be changed following a GR or IR. Do not select this, when you want no changes for the account assignment following a GR/IR.
- Ensure that the value A ('Asset') has been selected for 'Consumption posting' field. In case of sales-order-related production, this field determines whether the costs of sales-order-related production are collected under a sales order item. For that you need to select E (Accounting via sales order).
- The entry in the 'Distribution' field determines how the quantity and value of a PO item are to be distributed among the individual account assignment items: by quantity (1) or on a percentage basis (2) or) or by amount (3). The value you enter here will be pre-set on the multiple account assignment screen.
- Use the 'AA Chagble at IR' check-box to decide if you need the flexibility to change the account assignment of a PO item at the time of IR during invoice verification.
- Select 'Goods receipt' to specify if the item involves a GR.
- Select 'Invoice receipt' to specify if an IR is linked to the PO item. If not set, the goods are to be delivered free of charge.

- Select 'GR non-valuated' check-box, to determine if the GR for this item is to be valuated or not. When selected (= GR is valuated), the asset is capitalized at the time of the GR; when not selected (= GR is non-valuated), the asset is capitalized at the time of the IR.
- You may also make the required changes to the field status of any of the fields that is listed at the bottom of the screen: we have changed the field status of 'Business Area' and 'Cost Center' fields from 'Hidden' to 'Opt.Entry'.

The next step is to specify the asset class for creating asset form POs.

13.1.3 Specify Asset Class for Creating Asset from Purchase Order

As you can create an asset directly from the purchasing transaction for PO, you can enter an asset PO, without creating an asset beforehand in FI-AA. This asset, thus created, will, then, serve as the account assignment object for the PO. Here, in this configuration step, you can specify the asset classes that the system should use, as defaults, when you create an asset from within a PO. You need to specify the asset class for each of the material groups for fixed assets.

Use the menu path: SAP Customizing Implementation Guide > Financial Accounting > Asset Accounting > Transactions > Acquisitions > Specify Asset Class for Creating Asset from Purchase Order. You may also use Transaction OMQX.

On the resulting screen, enter the appropriate asset 'Class' against all the material groups ('Mat. Grp') for fixed assets (Figure 13.3).

Change View "Default Asset Class": Overview

Mat. Grp	Mat. Grp Descr.	Class	Short Text
YBFA05	Machinery Equipment	B2000	Plant
YBFA06	Fixtures Fittings	B4200	Furniture
YBFA07	Vehicles	B3000	Vehicles
YBFA08	Computer Hardware	B5100	Computer Hardware
YBFA09	Computer Software	B5200	Computer Software
YBFA10	Low Value Assets	B7000	LVA - Collective
YBFA11	Other Intangibles	B8000	Intangible Assets
YBFA12	Office Equipment	B4100	Office Equipment

Figure 13.3: Asset Class Specification for Creating Asset from PO

The next step is to assign the G/L accounts for asset acquisitions.

13.1.4 Assign Accounts

Use the menu path: SAP Customizing Implementation Guide > Financial Accounting > Asset Accounting > Transactions > Acquisitions > Assign Accounts, or Transaction AO85 to assign the appropriate G/L accounts for posting acquisition-related asset transactions:

    i.   Maintain the chart of depreciation (BEUS), and select the chart of accounts (BEUS) on the resulting screen.

    ii.   Select an 'Account Determination' (say, B1000 Buildings) and double-click on 'Balance Sheet Accounts' on the left-hand side 'Dialog Structure'.

    iii.   On the next screen, double-click on the depreciation area (say, 01) and maintain the required G/L accounts on the next screen. We have already completed assigning of accounts for acquisitions in Chapter 8.4.2 when we discussed the FI-AA integration with SAP G/L Accounting. Here, in this activity, you may add the G/L accounts for 'Account assignment of cost portions not capitalized' which we did not set up earlier.

    iv.   Repeat assigning the G/L accounts for 'Account assignment of cost portions not capitalized', for all the account determinations.

The next configuration activity is to define the technical clearing account for integrated asset acquisition.

13.1.5 Define Technical Clearing Account for Integrated Asset Acquisition

We have completed this setting in Chapter 8.4.3 when we discussed the FI-AA integration with SAP G/L Accounting. However, you may use the menu path: SAP Customizing Implementation Guide > Financial Accounting > Asset Accounting > Transactions > Acquisitions > Technical Clearing Account for Integrated Asset Acquisition > Define Technical Clearing Account for Integrated Asset Acquisition, to verify the same.

With this, let us see how to configure a different technical clearing account for required field control, in the next Section.

13.1.6 Define Different Technical Clearing Account for Required Field Control

We have already seen, vide Chapter 8.4.3, that in an integrated asset acquisition posting, the system divides the business transaction into an operational part and a valuating part. When you enter the posting, initially, only the operational part (that is, the posting against the technical clearing account) is visible. The properties of the account assignment fields, such as cost center or profit center, are derived from the field control of the technical clearing account. Hence, if you require different field control behaviour, depending on the asset balance sheet account to be posted to, you, then, need to reflect this using different technical clearing accounts for integrated asset acquisition.

We have, vide the pervious Section 13.1.5, already defined a technical clearing account of integrated asset acquisition. Here, in this activity, you differentiate between technical clearing accounts for integrated asset acquisition using their account determination. You can then assign the required field status variant to the different technical clearing accounts for integrated asset acquisition. In the process, you also need to make sure that the FSV of the technical clearing accounts and the relevant asset accounts (that are posted to in the valuating part of the transaction) match. Especially in the field control of the technical clearing account, you need to ensure that no 'required entry' fields of asset accounts are with 'hidden' field status.

For example, when you want the system to post the asset in, say, 'Independent AuC' asset class with the account assignment to the 'Order' field, then, that field is to be set to 'required entry' status; for all other asset classes it is to be set as 'optional entry' status. Here, as you need different field control behaviour, you need to make the required configuration settings. To achieve this, you need two G/L accounts, defined, to be used as technical clearing accounts for integrated asset acquisition: for the first account, you enter a field status with the setting 'optional entry' for the 'Order' field, and for the second account, you enter a field status with the setting 'required entry' for the 'Order' field.

You may achieve this configuration by using the menu path: SAP Customizing Implementation Guide > Financial Accounting > Asset Accounting > Transactions > Acquisitions > Technical Clearing Account for Integrated Asset Acquisition > Define Different Technical Clearing Account for Required Field Control.

On the resulting screen, you assign an FSV with 'Order' field set to 'optional entry' to the G/L account that you have already defined in the previous configuration activity 'Define Technical Clearing Account for Integrated Asset Acquisition' (Section 13.1.5). Now, create another entry, enter another G/L account for the specific asset class ('Independent AuC') and assign another FSV with the field status of 'Order' set to 'required entry'.

Project Dolphin

In the case of integrated asset accounting, BESTM does not want to use differing technical clearing accounts, but wants the system to use the one defined at the chart of accounts level. Accordingly, the project team has decided not to configure the IMG node 'Define Different Technical Clearing Account for Required Field Control'.

The next configuration is to make the required settings for allowing down payment transaction types in the appropriate asset classes.

13.1.7 Allow Down Payment Transaction Types in Asset Classes

Using this configuration step, you can determine the asset classes, like AuC, for which down payments made may be capitalized in the system.

Use the menu path: SAP Customizing Implementation Guide > Financial Accounting > Asset Accounting > Transactions > Acquisitions > Allow Down Payment Transaction Types in Asset Classes. You may also use Transaction OAYB.

On the resulting screen, for each of the transaction type groups ('TTG) like 15 (down payment), 16 (down payment balance from previous years), 38 (retirement transfer previous year acquisition - AuC summary) and 39 (retirement transfer current year acquisition - AuC summary), you need to specify the asset classes. Select a 'TTG' (say, 15), double-click on 'Specification of asset classes' on the left-hand side 'Dialog Structure' and specify the asset class(es) on the next screen (say, B6000), by clicking on 'New Entries' (Figure 13.4). And, repeat this for all the transaction type groups, and 'Save' your details.

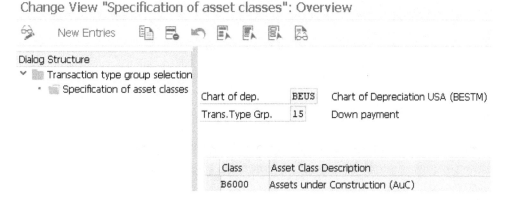

Figure 13.4: Specification of Asset Classes for allowing Down Payment Transaction Types

The next task is to make the appropriate configuration to prevent subsequent capitalization of discounts.

13.1.8 Prevent Subsequent Capitalization of Discounts

When an asset acquisition posting has been integrated with FI-A/P, you can specify, through the appropriate document type, if the invoice should be posted 'gross' (without deducting discount) or 'net' (with discount deducted). In 'net' posting, the system automatically determines the cash discount to be deducted (on the basis of the payment terms), capitalizes the invoice amount (less tax and cash discount), on the fixed asset. However, should there be a difference in discount (too much or too little), which you find out later during the payment run, you can subsequently adjust / correct the APC (through collective processing) in SAP G/L

Accounting. But, using this configuration step, and selecting the 'No Discount' check-box, you can prevent these subsequent adjustments to APC.

Project Dolphin

BESTM wants the project team to configure the system to prevent subsequent adjustments made to APC of an asset arising out of incorrect discount charged in 'net' invoice posting, relating to assets, in FI-A/P and the resulting capitalization.

Use the menu path: SAP Customizing Implementation Guide > Financial Accounting > Asset Accounting > Transactions > Acquisitions > Prevent Subsequent Capitalization of Discounts.

On the resulting screen, select the 'No Discount' check-box for all the required company codes to prevent subsequent adjustments to APC on account of incorrect discount during 'net' posting capitalization (Figure 13.5).

Change View "Prevent Subsequent Capitalization of Discounts": Overview

Prevent Subsequent Capitalization of Discounts

Company Code	Company Name	No Discount	
1110	BESTM Farm Machinery	✓	
1120	BESTM Garden & Forestry E	✓	

Figure 13.5: Preventing Subsequent Capitalization of Discounts

This completes our discussion on configuration for acquisition transactions. Let us move on to discuss the settings required for asset retirement, in the next Section.

13.2 Retirements

The '*asset retirement*' is the removal of an asset or part of an asset from your asset portfolio. The asset retirement ca be complete or partial. It can happen with or without revenue. Based on the organizational considerations, or business transaction leading to asset retirement, you will come across with the following types of asset retirement in the system:

- You sell an asset and realise some revenue. You post the sale with a customer.
- You sell an asset and realise some revenue. You post the sale against a clearing account.
- You scrap an asset and do not realise any revenue.
- You sell an asset to your affiliated company (manual posting).

SAP provides you with the standard transaction types to take care of asset sale (with or without customer) and asset retirement due to scrapping. Let us understand each of the asset retirements in brief:

- *Asset Sale with Customer*
  In cases of *'asset sale with customer'*, the system enables posting the entry to FI-A/R, the revenue posting and asset retirement in one step. During posting, first, you need to enter the revenue posting (debit A/R, credit revenue from asset sale), and, then, enter the asset retirement. An indicator in the posting transaction denotes that the system posts the asset retirement with the revenue posting. The system posts a separate accounting-principle-specific document, per posting depreciation area, provided that the depreciation area manages APC.

- *Asset Retirement without Revenue*
  When you use the *'asset retirement without revenue'* (for example, asset scrapping) posting option, the system does not create revenue and gain/loss postings; instead, it creates a 'loss made on asset retirement without revenue' posting in the amount of the NBV of the asset that is getting retired.

- *Complete / Partial Retirement*
  The asset retirement can refer to an entire fixed asset (*'complete retirement'*) or part of a fixed asset (*'partial retirement'*). In both cases, the system automatically determines, using the asset retirement dates entered, the amounts to be charged off for each depreciation area. You can initiate the partial retirement of a fixed asset by entering (a) the APC that is being retired or (b) a retirement percentage or (c) a quantity:

  - When you enter the amount of APC that is being retired, the system determines, per accounting principle, the percentage to be retired from the asset using the first depreciation area of the respective ledger group in which posting is to take place. It, then, uses the same percentage for other depreciation areas. You can enter a quantity, provided that you have not specified a retirement amount or percentage rate: then, the system interprets the quantity as a ratio to the total quantity of the asset and thereby determines the asset retirement percentage rate.
  - The complete retirement of a fixed asset is only possible if all transactions to the asset were posted with a value date before the asset value date of asset retirement. You must clear or reverse down payments and investment support measures, which are in the same posting year as the retirement, before you post the complete retirement.

> **i** Select the correct transaction type, for both partial and complete retirement. For the complete retirement of a fixed asset acquired in previous years, always select a transaction type intended for prior-year acquisitions. A partial retirement can always relate either to prior-year acquisitions or to current-year acquisitions. The system shows prior-year asset acquisitions and current-year acquisitions, separately from one another in the document.

- *Retirement of LVAs*
  It is not necessary to actually post the retirement of LVAs, due to the large number of assets that are being retired, in order for the assets transactions to be displayed correctly in the asset history sheet. You can simulate the retirements during a time period that you specify in the initial screen of the asset history sheet. However, if you want to actually post the retirement of LVAs, use the usual procedure for asset retirements. Refer Section 14.7 for details on asset history sheet.

- *Simultaneous Retirement of Several Asset Subnumbers*
  You can post the complete retirement of several subnumbers of a fixed asset in one step by using the generic entry using an * in the 'Subnumber' field.

- *Mass Retirement*
  When you sell a large portion of its fixed assets (such as a plant or a building), it is necessary to post the retirement of all the individual assets which make up the whole asset. Since the number of affected assets can be very large, FI-AA enables making the necessary postings using mass processing. For the selection of the assets involved and the basic procedure for mass retirement, you will be using the same functions as that of 'mass change' to asset master data. When you create a worklist for mass retirement, enter the purpose as either 'retirement with revenue' or 'retirement without revenue (scrapping)'. Besides you also need to make the entries including the posting date, transaction type, revenue and type of revenue distribution.

> **i** When you retire an asset, the system records the value date of the retirement in the asset master record. Once this is done, you cannot, then, post any transactions with a value date before the value date of the last retirement. However, if need to post such a transaction, you must first reverse all retirements that lie after the value date of the belated posting, post the belated transaction, then, finally then re-post the asset retirements.

With this background in asset retirement, let us now understand the configuration that is required to use the retirement functionality in the system.

Let us start with the transaction types for asset retirements.

13.2.1 Define Transaction Types for Retirements

Use the menu path: SAP Customizing Implementation Guide > Financial Accounting > Asset Accounting > Transactions > Retirements > Define Transaction Types for Retirements. On the resulting 'Select Activity' pop-up, double-click on 'Define Transaction Types for Retirements'. You will see the standard transaction types, for asset retirement transactions, on the next screen (Figure 13.6). You may also use Transaction AO74 to reach this screen directly.

Change View "FI-AA: Transaction types": Overview

⬦ ⬦   New Entries   ▤ ▤ ↰ ▤ ▤ ▤

Transact. type	Transaction Type Name
200	Retirement without revenue
201	Retirement due to catastrophe, without revenue
202	CZ Retirement due to scrapping
206	Retirement without revenue - Finnland EVL
209	Retmt. of prior-yr acq. from inv.meas. w/o revenue
210	Retirement with revenue

Figure 13.6: Transaction Types for Asset Retirement

When you double-click on a particular transaction type (say, 210), you will be able to see the detailed settings on the next screen (Figure 13.7):

- You will notice that the 'Deactivate Fixed Asset' check-box has been selected under 'Account assignment'. This indicates that the asset will be deactivated when you make a posting that results in an acquisition value = zero. The system sets the asset retirement date and the status.
- Under 'Transfer / retirement / current-yr. acquis.' data block, you will see that the 'Retirement with Revenue' check-box has been selected indicating that you must enter revenue when posting a retirement of a fixed asset using this transaction type.
- The 'Repay Investment Support', when selected, results in the system automatically posting the repayment of the investment support, if any, that has been claimed, when the asset is retired. However, if you claimed the investment support in the same year in which the asset is retired, you have to reverse the investment support before posting the retirement.
- The 'Post gain/loss to asset' check-box, when selected, denotes that the gain/loss made on an asset retirement will not assigned to a P&L account, but to a specific asset as a value adjustment.

Change View "FI-AA: Transaction types": Details

🖉 New Entries 📄 📑 🔙 ↩ 📤 ➡

| Trans. Type | 210 | Retirement with revenue |
| Transaction Type Grp | 20 | Retirement |

Account assignment

☑ Deactivate Fixed Asset

Document type   `AA`   Asset Posting

Transfer/retirement/current-yr acquis.

☑ Retirement with Revenue

☑ Repay Investment Support

☐ Post gain/loss to asset

Acquisition in Same Year   `260`   Retirement of current-year acquis. with reven

Posting type

◯ Post to affiliated company   ◯ Post Gross

◉ Do not post to affiliated co.   ◉ Post Net

Other features

☐ Cannot Be Used Manually

☐ Call up individual check   ☐ Trans. Type Obsolete

Consolidation Transaction Type   `930`   Decrease/ Disposal

Asst Hist Sheet Grp   `20`   Retirement

Figure 13.7: Transaction Type 210: Detailed Settings

You may go back to the initial pop-up, and double-click on 'Define Transaction Types for Subsequent Costs/Revenues' to view the associated transaction types (285 and 286) for subsequent costs and revenues (Figure 13.8). You can reach this screen directly by using Transaction AO81.

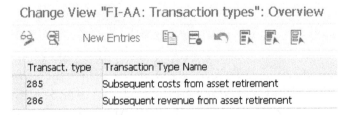

Change View "FI-AA: Transaction types": Overview

🖉 🗐 New Entries 📄 📑 🔙 📊 📊 📊

Transact. type	Transaction Type Name
285	Subsequent costs from asset retirement
286	Subsequent revenue from asset retirement

Figure 13.8: Transaction Types for Subsequent Costs / Revenues from Asset Retirement

The next activity is to determine the posting variants for gain/loss posting, arising out of asset retirements.

13.2.2 Determine Posting Variants

Here, you define how to manage gain/loss with asset retirement for each depreciation area. The standard asset retirement transaction types use variant 0, and is the variant prescribed by tax/commercial law in most countries. The variants 1 and 2 are, for example, necessary for *group assets* in USA, to meet the with American ADR legislation.

Use the menu path: SAP Customizing Implementation Guide > Financial Accounting > Asset Accounting > Transactions > Retirements > Gain/Loss Posting > Determine Posting Variants. You may also use Transaction OAYS.

On the resulting screen, select the transaction type (say, 210) and double-click on 'Special treatment of retirement' on the left-hand side 'Dialog Structure'. On the next screen, select the depreciation area, and enter the appropriate posting variant for that. We have selected the variant 0 for the 'Ret.type' field which is suitable for most of the countries (Figure 13.9). Repeat and assign the variant for all the required transaction types / depreciation areas.

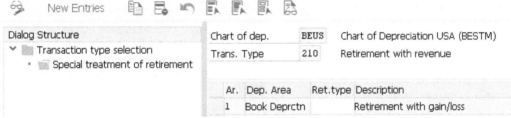

Figure 13.9: Posting Variant for Transaction Type 210

With this, let us move to define the transaction types for write-up due to gain/loss.

13.2.3 Define Transaction Types for Write-Up Due to Gain/Loss

You need to configure this step only if you do not post gain/loss to P&L accounts, instead want to collect gain/loss on *'special assets'* (as in USA). The system uses the transaction types, you define here, to post gain/loss to specified assets as a write-up. You can use SAP supplied standard transaction type 770, without making any changes. This is not required for BESTM.

Project Dolphin

As BESTM uses P&L accounts to post the gain/loss arising out of asset retirements, the project team has been asked not to configure the transaction types to collect gain/loss on an asset itself. Also, BESTM does not want to configure this for asset classes as well.

The next step is to determine the asset for gain/loss posting per asset class

13.2.4 Determine Asset for Gain/Loss Posting per Class

Similar to the previous activity, you will need this implementation step only when you do not post gain/loss to profit and loss accounts, but instead want to collect gain/loss on *'special assets'* (using asset retirement variant 3) In that case, you enter the asset ('Asset No.' and 'SNo.'), for each asset class, to which the system should post gain/loss from asset retirement. Not required for BESTM.

Let us now define the how to distribute the revenue for asset retirement.

13.2.5 Define Revenue Distribution for Fixed Asset Retirement

You can specify, here, at company code level, how the system is to distribute revenue arising from asset retirements: whether it is to be distributed based on APC or based on NBV. However, when you create a worklist of mass retirement, you can still opt for an alternative type of revenue distribution, irrespective the settings you make here.

Project Dolphin

BESTM has indicated that the revenue distribution method, in company code, should be based on NBV instead of APC, for all the company codes, both in US and India.

Use the menu path: SAP Customizing Implementation Guide > Financial Accounting > Asset Accounting > Transactions > Retirements > Gain/Loss Posting > Determine Posting Variants, to configure the settings.

On the resulting screen, select the appropriate value ('By Net Book Value') for 'Rev. Dist.' field (Figure 13.10). The other option is 'By APC'.

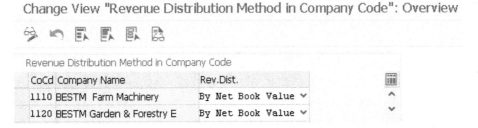

Figure 13.10: Revenue Distribution Method per Company Code

The last configuration activity under asset retirement is to assign the G/L accounts.

13.2.6 Assign Accounts

Use the menu path: SAP Customizing Implementation Guide > Financial Accounting > Asset Accounting > Transactions > Retirements > Assign Accounts or Transaction AO86, to enter the appropriate G/L accounts for posting asset retirements. On the resulting screen:

i. Select the chart of accounts (say, BEUS) and double-click on 'Account Determination' on the left-hand side 'Dialog Structure'.

ii. On the next screen, select an 'Account Determination' (say, B1000) and double-click on 'Balance Sheet Accounts' on the left-hand side 'Dialog Structure'

iii. On the resulting screen, double-click on the depreciation area ('Area') and maintain the appropriate G/L accounts, under 'Retirement account assignment' data block, on the next screen (Figure 13.11).

iv. Repeat for all the account determinations and appropriate depreciation areas.

Change View "Balance Sheet Accounts": Details

Dialog Structure
- Chart of Accounts
  - Account Determination
    - Balance Sheet Accounts

Chart of Accts	BEUS	BESTM - US Standard Chart of Accounts
Account Determ.	B1000	Buildings
Deprec. area	1	Book Depreciation

Retirement account assignment

Loss Made on Asset Retirement w/o Reven.	71010900	Loss frm Asset Retir
Clearing Acct. Revenue from Asset Sale	70030000	Clear ass.disp.
Gain from Asset Sale	71010100	Gain asset transactn
Loss from Asset Sale	71010300	Loss Asset Trns
Clear.revenue sale to affil.company	70050000	Clrg aff assettransf

Figure 13.11: Assigning G/L Accounts for Asset Retirements

This completes our discussion on configuring the settings for asset retirements. Let us move on to discuss the settings for asset transfers.

13.3 Transfer Postings

In this Section, we shall be discussing the configuration settings for asset transfers. The first activity is to define the transaction types for such transfers.

13.3.1 Define Transaction Types for Transfers

You need two transaction types for transfers between assets: (a) a transaction type for retirement from the sending asset and (b) a transaction type for the acquisition on the receiving asset. The system performs the posting transaction from the point of view of the sending asset.

We recommend using the SAP supplied standard transaction types which you can view using the menu path: SAP Customizing Implementation Guide > Financial Accounting > Asset Accounting > Transactions > Transfer Postings > Define Transaction Types for Transfers.

You will see the 'Select Activity' pop-up screen, when you enter the transaction. Double-click on the 'Define Transaction Types for Retirement Transfers' activity to view the list of standard transaction types (300, 306, 320, 338, 339, 340 etc) for retirement transfers (Figure 13.12). You can also reach this screen, directly, by using Transaction AO76.

Change View "FI-AA: Transaction types": Overview

New Entries

Transact. type	Transaction Type Name
300	Retirmt transfer of prior-yr acquis. frm cap.asset
306	Retmt transfer prior-yr acquis. from cap.asset FI
320	Retirmt transfer of curr-yr acquis.
338	Retirmt transfer of prior-yr acquis from inv.meas.
339	Acquirg transfer of curr-yr acquis from inv.meas.
340	Retmt transfer of prior-yr acquis f. AuC, line itm
345	Retmt transfer of curr-yr acquis f. AuC, line itm
348	Retmt transfer of prior-yr acquis from AuC,summary

Figure 13.12: Standard Transaction Types for Retirement Transfers

When you go back to the initial pop-up and double-click on 'Define Transaction Types for Acquisition Transfers', you will be taken to another set of standard transaction types (310, 330, 331, 336 etc) for acquisition transfers. You may reach this screen (Figure 13.13), directly, using Transaction AO75.

Change View "FI-AA: Transaction types": Overview

New Entries

Transact. type	Transaction Type Name
310	Acquirg transfer of prior-yr acquis. frm cap.asset
330	Acquiring transfer of curr-yr acquis.
331	Acquirg transfer of prior-yr acquis from inv.meas.
336	Acquirg transfer of curr-yr acquis from inv.meas.
341	Acquirg transfer of prior-yr acquis from AuC
342	Bal.forward AuC after partial settlmt pr-yr acquis
346	Acquirg transfer of curr-yr acquis. from AuC

Figure 13.13: Standard Transaction Types for Acquisition Transfers

The next step is to specify the posting variant for retirement transfers.

13.3.2 Specify Posting Variant for Retirement Transfers

Here, in this step, you shall define the way retirement transfers are to be treated in the system, per depreciation area, whether to:

a) Transfer of APC and proportional value adjustments, or
b) Transfer of APC <u>without</u> proportional value adjustment.

In most of the countries, you will use the option (a) unless you need to take care of group assets in accordance with ADR legislation in USA wherein you will use the option (b).

Use the menu path: SAP Customizing Implementation Guide > Financial Accounting > Asset Accounting > Transactions > Transfer Postings > Specify Posting Variant for Retirement Transfers, or Transaction OAY1:

i.   On the resulting screen, per transaction type ('Tra'), you need to specify how to handle the retirement transfers. Select the transaction type and double-click on 'Special handling of transfer posting' on the left-hand side 'Dialog Structure'.

ii.   On the next screen, ensure that you do not select 'Trans. APC Only' check-box, for the depreciation areas, if you want to transfer APC and proportional value adjustments (Figure 13.14). If you select this check-box, then, the system transfers only the APC and <u>not</u> the proportional value adjustments. You will select the check-box only when you want to take care of *group assets* in accordance with ADR legislation in USA.

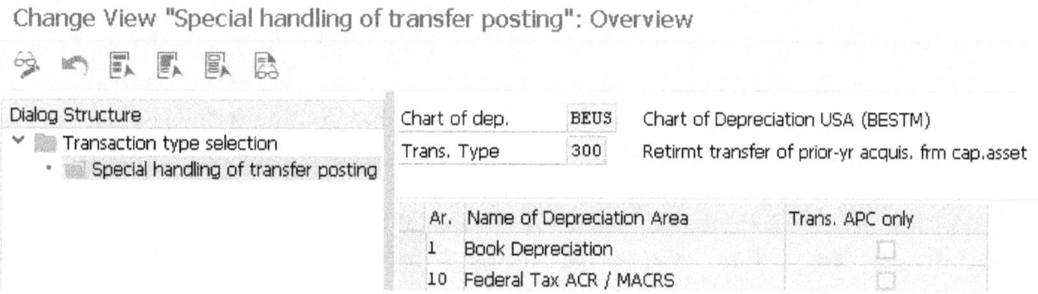

Figure 13.14: Posting Variant for Retirement Transfers

Let us, now, discuss the configuration settings for intercompany asset transfers.

13.4 Intercompany Asset Transfers

You use *'intercompany asset transfer'* to carry out asset transfers between company codes. In the case of individual companies, an intercompany transfer represents a retirement for one company code and an acquisition for the other. However, from corporate groups' view point, it represents a transfer that balances to zero in the group asset history sheet. Refer Chapter 14.7 for details on asset history sheet.

An intercompany asset transfer results when (a) there is a change in the physical location of the asset which leads to assigning of the asset to a new company code and/or (b) there is a change in the organizational structure of the corporate group calling for re-assigning the asset to a different company code.

You cannot just change the organizational assignment of the asset by changing the asset master record: for each asset that you want to transfer, you have to create a new master record in the target company code, or you use an existing asset master record. This way, the system preserves the unique identity of the asset using the inventory number in the asset master record.

The intercompany asset transfers can be of the following types:

- *Client-internal transfer*
  Also known as *'automatic intercompany transfer'*, here, you post the retirement transfer and the acquisition transfer in a single step.

  You can reverse automatic intercompany asset transfers, using the normal reversal functions in FI-AA: the system reverses the 'retirement document' in the sending company code and the 'acquisition document' in the target company code. If the transfer has resulted in a new asset creation in the target company code, you can block the asset for any additional acquisition postings.

- *Cross-client transfer*
  Also known as the *'manual intercompany transfer*, here, you process the transfer across clients / systems; you post the retirement transfer and the acquisition transfer in two separate steps. While you can integrate the posting with FI-A/P and FI-A/R in the manual transfer, you cannot do so in the automatic transfer.

  In the case of manual intercompany asset transfer, you can reverse the retirement and the acquisition, separately, in the company code in which you made the respective postings.

With this background, let us understand the control parameters that you need to define for intercompany asset transfer (both automatic and manual).

Let us understand first, the settings, for automatic transfer.

13.4.1 Automatic Intercompany Asset Transfers

Towards automatic intercompany asset transfer, you need to complete the following tasks:

- Define Cross-System Depreciation Areas
- Define Transfer Variants

Let us start with the first activity of defining the cross-system depreciation areas.

13.4.1.1. Define Cross-System Depreciation Areas

Using 'cross-system depreciation areas', you can assign a meaning to the local depreciation areas that is then valid in all charts of depreciation throughout your system. The cross-system depreciation area makes this possible, although the different depreciation areas have different keys in different charts of depreciation. For each cross-system depreciation area, you can specify its own transfer methods in a transfer variant.

Project Dolphin

BESTM does not need a cross-system depreciation areas to handle intercompany asset transactions, when asset transfer happens among the company codes situated either within US or within India, as all the US-based company codes use the same chart of depreciation BEUS and all the company codes in India use the same chart of depreciation BEIN. In each case, the chart of depreciation is the same and the depreciation areas have the same numbering and meaning (Figure 13.15).

However, BESTM requires the cross-system depreciation areas, to facilitate intercompany asset transfers between a company in US and another in India, as these company codes use two different charts of accounts (BEUS for US-based company codes and BEIN for India-based company codes). In this case, the depreciation areas, though have the same keys (for some of the areas), their meaning are different across the systems.

You do not need cross-system depreciation areas, if all company codes in your client use the same chart of depreciation, or if the depreciation areas (in your charts of depreciation) have the same purpose and meaning, across the system, and also have the same keys.

You need global cross-system depreciation areas only when (a) you use different charts of depreciation (with the individual depreciation areas having the same meaning), or (b) a depreciation area that is not intended to be transferred during intercompany transfer, or (c) you have individual depreciation areas with the same name, but their meanings are different.

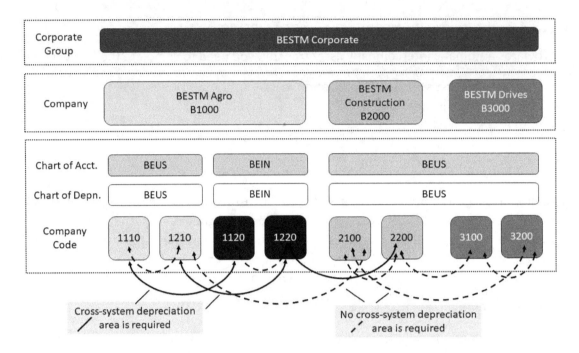

Figure 13.15: BESTM - Intercompany Asset Transfer: Overview

Use the menu path: SAP Customizing Implementation Guide > Financial Accounting > Asset Accounting > Transactions > Intercompany Asset Transfers > Automatic Intercompany Asset Transfers > Define Cross-System Depreciation Areas.

On the resulting 'Select Activity' pop-up screen, double-click on 'Define Cross-System Depreciation Areas'. On the next screen, click on 'New Entries' and define the new cross-system depreciation area (Figure 13.16).

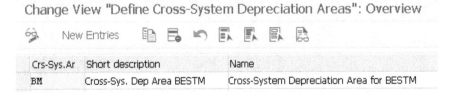

Figure 13.16: New Cross-System Depreciation Area for BESTM

Now, go back to the initial pop-up screen, and double-click on 'Assign Local to Cross-System Depreciation Areas'. On the next screen (you can reach here, directly, by using Transaction OATB), for your chart of depreciations (say, BEUS and BEIN) enter the cross-system depreciation area's key in the 'Crs-Sys.Ar' field against the appropriate depreciation area(s), and 'Save' the details (Figure 13.17).

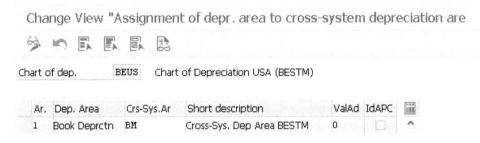

Figure 13.17: Assigning Depreciation Area to Cross-System Depreciation Area

The next step is to define the transfer variants.

13.4.1.2. Define Transfer Variants

Here, in this step, you will define the *'transfer variants'*. These variants contain the appropriate control parameters for intercompany asset transfers including (a) the transaction types for posting the transactions that belong to an intercompany transfer (retirement / acquisition) and (b) the transfer method for the capitalization of the transferred assets in the target company code. Besides these two, you can also specify, in each transfer variant, which master data fields should be copied from the transferred asset to the target asset, if a new asset has to be created in the target company code.

> **i** You can use SAP supplied standard transaction types without creating your own. The retirement transaction type specifies whether the retirement affects current-year acquisitions or prior-year acquisitions. Accordingly, you need two different transfer variants (with different transaction types, such as 230 and 275) for the transfer of prior-year acquisitions and current-year acquisitions.

Use the menu path: SAP Customizing Implementation Guide > Financial Accounting > Asset Accounting > Transactions > Intercompany Asset Transfers > Automatic Intercompany Asset Transfers > Define Transfer Variants.

On the resulting screen, you will see a 'Select Activity' pop-up screen, with three activities listed there on (Figure 13.18).

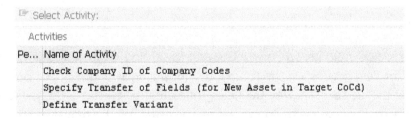

Figure 13.18: 'Select Activity' Pop-up Screen for defining Transfer Variants

i.   Double-click on the 1st activity ('Check Company ID of Company Codes'). The system takes you to the next screen wherein you can view / change company code global parameters. You can also reach this screen directly using Transaction OAY6. We have already configured the company code global parameters in Section 6.8 of Chapter 6.

ii.   Go back to the initial pop-up screen, and double-click on the 2nd activity, 'Specify Transfer of Fields (for New Asset in Target CoCd)'.

a)   On the resulting screen, you will see the list of variants (Figure 13.19).

Display View "Transfer variant": Overview

Variant	Name
1	Gross method
2	Net method
3	Revaluation method
4	Transfer within a company code

Figure 13.19: List of Transfer Variants

b)   Select a variant (say, 2 Net method) and double-click on 'Logical field group master data' on the left-hand side 'Dialog Structure'. The system will bring up the logical field groups, on the next screen (Figure 13.20).

Display View "Logical field group master data": Overview

Log.Fld.Gr	Log.Field Group Name
1	General data
2	Posting information
3	Time-dependent data
4	Allocations
5	Leasing
6	Net worth valuation
7	Real estate and similar rights

Figure 13.20: List of Logical Field Groups

c)   Select a logical field group (say, 1 General Data) and double-click on 'Field transfer of field groups' on the left-hand side 'Dialog Structure'. The system brings up the next screen, with the field group details. Select the 'Copy' check-box against the required field groups, if you want the system to copy the contents of fields, of the corresponding field group, from the asset being retired to the new asset, during intercompany asset transfer (Figure 13.21).

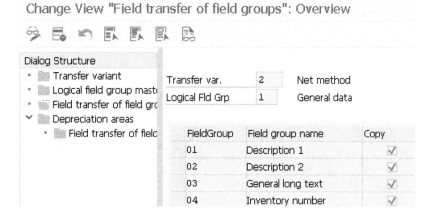

Figure 13.21: List of Field Groups

d) Now, select a field group (say, 04 Inventory number) and double-click on 'Depreciation areas' on the left-hand side 'Dialog Structure'. The system brings up the 'Change View "Depreciation Areas": Overview' screen. Notice that there are two entries: one with * and another with BM (Figure 13.22).

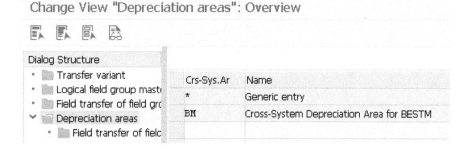

Figure 13.22: Cross-System Depreciation Area

e) Now, select the BM row and double-click on 'Field transfer of field groups' (under 'Depreciation areas') on the left-hand side 'Dialog Structure'. You will reach the 'Change View "Field transfer of field groups": Overview' screen. Select the 'Copy' check-box against the required field groups and 'Save' your settings (Figure 13.23). The 'Copy' check-box, when selected, enables the system to copy the field content, of the corresponding fields in the field group, from the asset being retired to the new asset, during intercompany asset transfer.

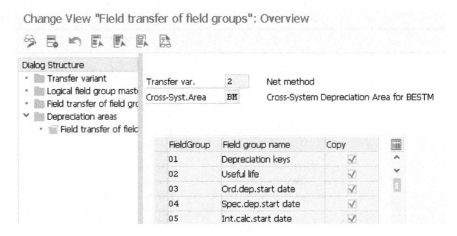

Figure 13.23: Field Group Activation for Cross-System Depreciation Area BM

    f)   Repeat the steps (a) to (e) for the other variants / logical field groups / field groups for the cross-system depreciation area BM and 'Save' the details.

iii.   Now, again, go back to the initial pop-up screen, and double-click on 3rd activity, 'Define Transfer Variant':

    a)   On the resulting screen, the system brings up all the transfer variants (Figure 13.24).

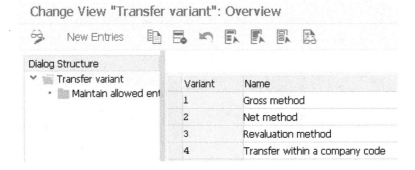

Figure 13.24: Transfer Variants

    b)   Select the variant (say, 2 Net method) and double-click on 'Maintain allowed entries' on the left-hand side 'Dialog Structure'. The system will, now, bring up the next screen, 'Change View "Maintain allowed entries": Overview' screen, with two generic entries. Copy those two * entries and create the new entries for BM (Figure 13.25).

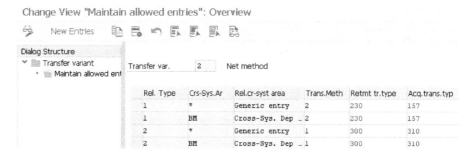

Figure 13.25: Maintaining Allowed Depreciation Areas for Transfer Variant 2

c) Repeat the steps (a) and (b) and complete the configuration for the other transfer variants also.

This completes our settings for automatic intercompany asset transfer. The next configuration is to specify gross/net transfer method for manual intercompany transfer.

13.4.2 Specify Gross or Net Transfer Method for Manual Transfer

You need to make the system settings, here in this step, only if you plan to post intercompany asset transfers manually between systems or clients, as in the case of BESTM when asset transfer happens between a US-based company code and an India-based company code. In all other cases intercompany asset transfers for BESTM, that is between company codes within US / India, you can use the automatic intercompany transfer procedure that we have described in the previous Section 13.4.1.

You are already aware that the intercompany transfers between systems or clients are posted in two steps: (a) retirement of the sending asset and (b) acquisition on the receiving asset. Now, using this configuration step, you shall define the features of the transaction types that you will use in these manual asset transfers. You will specify (a) a sending or receiving company for the postings belonging to a transfer (posting with affiliated company), and (b) that cumulative value adjustments can be entered along with the APC being acquired, when making the acquisition posting (gross posting). You can also specify that the affiliated company can be entered in receiving transfers from affiliated companies, but that accounting transaction, however, will be posted net in all areas (regardless of the indicator in the area definition).

Use the menu path: SAP Customizing Implementation Guide > Financial Accounting > Asset Accounting > Transactions > Intercompany Asset Transfers > Specify Gross or Net Transfer Method for Manual Transfer:

i. On the resulting 'Select Activity' pop-up screen, double-click on 'Define Characteristics of Transfer Transact. Types (Acquis.)'.

ii.   The system takes you to the 'Change view "FI-AA: Transaction types": Overview' screen. You can also reach this screen directly using Transaction AO67. You will see a list of asset acquisition transaction types on this screen.

iii.   Double-click on a transaction type (say, 151), and ensure that the standard settings are correct (Figure 13.26).

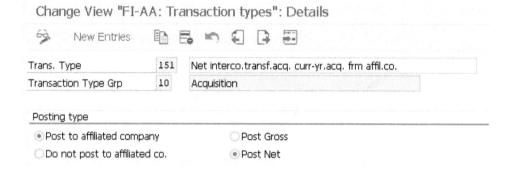

Figure 13.26: Posting Type Specification for Transaction Type 151

iv.   Now, go back to the initial pop-up screen, and double-click on 'Define Characteristics of Transfer Transact. Types (Retirmt)'. You will see the list of transaction types associated with asset retirement, on the next screen (you can also reach this screen, directly, through Transaction AO68).

v.   Double-click on a specific transaction (say, 230) to view the settings for intercompany retirement posting on the next screen (Figure 13.27).

Figure 13.27: Posting Type Specification for Transaction Type 230

This completes our discussion on configuring the system for intercompany asset transfers. Let us, now, move on to discuss how to configure the transactions for AuC.

13.5 Capitalization of Assets under Construction (AuC)

We have already seen in Chapter 7.1, that AuC is a special form of tangible asset that you usually display as a separate B/S item and therefore it needs a separate account determination in the asset class.

The AuC that you produce in-house has two stages in its life that are relevant for accounting: (a) under construction phase and (b) useful life (Figure 13.28). You need to show AuC as an in different B/S items, based on the phase that it is in. Hence, you need to manage this asset as a separate object or asset master record during the construction phase. The transition from the construction phase to the other phase is called as the 'capitalization of AuC'.

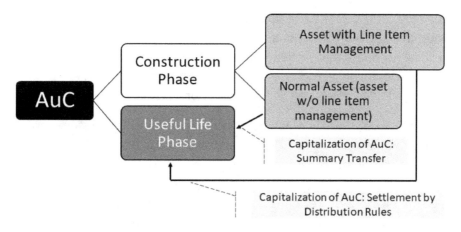

Figure 13.28: AuC: Phases and Settlement Overview

During the under *'construction phase'*, you can manage these assets either in a normal asset master record or in an asset master record with line item management. As a result, you can handle the transfer from the AuC to completed fixed assets in one of two ways: (a) summary transfer from a normal asset master record to the receiver assets (transaction type 348/349) or (b) as an asset master record with line item management, that you settle by line item to the receivers.

Let us understand more on AuC with line item management / without line item management (*summary transfer*):

- *AuC without Line Item Management (Summary Transfer)*
  The procedure corresponds to the procedure for the transfer between two assets within the same company code. Before carrying out a full transfer of an AuC, reverse any down payments that you have already posted in the current fiscal year. You can ignore down payments for a partial transfer. To display transfers in asset history sheet as acquisitions, you need to use special transaction types for the transfer of AuC.

- *AuC with Line Item Management (Collective Management)*
  As FI-AA allows you to accumulate costs, under purely technical aspects, in an AuC, you do not need to consider the later creation of fixed assets at this point, during construction. Accordingly, you can accumulate all acquisitions for an investment in a single asset, during the construction phase. These acquisitions can include (a) external activity (acquisition from vendor), (b) internal activity (internal order) and/or (c) stock material (withdrawal from warehouse).

  When you use this *'collective management'* of AuC, it is possible that you can manage the individual acquisitions as open items over the course of several fiscal years. However, at completion, you need to clear these line items and distribute them to the various receivers. The system activates open item management when you create AuC, if you have set the corresponding indicator in the asset class (Refer Chapter 7.4.4). Besides, for open item settlement, you need to assign a settlement profile to the company codes involved (Refer Section 13.5.4); using the settlement profile, you can specify the allowed receivers (such as, assets or cost centers).

During the *'settlement phase'*, for AuCs with line item settlement, the system carries the settlement by using *'distribution rules'*. These are asset-specific, and they contain a distribution key and a receiver. You can bundle several distribution rules to form a *'distribution rule group'*. You can, then, assign these groups to one or more line items of an asset. You can have the distribution key either as equivalence numbers or percentage rates, so that you can distribute any number of combinations of line items to any number of combinations of receivers.

> **ℹ** You can set up the settlement rules at a given point in time, and then carry out the corresponding update of the line items at a later point in time, since a separate transaction exists for the actual settlement (Transaction AIBU). This transaction triggers the settlement posting for the selected AuC, and creates the necessary posting documents. Here, the system automatically separates the transfer of asset acquisitions from prior fiscal years from acquisitions that took place in the year of capitalization. When the system transfers the prior-year acquisitions, it also transfers the (special) depreciation and investment support proportionally. The system automatically generates carryforward postings for partial capitalization.

With this background on AuC, let us understand the configuration settings that are required for setting up the system for capitalizing AuC. Let us start with the first task of defining the transaction types.

13.5.1 Define Transaction Types

Here, using this configuration step, you shall define the transaction types for capitalizing AuC. As in other cases of asset transaction types, here also, you can use the standard ones supplied by SAP without defining a new transaction type.

Use the menu path: SAP Customizing Implementation Guide > Financial Accounting > Asset Accounting > Transactions > Capitalization of Assets under Construction > Define Transaction Types. You may also use Transaction OAXG.

On the resulting screen, you will see the list of standard transactions (like 331, 336, 338 etc) associated with AuC (Figure 13.29). You may select any of the transaction types and view the detailed settings.

Change View "FI-AA: Transaction types": Overview

New Entries

Transact. type	Transaction Type Name
331	Acquirg transfer of prior-yr acquis from inv.meas.
336	Acquirg transfer of curr-yr acquis from inv.meas.
338	Retirmt transfer of prior-yr acquis from inv.meas.
339	Acquirg transfer of curr-yr acquis from inv.meas.
340	Retmt transfer of prior-yr acquis f. AuC, line itm
341	Acquirg transfer of prior-yr acquis from AuC

Figure 13.29: AuC - Transaction Types

We can, now, move on to specify the asset classes for enabling transfer posting, from AuC to completed assets, in the next step.

13.5.2 Allow Transfer Transaction Types for Asset Classes

In this step, you will specify the asset classes, in which posting is allowed using the transaction type groups, for transfers from AuC to completed assets.

Use the menu path: SAP Customizing Implementation Guide > Financial Accounting > Asset Accounting > Transactions > Capitalization of Assets under Construction > Allow Transfer Transaction Types for Asset Classes. You may also use Transaction OAYB:

i.   On the resulting screen, select a transaction type group (say, 15 Down payment) and double-click on 'Specification of asset classes' on the left-hand side 'Dialog Structure'.

ii.   On the resulting screen (Figure 13.30), you will see that the system has already populated the asset class B6000 (AuC) as the specified asset class for allowing transfer postings for AuC.

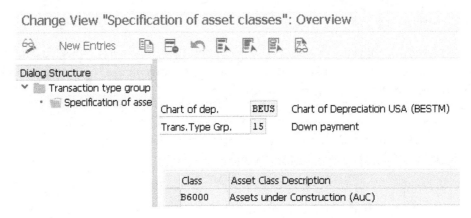

Figure 13.30: AuC - Specification of Asset Classes for Transaction Type Group 15

iii.   Go back to the previous screen and select another transaction type group (say, 38) and double-click on 'Specification of asset classes' on the left-hand side 'Dialog Structure'.

iv.   Click on 'New Entries' on the next screen, and enter the appropriate asset classes (Figure 13.31).

v.   Repeat the steps for the other two transaction type groups (16 and 39), if required.

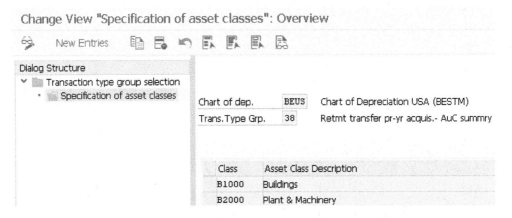

Figure 13.31: AuC - Asset Classes for Transfer Posting for Trans. Type Group 38

The next step is to specify the cost element for AuC's settlement to CO receiver.

13.5.3 Determine Cost Element for Settlement to CO Receiver

When you settle AuC with line item management, you can settle debits to CO receivers (particularly, cost centers). You may need this if debits were capitalized to the AuC by mistake. To make this settlement to CO receivers, the system requires a cost element that you will define in this step.

Use the menu path: SAP Customizing Implementation Guide > Financial Accounting > Asset Accounting > Transactions > Capitalization of Assets under Construction > Determine Cost Element for Settlement to CO Receiver. You may also use Transaction AO89:

i.   On the resulting screen, select the chart of accounts (say, BEUS) and double-click on 'Account Determination' on the left-hand side 'Dialog Structure'.

ii. Select an account determination (say, B1000) and double-click on 'Assign Accounts to Areas' on the left-hand side 'Dialog Structure'.

iii. Now, double-click on the depreciation area (say, 01) on the resulting screen, and enter the cost element for settlement of AuC to Co objects on the next screen.

The next step is to define / assign settlement for profiles.

13.5.4 Define/Assign Settlement Profiles

Here, in this step, you can define the *'settlement profiles'* for settling AuC. You can store one profile in the Customizing definition of each asset company code. The system, then, uses this key when there is an AuC to be settled in that company code. SAP provides the settlement profile 'AI' as the default one which you can use as such, or you can create a new one by copying this and changing settings appropriately.

Project Dolphin

The project team has suggested to the BESTM management to copy the standard profile and create a new one so that settlement is made optional to some of the CO receivers like cost center, order etc. This is required to take care of settling debits to these receivers when debits were capitalized to AuC by mistake. Also, BESTM wants to have the flexibility of settling by percentage, equivalence numbers and amount. Besides, it was suggested to have a validation to ensure that the settlement does not exceed 100% in a percentage settlement; above, or below, the system should issue a warning accordingly.

Use the menu path: SAP Customizing Implementation Guide > Financial Accounting > Asset Accounting > Transactions > Capitalization of Assets under Construction > Define/Assign Settlement Profiles:

i.   On the resulting pop-up screen, double-click on the 'Define Settlement Profile' activity.

ii. On the next screen, you will see the standard settlement profile, AI, supplied by SAP (you may directly reach this screen using Transaction OKO7). Select that row and click on 'Copy As' and create a new one (B1) for BESTM.

iii. Double-click on B1 to change the default settings, appropriately, on the next screen (Figure 13.32):

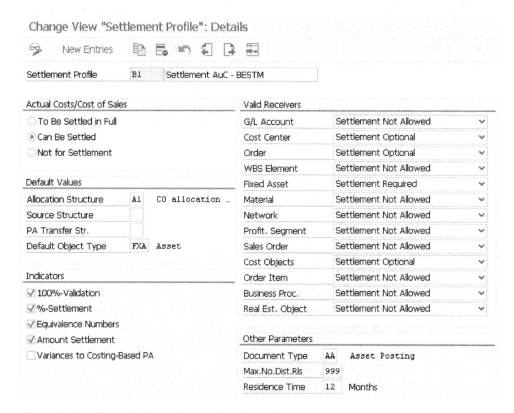

Figure 13.32: AuC - Settlement Profile B1 for BESTM

a. Under 'Actual cost/ Cost of Sales', endure that you have selected the default 'To be settled in full' radio-button. If you try to close the object, or set the delete flag, the system displays an error message if the balance in the object is not zero.

a. Under 'Valid Receivers', the default setting is 'Settlement Required' for 'Fixed Asset'. As we want to settle the debits that would have been mistakenly capitalized to AuC, you need to select the value 'Settlement Optional' for 'Cost Center' and 'Order'.

b. Under 'Indicators':

- When you select '100%-Validation', if you have defined percentage distribution rules for a particular settlement rule, then, the system checks the total percentage either when you save the settlement rule or when you use the percentage check function. The indicator only affects periodic settlement. In overall settlement, the percentage must always be 100%.

  When set, the system issues a warning, if the total is <> 100%. When NOT set, the system issues a warning only when the total is >100%.

In both cases, you can ignore the warning and save the settlement rule. However, to run the settlement, you must first correct the settlement rule.

- When you select '%-Settlement', then, you can use the settlement rule to determine the distribution rules governing the percentage costs to be settled.
- When you select 'Equivalence Numbers', then, you can define distribution rules in the settlement rule, according to which costs are settled proportionally.

> **i** For example, if you have a settlement rule to distribute to four cost centers, in the ratio of 1:2:3:4, then as per equivalence, the first cost center will receive 1/10 of the costs, the second cost center at 2/10, and so on.

- Select 'Amount Settlement' check-box, so as to define distribution rules in the settlement rule, which allow costs to be settled by amount.

iv.   Now, go back to the initial pop-up screen, and double-click on 'Assign Settlement Profile to Company Code'.

v.   On the resulting screen, enter the settlement profile ('SProf.') against the asset accounting company codes and 'Save' the details (Figure 13.33). You may also reach this screen, directly, by using Transaction OAAZ.

Change View "FI-AA: Settlement profile": Overview

CoCd	Company Name	SProf.	Text
1110	BESTM Farm Machinery	B1	Settlement AuC - BESTM
1120	BESTM Garden & Forestry E	B1	Settlement AuC - BESTM

Figure 13.33: AuC - Assignment Settlement Profile

The next task is to specify the depreciation areas for capitalization of AuC / down payment.

13.5.5 Specify Capitalization of AUC/Down-Payment

Here, you can determine how the system deals with down payments on AuCs, and their closing invoice during capitalization (=settlement) of the AuC. The settings you make here are particularly relevant for representing the down payments, from previous years, in the asset history sheet.

> **i** In the standard system, when you capitalize down payment (from the previous year), and the closing invoice (from the current year) together, the system transfers (a) the down payment amount, with the transaction type for old asset data from previous years, and (b) only the difference between the closing invoice and the down payment, with the transaction type for current (new) acquisitions.

Project Dolphin

BESTM, in AuCs, does not want to ignore the down payments during line item settlement. Instead, they want capitalization of down payments from the previous year, and the closing invoice from the current year, together.

Use the menu path: SAP Customizing Implementation Guide > Financial Accounting > Asset Accounting > Transactions > Capitalization of Assets under Construction > Specify Capitalization of AUC/Down-Payment, or Transaction OAYU:

   i.   On the resulting screen, select the company code (say, 1110), and double-click on the 'Capitalization rule' on the left-hand side 'Dialog Structure'.

   ii.   On the next screen, the system displays all the depreciation areas with the 'Trans DP' check-box selected against them, by default.

        With this setting, the system ignores down payments during the line item settlement of AuC. The total amount of the closing invoice is, then, transferred to the capitalized asset using the transaction type based on the year of the closing invoice. However, if you want to capitalize down payment (from the previous year), and the closing invoice (from the current year) together, as in for BESTM, then, you should de-select the 'Trans DP' check-box for the appropriate depreciation areas (Figure 13.34).

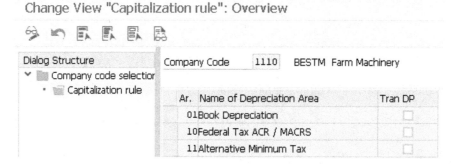

Figure 13.34: AuC - Capitalization Rule

   iii.   Repeat the settings for other company codes, and 'Save' the details.

The next task is to maintain the number ranges for line item settlement documents.

13.5.6 Maintain Number Ranges for Documents for Line Item Settlmt

As in the case of every settlement (in cost accounting) that is uniquely numbered by a settlement document, under a separate number (per settlement), the system creates a CO settlement document in the CO area, to which the asset or the investment measure belongs, for the line item settlement of an AuC. Hence, if you plan to use line item settlement of AuC (or investment measures), then, you need to define the number range intervals for the settlement documents in one or more CO areas.

> **i** Define separate number range intervals for settlement documents for each CO area, if you use more than one CO area, so as to improve performance when you carry out settlements in different CO areas simultaneously.

Use the menu path: SAP Customizing Implementation Guide > Financial Accounting > Asset Accounting > Transactions > Capitalization of Assets under Construction > Maintain Number Ranges for Documents for Line Item Settlmt:

i. On the resulting 'Select Activity' pop-up screen, double-click on the first activity: 'Maintain Number Ranges for Controlling Documents'.

    a. On the next screen, enter the controlling area (say, B100). You can come to this screen directly by using Transaction KANK.

    b. Now, click on 'Change Groups' and click on 'Create Group' on the next screen.

    c. On the resulting screen, enter the details to create a new group and assign the appropriate number ranges (Figure 13.35).

Edit Intervals: CO Document, Object RK_BELEG, Subobject B100

Group	CO - Number Range for Line Item Settmnt for CO Area B100

Object	RK_BELEG
Subobject	B100

Ranges

N..	From No.	To Number	NR Status	Ext
01	0000000001	2999999999	0	☐

Figure 13.35: Number Range for CO Documents

    d. Go, back to the initial 'Edit Intervals: CO Document, Object RK_BELEG' screen, and click on 'Change Groups'.

e. On the next screen, you will see the 'Non-Assigned Elements' for the controlling area B100 (Figure 13.36).

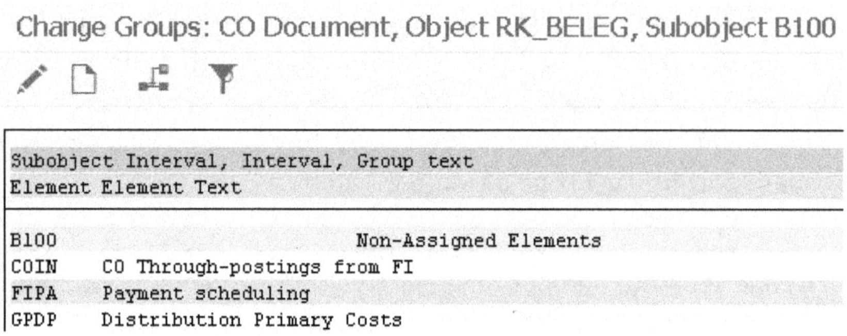

Change Groups: CO Document, Object RK_BELEG, Subobject B100

✏ ▯ ⬚ ▼

Subobject Interval, Interval, Group text Element Element Text	
B100	Non-Assigned Elements
COIN	CO Through-postings from FI
FIPA	Payment scheduling
GPDP	Distribution Primary Costs

Figure 13.36: Non-Assigned Elements for CO Area B100

f. Place the cursor on an 'Element' and click on 'Assign Element to Group', to add the appropriate elements to the newly created number interval group for CO area B100.

ii. Go back to the initial pop-up screen, double-click on 'Change Number Ranges for Settlement Document':

   a. On the resulting screen (you can also reach this screen using Transaction SNUM), click on 'Change Groups'. On the next screen, click 'Create Group' and define a new number range group (say, B1) for settlement documents.

   b. Once defined, assign this group the CO area B100.

   c. Now, from the 'Edit Intervals: CO object Settlement, Object CO_ABRECHN' screen, you can click on 'Change Intervals' and see the newly added group B1 (Figure 13.37).

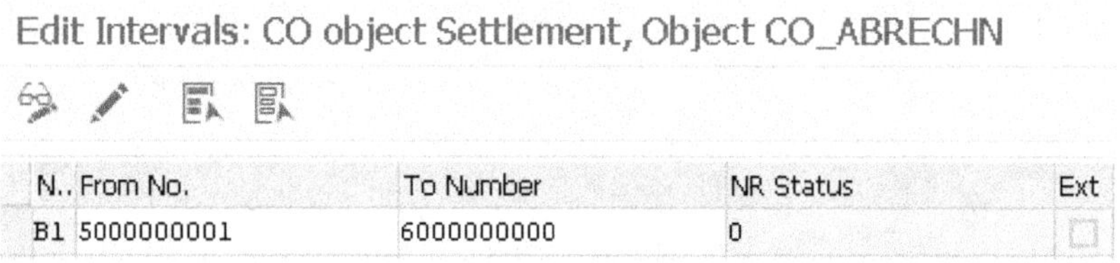

Edit Intervals: CO object Settlement, Object CO_ABRECHN

⇱ ✏ ▤ ▤

N..	From No.	To Number	NR Status	Ext
B1	5000000001	6000000000	0	☐

Figure 13.37: Number Ranges for Settlement Document

iii. Again, go back to the initial pop-up and double-click on 'Check Assignment of Controlling Area to Company Code':

   a. On the resulting screen (you can reach here directly by using Transaction OKKP), select the controlling area (say, B100) and double-click on 'Activate components/control indicators' on the left-hand side 'Dialog Structure'.

b. On the resulting screen, you will see the CO components that have already been activated. You can reach this screen (Figure 13.38), directly, by using Transaction OKKP.

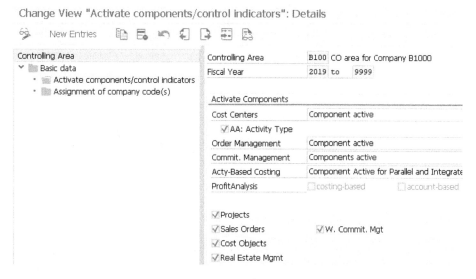

Figure 13.38: Activation of CO Components / Control Indicators – CO Area B100

c. Now, double-click on 'Assignment of company code(s)', and you will see the company codes assigned to the controlling area B100 on the next screen (Figure 13.39). We have already completed this, when we did the 'CO Area-Company Code' assignment while configuring the enterprise structure.

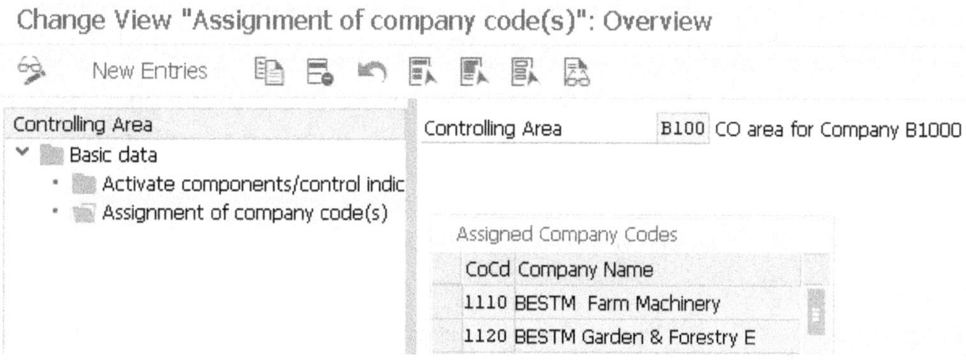

Figure 13.39: Assignment of Company Codes to CO Area B100

iv.   Repeat and complete the above steps, for all other controlling areas of BESTM.

This completes our discussion on configuring the system for capitalizing AuC. Let us now look at a few more settings that are required for putting through some of the asset transactions. Let us start with the transaction types for post-capitalization

13.6 Define Transaction Types for Post-Capitalization

Here, you will define the transaction types for post-capitalization activities. If you plan to use SAP's standard transaction types, you do not need to define anything new here. You can view the standard transaction types for post-capitalization (Figure 13.40) by using the menu path: SAP Customizing Implementation Guide > Financial Accounting > Asset Accounting > Transactions > Define Transaction Types for Post-Capitalization, or Transaction AO77.

Change View "FI-AA: Transaction types": Overview

🔩 🔩   New Entries   🗅 🗟 🔊 🗐 🗐 🗐

Transact. type	Transaction Type Name
400	Post-capitalization
401	Post-capitalization in following year
490	Post-capitalization: TTY for proportional values

Figure 13.40: Standard Transaction Types for Post-Capitalization

The next step is to define the transaction types for manual depreciation.

13.7 Define Transaction Types for Manual Depreciation

You already know that you can use manual postings to correct the value of assets, for example, when there is a need for unplanned depreciation, or write-ups or handling other manually scheduled depreciation (ordinary or special depreciation). Here in this step, you can define the transaction types for handling manual depreciation. As in other cases of transaction types, here also, you can use SAP supplied standard transaction types.

You can use the menu path: SAP Customizing Implementation Guide > Financial Accounting > Asset Accounting > Transactions > Define Transaction Types for Manual Depreciation or Transaction AO78, to view the standard transaction types (Figure 13.41).

Change View "FI-AA: Transaction types": Overview

🔩 🔩   New Entries   🗅 🗟 🔊 🗐 🗐 🗐

Transact. type	Transaction Type Name
600	Manual ordinary depreciation on prior-yr acquis.
610	Manual ordinary depreciation on current-yr acquis.
620	Manual spec. dep. on prior-yr acquis per dep. key
630	Manual spec. dep. on curr-yr acquis per dep. key
640	Unplanned depreciation on prior-year acquisitions
650	Unplanned depreciation on current-yr acquisition

Figure 13.41: Standard Transaction Types for Manual Depreciation

With this, let us specify the default transaction types for FI-AA postings.

13.8 Specify Default Transaction Types

Here, in this step, you can determine the transaction types that the system defaults to, for the standard posting transactions in FI-AA. Again, go with SAP's standard settings unless you have a very specific reason to change the transaction type for a given asset transaction.

If you have defined any new transaction type, then you may need to change the defaults in the "TType' field. Else, you do not need to take any action here, except viewing the details (Figure 13.42) using the menu path: SAP Customizing Implementation Guide > Financial Accounting > Asset Accounting > Transactions > Specify Default Transaction Types.

Change View "Default transaction types for FI-AA posting transactions"

New Entries

Default transaction types for FI-AA posting transactions

Acct. transact. ID	Description	TType	Transact. Type Text
ABAA	Unplanned depreciation	640	Unplanned depreciation on prior-year acquisitions
ABA0	Asset sale without customer	210	Retirement with revenue
ABAV	Asset retirement by scrapping	200	Retirement without revenue
ABAW	Balance sheet revaluation	800	Post revaluation gross
ABGF	Credit memo in year after invoice	160	Credit memo in following year
ABGL	Enter credit memo in year of invoice	105	Credit memo in invoice year
ABMA	Manual depreciation	600	Manual ordinary depreciation on prior-yr acquis.

Figure 13.42: Default Transaction Types for FI-AA Posting Transactions

The next step is to determine the default transaction types for internal transactions.

13.9 Determine Transaction Types for Internal Transactions

Here, in this step, you can determine the default transaction types that the system uses for postings that are initiated (a) in other SAP modules / applications (like, SAP MM), and (b) automatically (like, depreciation). You can, of course, go along with the defaults from SAP.

Change View "Default transaction types": Overview

Transaction Name	Tra	Transaction Type Name
Retirement w/o revenue	200	Retirement without revenue
Clearing downpayment curr. fiscal year	181	Clearing of down payment from current fisca
Bal. downpaymt par.stlmt.	185	Bal. carried over from prev. year for part. ca
Retirement to affil.co.	230	Retirement to affiliated company with reven
Down payment to affiliated company	188	Down payment from affiliated company

Figure 13.43: Default Transaction Types for Internal Transactions in FI-AA

You can use menu path: SAP Customizing Implementation Guide > Financial Accounting > Asset Accounting > Transactions > Determine Transaction Types for Internal Transactions, to view the standard settings, and change, if required (Figure 13.43). Note to make an entry here in 'Tra' field, if you have defined your own transaction type for any of the transaction postings.

With this, let us understand the last configuration activity of specifying how the system should determine the default value date for an asset.

13.10 Specify How Default Asset Value Date is Determined

The default asset value date is particularly important for transactions that are initiated in applications that are integrated with FI-AA (such as, acquisition from GR, from SAP MM). In those transactions, the default asset value date is not displayed, and you cannot, therefore, manually change that, when you post.

Normally, you do not need to configure this step unless you have some special needs in regard to the asset value date, since the standard rules, in the system, can meet most the needs for setting the asset date. In case you need to define, you will define the 'value date variant' (per company code) which contains the rules for determining the default asset value date.

You can use menu path: SAP Customizing Implementation Guide > Financial Accounting > Asset Accounting > Transactions > Specify How Default Asset Value Date is Determined, to make the required settings.

First, you will assign a value date variant for each of the company codes. Later, for the variant entered, you will define the business transactions with the primary / alternate rules for determining the asset value date (Figure 13.44). For example, for the transaction 'Current-value depreciation' the primary rule determines the default asset value data as 'capitalization date' (9) and the alternate rule as 'earlier of either the document or posting date' (4); for the transaction 'retirement', the primary rule stipulates that the asset value date to be entered manually (1).

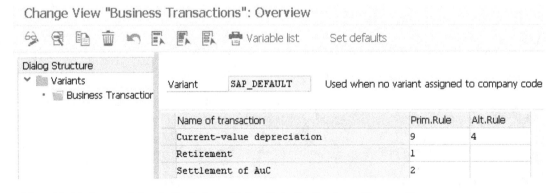

Figure 13.44: Determining Default Asset Value Date for Business Transactions

> **i** SAP supplies the value date variant SAP_DEFAULT, that contains the rules for determining the asset value date for all Asset Accounting transactions. The system uses this variant, in all company codes, to which you do not assign a specific value date variant.

This completes our discussion on configuring the system for FI-AA transactions.

13.11 Conclusion

You learned that the 'transactions' component, in FI-AA, helps in carrying out all accounting transactions that occur during the life of a fixed asset (like acquisitions, retirements, intracompany / intercompany transfers, capitalizations of AuC etc) in your organization. You learned that you can use the asset 'transaction types' to identify individual business transactions. You learned that, besides controlling the account assignment (debit / credit entry, document numbering etc), the transaction type also takes care of posting type (gross or net, for example) and other features. You learned that you can assign the business transactions to an 'asset history sheet' using these transaction types. You learned that each transaction type is assigned exactly to one 'transaction type group' which determines, among others, which value fields are updated in year segments, whether the transaction refers to the past (or to the current fiscal year), whether the total of transactions of a group is positive or negative with reference to a fiscal year, and so on. You learned that you cannot change either the number of transaction type groups or their characteristics, in the standard system.

You learned that, on the basis of transaction type groups, you can segregate the asset business transactions into various categories, like transactions that influence the APC of fixed assets (acquisitions, retirements, transfer postings etc), down payments, investment support measures, manual depreciation and write-ups.

You learned that the 'acquisition' is the primary business process in FI-AA relating to the purchase of assets and/or the capitalization of in-house produced goods or services, and that the system supports three distinct methods of asset acquisition. You learned that the 'asset retirement' is the removal of an asset or part of an asset from your asset portfolio, and that the asset retirement can be complete or partial, and that it can happen with or without revenue. You learned that you need two transaction types for transfers between assets: (a) a transaction type for retirement from the sending asset and (b) a transaction type for the acquisition on the receiving asset, and that the system performs the posting transaction from the point of view of the sending asset. You learned how to use 'intercompany asset transfer' to carry out asset transfers between company codes. You learned that, in the case of individual companies, an intercompany transfer represents a retirement for one company code and an acquisition for the other, but from corporate groups' view point, that it represents a transfer that balances to zero in the group asset history sheet.

You learned that the AuC you produce in-house has two stages in its life that is relevant for accounting: (a) under construction phase and (b) useful life. You understood that you need to show AuC as a different B/S item, based on the phase that it is in, and accordingly, you need to manage this asset as a separate object or asset master record during the construction phase. You learned that the transition from the construction phase to the other phase is called as the 'capitalization of AuC', and you learned how to capitalize an AuC by summary transfer or settlement by distribution rules.

You learned about the various standard transaction types for post-capitalization activities, manual depreciation and internal asset transfers. You understood that you can determine the transaction types that the system defaults to, for the standard posting transactions in FI-AA.

We are now ready to discuss the settings relating to FI-AA information system, in the next Chapter.

14 Information System

T he *Information System* component, of FI-AA, contains several standard reports and functions to meet your specific reporting needs. The reports are offered in the form of a *report tree*. You can freely define the hierarchical structure of the report tree through Customizing. The system makes use of the logical database ADA for these reports.

You can pre-define all of the reports, in the standard report selection tree, using the report variants. All the standard report variants begin with 'SAP...'; you can copy them, if needed, and make the required changes. Or, you can create new variants, from scratch, and enter them in the report tree.

Here, in this Section, we shall define (a) the report selection in FI-AA Information System, (b) sort versions for the asset reports, (c) the structure of the asset history sheet, (d) currency translation methods and (e) any other system configurations, for reporting.

Let us start with the sort versions for asset reports.

14.1 Define Sort Versions for Asset Reports

You use *'sort versions'* for sorting and totalling the data records in report lists in FI-AA. You need to enter the sort version, as a parameter, before running the report. The system offers a standard sort as a default for each report; you can, of course, change this default. When you choose the 'input help' on the 'Sort version' field, the system displays an overview of the existing sort versions from which you can select the required one.

You may use SAP-delivered standard sort versions, as such. Or you can use them as reference to create your own sort versions. The standard ones include:

- Classification for Transaction Data Reports
- Book Depreciation Classification
- Cost-Accounting Classification
- Net Worth Tax Classification
- Classification for Insurance Values

Project Dolphin

BESTM wants to use the standard sort versions without defining anything new.

Use the menu path: SAP Customizing Implementation Guide > Financial Accounting > Asset Accounting > Information System > Define Sort Versions for Asset Reports, to view the standard sort versions (Figure 14.1) or create your own (starting with X, Y or Z). You can also use Transaction OVAI.

Figure 14.1: Standard Sort Versions

You may double-click on a row (say, 0001), to view detailed settings of a sort version (Figure 14.2):

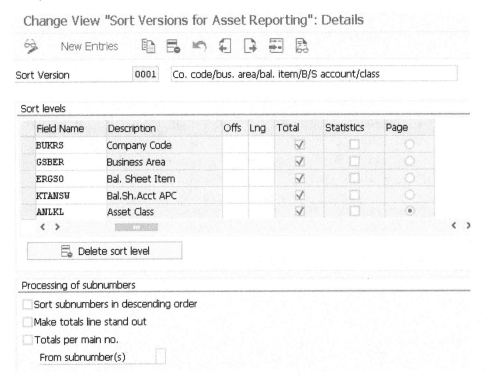

Figure 14.2: Standard Sort Version 0001 – Details

i. The 'Total' check-box, when selected, indicates that values will be totalled at this sort level for, reports using this sort version.

ii. Select the 'Page' radio-button, against a field name, at which you want a page break to occur, in the printed report. The system, then, makes a page break as soon as the sort level has new field contents. This setting guarantees that a page break occurs after high sort levels (such as, plant or business area), and that there is no page break after lower sort levels (such as, asset class).

iii. The other parameters, under 'Processing subnumbers', help you to, for example, sort the asset subnumbers in the reverse order, making the totals line to stand out from the rest, and enabling totals per main number.

iv. You can use the 'From subnumber(s)' field to control the totals of the values of subnumbers per asset. In this field, you can specify the number of subnumbers after which the system should provide a total. For example, if you enter 3 here in this field, then the system totals assets with more than 2 subnumbers; you can enter a value between 0 and 9.

The next step is to define simulation variants for depreciation reports.

14.2 Define Simulation Variants for Depreciation Reports

SAP offers two simulation options with which (a) you can execute standard reports with simulated depreciation terms and (b) you can analyze changes in the value of individual assets using simulated depreciation terms and transactions. The simulation enables planning the future development value your fixed assets portfolio.

When starting a standard list report, you can enter a defined *'simulation version'* to generate the list using simulated depreciation terms. For example, you can simulate how depreciation would look like if you used declining-balance depreciation instead of straight-line depreciation for your assets.

All depreciation lists that allow the use of simulation versions show the simulation version that was used, in the page header of the list. You can also request a list of all the replacement rules that were used in the simulation by pressing F2.

You can define these simulation versions anew, specifying the rules for the simulation. In this case, you need to specify (a) the depreciation area for the simulation, (b) the asset class (generic entry from right to left with '+'), (c) the depreciation key to be replaced in the simulation, and (d) a valid-to date, which means that for an asset to be included in the simulation, it has to have a capitalization date on or before this date.

Project Dolphin

BESTM wants to create a new simulation version to simulate the depreciation in all asset classes, for book depreciation, to understand what happens when the depreciation key is LINS and the useful life is increased by 10% across asset classes.

Use the menu path: SAP Customizing Implementation Guide > Financial Accounting > Asset Accounting > Information System > Define Simulation Variants for Depreciation Reports or Transaction OAV7, to define a simulation version:

i.   On the resulting screen, click on 'New Entries' and enter the identifier for the simulation version (say, B1) and provide a description in 'Simulation Version'. 'Save'.

ii.   Select this row B1, and double-click on 'Simulation Rules' on the left-hand side 'Dialog Structure'.

iii. On the next screen (Figure 14.3), click on 'New Entries' and make the required settings:

Figure 14.3: New Simulation Version B1

- Enter the depreciation area ('Area'); let that be 01.
- Enter the asset class in 'Class'. You can make a generic entry here instead of specifying the individual asset classes.

> **i** You can use the generic entry in several ways: enter a '+' sign, starting from the right and moving to the left. The '+' sign always represents a single character.
>
> Asset Class: B++++: B1000 to B8000
> Asset Class: B4+++: B4100 to B4200

- Enter the actual depreciation terms. Here also, you may use a generic entry.
- Enter 'Valid To' and 'Valid From' dates.
- Enter the simulation depreciation key (say, LINS).

- Enter the percentage by which you want to increase the useful life of assets in 'Diff.%rate UL' field. When you enter, 110, it means that the useful life will be increased by 10% during the simulation.
- 'Save' the settings. You have now created a simulation version (B1) with the required simulation rules.

When you execute the simulation, if the system finds several possible entries, it follows the following logic: (a) all the unmasked entries always take precedence, (b) when there is more than one masked entry, the system uses the first appropriate entry and finally (c) if the system finds only masked entries and no unmasked entries, it uses the entry that has the least number of masks.

With this, let us move on to discuss the SAP Queries.

14.3 Define SAP Queries

Some of the FI-AA reports, in the report tree, have been created using *ABAP Query*. SAP provides you with several standard queries (Figure 14.4) that you can use as such, or copy / modify them to meet your specific requirements. All these standard queries for FI-AA are provided in the global application area, and hence are not client-specific; you do not have to transport them.

Closing Preparation	Cost Accounting	P&L Explanations	Asset Balances
Gain for transfer of reserves	Revaluation and backlog Post depreciation (related to cost center)	Ordinary depreciation Write-ups Gain for transfer of reserves Depreciation posted per asset and posting period	Inventory list Real estate & similar rights Transportation equipment Leased asset Sample for address data for an asset

Figure 14.4: Standard SAP Queries in FI-AA - Categorization

> **i** ABAP or *SAP queries* are either limited to a given client, or are not client-specific. Whether they are client-specific or not depends on where you define them: in the standard application area or in the global application area. When you define them in the standard application area, then, you need to transport them (Transaction SQ02) as they are client-specific queries, so that they are available in other clients.

Use the menu path: SAP Customizing Implementation Guide > Financial Accounting > Asset Accounting > Information System > Define SAP Queries, to view the standard queries (Figure 14.5) and/or creating your own. You may also use Transaction SQ01.

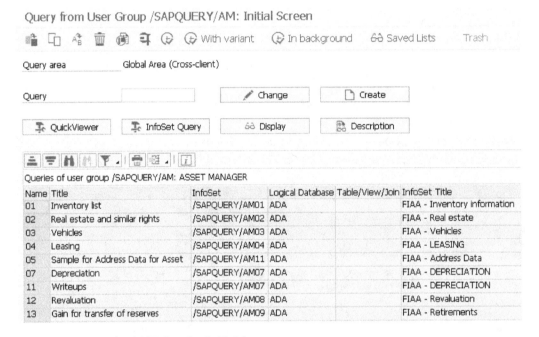

Figure 14.5: Standard SAP Queries in FI-AA

The table shown in the figure:

Name	Title	InfoSet	Logical Database	Table/View/Join	InfoSet Title
01	Inventory list	/SAPQUERY/AM01	ADA		FIAA - Inventory information
02	Real estate and similar rights	/SAPQUERY/AM02	ADA		FIAA - Real estate
03	Vehicles	/SAPQUERY/AM03	ADA		FIAA - Vehicles
04	Leasing	/SAPQUERY/AM04	ADA		FIAA - LEASING
05	Sample for Address Data for Asset	/SAPQUERY/AM11	ADA		FIAA - Address Data
07	Depreciation	/SAPQUERY/AM07	ADA		FIAA - DEPRECIATION
11	Writeups	/SAPQUERY/AM07	ADA		FIAA - DEPRECIATION
12	Revaluation	/SAPQUERY/AM08	ADA		FIAA - Revaluation
13	Gain for transfer of reserves	/SAPQUERY/AM09	ADA		FIAA - Retirements

> **i** When you define your own queries, you can decide if you want to create them in the global application area (not client-specific) or in the standard application area (client-specific). However, we recommend that you define your own queries in the global application area (not client-specific). However, you should use your own user group. To create your own user group, copy the user group AM with all of its queries, and then, name your user group using a name in the allowed name range (with X, Y or Z).

With this, let us understand some of the settings for Fiori apps for FI-AA.

14.4 Display Key Figures for Asset Accounting (Fiori)

SAP provides all the required *'key figures'* for use in SAP Fiori apps in FI-AA. You can use this step to display them (you cannot define new key figures). Additionally, you can display, which analytical transaction type categories and subledger line item types, are assigned to a key figure. This assignment determines which line items are combined in a key figure. You can assign the key figures to a *'key figure group'*. With the assignment of the key figures to the key figure group, you define which key figures are displayed in an analytical Fiori app of FI-AA, such as Asset History Sheet or Asset Transaction List.

Use the menu path: SAP Customizing Implementation Guide > Financial Accounting > Asset Accounting > Information System > Display Key Figures for Asset Accounting (Fiori), to display the key figures and also the assigned business transactions per key figure.

On entering the Transaction, you will see the list of key figures (Figure 14.6).

Display View "Key Figure": Overview

Dialog Structure	Key Figure	
∨ 📖 Key Figure	Key Figure	Key Figure Name
• 📁 Assigned Business Transactions	700000	APC FY Start
	700100	Down Payments FY Start
	700110	APC Incl. Down Payments FY-Start
	700120	APC Including Revaluations and Down Payments FY Start
	700121	APC Including Revaluations and Down Payments FY Start, Planned
	700200	Investment Support FY Start

Figure 14.6: Key Figures for FI-AA (Fiori)

Select a key figure row (say, 700100), and double-click on 'Assigned Business Transactions' on the left-hand side 'Dialog Structure' to view the assigned business transactions for that key figure, on the next screen (Figure 14.7).

Key Figure	700100
KF Name	Down Payments FY Start

Assigned Business Transactions

Category	Analytical Trans. Type Category Name	Subldgr LItm Type	Subledger Line Item Type De...	VT AA	
00	Balance Carry Forward	7001	Cumulative Down Payments	Exclusive Planned Value	∨
87	Legacy Data Transfer AuC Down Payment	7001	Cumulative Down Payments	Exclusive Planned Value	∨
C7	Legacy Data Transfer FY Start	7001	Cumulative Down Payments	Exclusive Planned Value	∨
E7	Legacy Data Transfer FY Ending Balance	7001	Cumulative Down Payments	Exclusive Planned Value	∨

Figure 14.7: Assigned Business Transactions for the Key Figure 700100

The next step is to define the key figure groups for Fiori app 'Asset Balances'.

14.5 Define Key Figure Groups for Asset Balances (Fiori)

SAP provides all the necessary key figure groups for the asset balances. By default, these are the key figure groups ABS_DEF (asset balances, planned values) and ABS_POSTED (asset balances, posted values). These key figure groups are, then, available as parameters when you execute the Fiori app 'Asset Balances' (Figure 14.8).

Figure 14.8: Entry Screen of Fiori App 'Asset Balances'

Here, in this configuration step, you can define your own key figure groups for the Fiori app 'Asset Balances'. Essentially, you define the key figures and their sequence for the asset balances.

> **i** You do not, in general, need to define your own key figure groups. However, you may do that when you want to display key figure digits in the asset balances that are different to the standard or when you want a different sequence of key figure digits.

Project Dolphin

BESTM wants to use the default key figure groups, without going in for any new key figure group definition for the Fiori app 'Asset Balances' and 'Asset Transactions'.

Use the menu path: SAP Customizing Implementation Guide > Financial Accounting > Asset Accounting > Information System > Define Key Figure Groups for Asset Balances (Fiori):

i. On the resulting screen, you see the default key figure groups with their description (Figure 14.9).

Figure 14.9: Standard Key Figure Groups for the Fiori App 'Asset Balances'

ii. Select a 'KF Group' row, and double-click on 'Create/Change Key Figure Groups of Asset Accounting' on the left-hand side 'Dialog Structure' to view the key figures and their sort sequences, on the next screen (Figure 14.10).

Key Figure Group   ABS_DEF

Create/Change Key Figure Groups of Asset Accounting (ABS)

Key Figure	Key Figure Name	Sequence
10700110	APC at Reporting Date	1
10700300	Revaluation APC at Reporting Date, Posted	10
10700302	Revaluation APC at Reporting Date, to be Posted	11
10700400	Revaluation Ordinary Depreciation at Reporting Date, Posted	12
10700402	Revaluation Ordinary Depreciation at Reporting Date, to be Posted	13
10700500	Ordinary Depreciation at Reporting Date, Posted	2
10700502	Ordinary Depreciation at Reporting Date, to be Posted	3

Figure 14.10: Key Figures and Sort Sequence of Key Figure Group ABS_DEF

iii. In case you want a different sort sequence of the key figures in a key figure group, you can define a new one by copying from the standard ones.

The next step is defining the key figure groups for the Fiori app 'Asset Transactions'.

14.6 Define Key Figure Groups for Asset Transactions (Fiori)

As in the case of key figure groups for the Fiori app 'Asset Balances', SAP provides all the necessary key figure groups for the app 'Asset Transactions' (Figure 14.11). By default, this comprises the following key figure groups:

- Asset Acquisitions: TRANS_ACQ
- Asset Retirements: TRANS_RET
- Intracompany Asset Transfers: TRANS_TRN
- All Asset Transactions: TRANS_ALL

Figure 14.11: Entry Screen for Fiori App 'Asset Transactions'

Here also, you generally do not need to define your own key figure groups. However, if you want to have a display of transactions different to the standard, then, you may define your own key figure groups.

Use the menu path: SAP Customizing Implementation Guide > Financial Accounting > Asset Accounting > Information System > Define Key Figure Groups for Asset Transactions (Fiori):

i.   On the resulting screen, you will see the default key figure groups for the Fiori app 'Asset Transactions' (Figure 14.12).

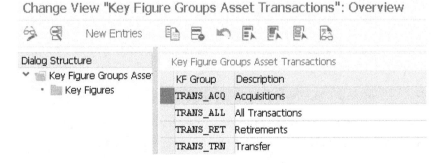

Figure 14.12: Standard Key Figure Groups for the Fiori App 'Asset Transactions'

ii.   Select a key figure group (say, TRANS_ACQ) and double-click on 'Key Figures' on the left-hand side 'Dialog Structure' to view the transaction types associated with this group, on the next screen (Figure 14.13).

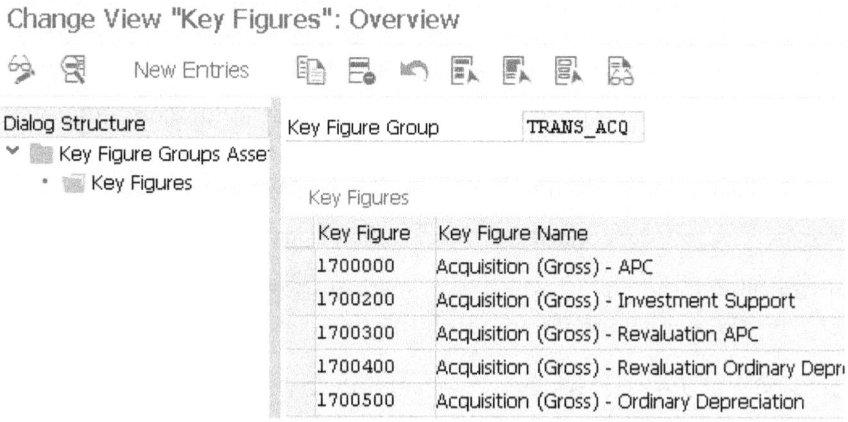

Figure 14.13: Key Figures of Key Figure Group TRANS_ACQ

iv.   In case you want to display transactions different to that of the standard, then you may define your own key figure groups and /or key figures.

With this, we are now ready to discuss how to configure asset history sheets.

14.7 Asset History Sheet

The *'asset history sheet'* is the most important and most comprehensive report, for the year-end closing or for an interim financial statement. Like other reports, you can set this up with any sort versions, and total on any group level. You can, also, create a compact totals list without individual asset information.

---

i SAP enables you to freely define the line and column structure of the asset history sheet, to meet your specific requirements. You can also define, which values should be displayed, in which lines of the report.

Let us now understand the different steps in configuring asset history sheet.

14.7.1 Define History Sheet Versions

The structure of the asset history sheet varies from country to country, depending on tax laws. Hence, SAP provides you with country-specific versions of the asset history sheet, known as *'asset history sheet versions'*; you also get additional history sheet versions. The system uses the asset history sheet version in the report, RAGITT01.

When you create an asset history sheet, the system notes (in the header of every screen) whether the asset history sheet version was created using a 'complete' or 'incomplete' version. An asset history sheet version is only complete when (a) every transaction type relevant to the asset history sheet is assigned to a 'history sheet group' and (b) the allocation indicator in column 1 to 5 is set (that is, contains either an X or a period) for every history sheet group except for the special groups YA, YY or YZ (more details in Section 14.7.2). When the asset history sheet version is complete, the indicator for completeness automatically appears in the definition for the version, on the overview screen. You can do a completeness check in Customizing, and see the log as to why the asset history sheet version is incomplete.

---

i The transactions relevant to the asset history sheet are the posting of acquisition and production costs, down payments, investment grants and write-ups.

The completeness of the asset history sheet version can only be guaranteed with the standard transaction types and groups provided by SAP. If you have defined your own transaction types, then, that could influence the completeness of the asset history sheet. Of course, an 'incomplete' history sheet version, from the system's point of view, does not necessarily mean that the asset history sheet is incorrect for accounting purposes.

Use the menu path: SAP Customizing Implementation Guide > Financial Accounting > Asset Accounting > Information System > Asset History Sheet > Define History Sheet Versions or Transaction OA79, to display standard asset history sheet versions and to define your own:

i. You can see the standard asset history sheet versions on the resulting screen (14.14). You can use them, as such without making any changes.

Choose Asset History Sheet Version

Details   New Entries

Asset hist. sheet versions

Language	Hist.Sht.Vers.	Asset History Sheet Name
EN	0001	In compl. w/EC directive 4 (13 col.,wide version)
EN	0002	In compliance with EC directive 4 (13 col.)
EN	0003	Depreciation by depreciation type
EN	0004	Acquisition values
EN	0005	Asset Register (Italy)
EN	0006	Cost-accouting w/revaluation (derived from HGB2)
EN	0007	Transferred reserves
EN	0008	History of res.for spec.depr.

Figure 14.14: Standard Asset History Sheet Versions

ii.   You may double-click on a version row (say, 0003), and see the detailed settings, on the next screen (14.15).

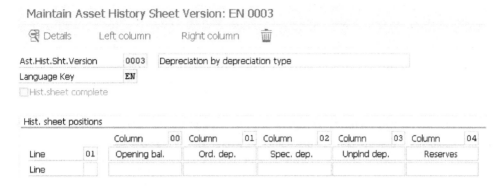

Figure 14.15: Initial Screen of Asset History Sheet Version 0003

iii. Let us understand the asset history sheet version 0003 (Figure 14.15), for example, before proceeding to discuss how to create a new one. On the initial 'Maintain Asset History Sheet Version: EN 0003' screen:
   - You will see the 4-digit identifier for the asset history sheet version (0003, in this case) and a description for the version
   - You will see the maintenance language as EN.

   > **i** A history sheet item created in another language, but which has not yet received a description in the maintenance language, will be marked with *.

   - You will also notice if the asset history sheet version is 'complete' or 'incomplete' ('Hist. sheet complete' check-box). This information appears in the header of every screen.
   - This particular asset history sheet version contains 6 columns; you see only 5 columns, 00 (Opening bal.) to 04 (Reserves) in the Figure 13.170; but, when you press 'Right column', the system scrolls to the right and shows the last column, that is 99 (Closing bal.). When you have scrolled to the right using the 'Right column' button, you need to press 'Left column' to come back to the initial position.

iv.   Let us understand more details about this asset history sheet version. Let us bring up the details, by double-clicking the column 01 (Ord. dep.). You can see these details on the next screen 'Maintain Items In Asset History Sheet Version 0003' (Figure 14.16):
   - What you see in the Figure 13.171, is actually the 2nd page of the details (you can press 'Previous page' to see the 1st page). If there are several pages, you can navigate across pages using 'Previous page' and 'Next page'.

- You will see that the column 01 (Ord. dep.) is made up of several *'history sheet groups'* viz., 70, 71...YA, YY and YZ. These groups control the sheet items into which the transaction amounts, their transaction types, and the proportional values flow. We shall discuss more about asset history sheet groups, in the next Section 14.7.2.
- Per group, you will see 8 subgroups (= indicators or flags) like 'Trn', 'Ord', 'Spc' etc, to the right of the group, that you need to configure for the flow of the transaction amount.
- A blank cell, in a subgroup, denotes that you have not allocated that transaction to the history sheet item; a '.' (period or dot) shows that the transaction has been allocated to another history sheet item, and X indicates that the transaction has been allocated to the current asset history sheet item.

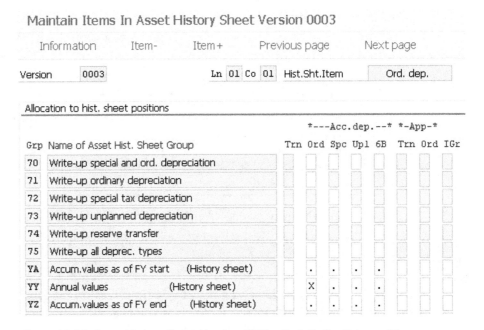

Figure 14.16: Asset History Sheet Version 0003 – Details for Column 01

v. If at all you need to create your own asset history sheet version, it is recommended that you copy an existing version and adapt the same suitably:

- To define a new asset history sheet version, you must first name it using a 4-digit identification code (starting with X, Y, or Z).
- When you define a new asset history sheet version, you need to set up the structure of the lines and columns of the asset history sheet. A maximum of 10 lines (rows) and 8 columns is possible, but a history sheet version must have at

least 2 columns. The first column is always 00, the last one 99. All other columns must be between 01 and 80.

- The first step is to consider which lines and columns you need; enter these into free line or column fields.
- If you need more than 5 columns, you must scroll to the right. When you press 'Enter', the lines and the columns are positioned correctly.
- To delete existing lines/columns, you have to over-write the line or column number with blanks.
- You can also duplicate lines/columns by over-writing the existing line or column number with the new number.
- You must enter all headings for the history sheet items that you have created.
- To define which asset transactions should flow into which history sheet items, you can go through the individual history sheet items one by one, using 'Edit > Choose' function.
- To check, if the asset history sheet version is complete, use 'Edit > Completion Check' or use F8. The system will bring up the log with the details (Figure 14.17).

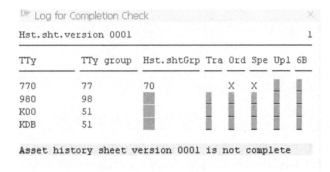

Figure 14.17: Asset History Sheet Version 0001 – Log for Completion Check

With this, we are ready to discuss (asset) history sheet groups.

14.7.2 Define History Sheet Groups

You will see a list of *'history sheet groups'* in the detail screen of each history sheet position. SAP delivers all the necessary history sheet groups for the standard version of the asset history sheet. In the standard system, these are all nothing but the transaction type groups that are relevant for the asset history sheet (every transaction type group corresponds to a history sheet group), and they bring in the values for APC, down payments, investment grants and write-ups. Besides, you will also notice three special history sheet groups: YA (values at the beginning of the fiscal year), YY (values during the fiscal year) and YZ (values at the end of the fiscal year).

Every history sheet group contains 8 indicators, with each of them representing a *'history sheet subgroup'*. By setting these indicators, in the selected history sheet position, you specify that the value fields associated with this group will flow into the selected history sheet position. The history sheet subgroups that are already allocated to a different (not the current one) history sheet position are identified with a period (.). You may press F7 on the indicator to determine the history sheet position into which the transaction type subgroup flows. The history sheet groups that are delivered with the standard system guarantee uniformity by ensuring that all transactions that belong to the same transaction type group are handled uniformly.

The meaning of the history sheet subgroups is not always uniform. The history sheet group YA (cumulative values at start of fiscal year), for example, has the following history sheet subgroups with the corresponding definitions:

- Trn = accumulated acquisition value, start of fiscal year
- Acc.dep-Ord = accumulated ordinary depreciation, start of fiscal year
- Acc.dep-Spc = accumulated special depreciation, start of fiscal year
- Acc.dep-Upl = accumulated unplanned depreciation, start of fiscal year
- Acc.dep-6B = accumulated transfer of reserves, start of fiscal year
- App-Trn = accumulated appreciation, start of fiscal year
- App-Ord = accumulated appreciation ordinary depreciation, start of fiscal year
- IGr = accumulated capital investment grants, start of fiscal year

Use the menu path: SAP Customizing Implementation Guide > Financial Accounting > Asset Accounting > Information System > Asset History Sheet > Define History Sheet Groups, to view the standard history sheet groups (Figure 14.18). You may also use Transaction OAV9.

Change View ""Asset History Sheet Group and Name"": Overview

New Entries

Grp	Name of Asset Hist. Sheet Group
10	Acquisition
12	Reverse acquisition in following years
15	Down payment
20	Retirement
25	Retirement of curr-yr acquisition
30	Retirmt transfer of prior-yr acquis.
31	Acquiring transfer of prior-yr acquis.

Figure 14.18: Standard History Sheet Groups

In general, you do not need to define your own asset history sheet groups. You should do this only if you want transaction types from the same transaction type group to flow into different positions of the history sheet. In this way, you can assign a newly defined transaction type to a special position in the asset history sheet, without having to define an individual transaction type group for it.

Click on 'New Entries' when you are in Transaction OAV9 (Figure 14.18) and define the new asset history sheet groups ('Grp') and ensure that you the group identifier starts with Z.

The last activity, under configuring asset history sheet, is to define the key figures for the Fiori app 'Asset History Sheet'.

14.7.3 Define Key Figure Groups for Asset History Sheet (Fiori)

SAP delivers all the necessary key figure groups for the standard version of the asset history sheet. By default, these are the key figure groups AHS (asset history sheet, book value) and AHS_PLAN (asset history sheet, planned values).

Use the menu path: SAP Customizing Implementation Guide > Financial Accounting > Asset Accounting > Information System > Asset History Sheet > Define Key Figure Groups for Asset History Sheet (Fiori), to view the default key figure groups for the Fiori app 'Asset History Sheet' (Figure 14.19). These key figure groups are available as parameters, when you execute the Fiori app, 'Asset History Sheet'.

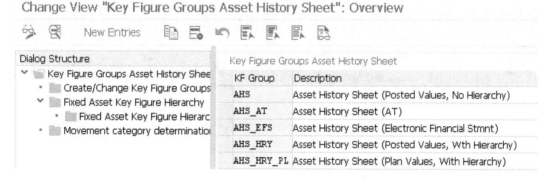

Figure 14.19: Key Figure Groups for Fiori App 'Asset History Sheet'

Select a 'KF Group' and double click on 'Create/Change Key Figure Groups of Asset Accounting' on the left-hand side 'Dialog Structure'. Now, on the resulting screen, you will see the key figures and their sequence (Figure 14.20).

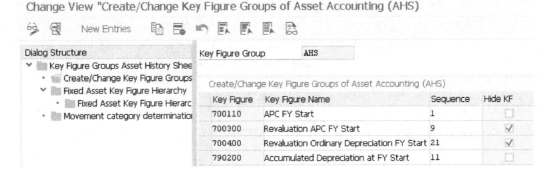

Figure 14.20: Details for Key Figure Group 'AHS'

Normally, you do not need to define your own key figure groups. However, you may need to define new key figure groups, when you want to display key figures in the asset history sheet that are different to the standard or when you want a different sequence of key figure digits. Use 'New Entries' or 'Copy As' on the initial screen to create your own key figure groups.

This completes our discussion on configuring the asset history sheet as a part of FI-AA Information System. There are a few more settings that we need to complete for FI-AA Information System, starting with the option to rename the value fields for asset explorer.

14.8 Rename Value Fields for the Asset Explorer

Here, in this step, you can change the default short texts of value fields that are displayed in the *Asset Explorer* (Transaction AW01N / AW01). You can specify this per depreciation area.

Project Dolphin

BESTM will not be renaming any of the value fields meant for the asset explorer. They are good with the short text supplied by SAP.

Use the menu path: SAP Customizing Implementation Guide > Financial Accounting > Asset Accounting > Information System > Rename Value Fields for the Asset Explorer. You may also use Transaction OAWT.

On the resulting screen, select the depreciation area (say, 01) and double-click on 'Value field texts' on the left-hand side 'Dialog Structure'. On the next screen (Figure 14.21), you will see the value fields along with their default short names and description. You may change the 'Short name' and 'Description', if required.

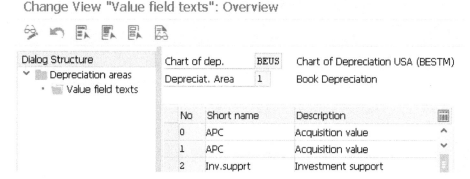

Figure 14.21: Renaming Value Field Texts

The next step is to define currency translation methods, for the asset reports.

14.9 Define Currency Translation Methods

You can specify the currency translation methods, when starting a report. The system, then, determines the asset values for the report, according to the defined method and in the corresponding currency. SAP delivers two translation methods as default, (a) historical conversion at the capitalization date and (b) key date translation. If these are not sufficient, you can define the new currency translation methods, in this configuration step.

Project Dolphin

BESTM will not be requiring any new currency translation methods as they will use the standard ones supplied by SAP as default.

Use the menu path: SAP Customizing Implementation Guide > Financial Accounting > Asset Accounting > Information System > Define Currency Translation Methods, or Transaction OAW3, to define new currency translation methods.

The last and final step in configuring FI-AA Information System is to define / assign forms (layout sets) for asset history sheet and asset labels.

14.10 Define or Assign Forms

Here, you can define layout sets (forms) for (a) the evaluation 'asset history' (*asset chart*) and (b) printing labels with asset information (*barcodes*) using the inventory list. The layout sets determine the layout of the list printout of reports.

You can store a separate layout set, per asset class, for the asset chart. The report then uses this layout set for the fixed assets of this class and creates a corresponding asset chart. You can enter the layout set for the inventory list when you start the report. SAP supplies the layout set FIAA_F001 as a default for the asset chart and the layout set FIAA_0003 for the inventory labels.

Project Dolphin

BESTM has decided to create new layout sets for both asset chart and asset information, and they will engage the ABAP development team to complete the task.

Use the menu path: SAP Customizing Implementation Guide > Financial Accounting > Asset Accounting > Information System > Define or Assign Forms, or Transaction SE71, to define the new forms. Once defined, you may use Transaction OAAY, later, to assign the new form (layout set), per asset class, for the asset chart.

This completes our discussion on configuring FI-AA Information System.

14.11 Conclusion

You learned that the FI-AA Information System component, contains several standard reports and functions to meet your specific reporting needs, and that the reports are offered in the form of a 'report tree', the hierarchical structure of which you can freely define through Customizing. You learned that the system makes use of the logical database ADA for these reports. You also learned that some of the FI-AA reports, in the report tree, have been created using 'SAP Query' (also known as, 'ABAP Query'), and that there are several standard queries that you can use as such, or copy / modify them to meet your specific requirements. You understood that all these standard queries for FI-AA, are provided in the global application area, and hence are not client-specific.

You learned that you can use 'sort versions' for sorting and totalling the data records in report lists in FI-AA, and that you need to enter the sort version, as a parameter, before running the report.

You learned that SAP offers two simulation options with which (a) you can execute standard reports with simulated depreciation terms and (b) you can analyze changes in the value of individual assets using simulated depreciation terms and transactions. You learned that the simulation enables planning the future development value your fixed assets portfolio.

You learned about the 'key figures' / 'key figure groups' that are used for some of the SAP Fiori apps like 'Asset History Sheet', 'Asset Transaction List', 'Asset Balances' and 'Asset Transactions'.

You learned that the 'asset history sheet' is the most important and most comprehensive report, for the year-end closing or for an interim financial statement, and that, like other reports, you can set this up with any sort versions, and total on any group level. You learned how to configure asset history sheet. In the process, you learned that the structure of the asset history sheet varies from country to country, depending on tax laws and that SAP provides you with country-specific versions of the asset history sheet, known as 'asset history sheet versions'. You also learned that there are several 'history sheet groups' in the detail screen of each history sheet position, and that SAP delivers all the necessary history sheet groups for the standard version of the asset history sheet. You understood that these groups are all nothing but the transaction type groups that are relevant for the asset history sheet (with every transaction type group corresponding to a history sheet group), and that they bring in the values for APC, down payments, investment grants and write-ups.

You also learned that you can define layout sets (forms) for (a) the evaluation of 'asset history' ('asset chart') and (b) printing of labels with asset information (barcodes) using the inventory list.

With this, let us move on to discuss asset data transfer, in the next Chapter.

15 Asset Data Transfer

The 'asset data transfer' or 'legacy data transfer' refers to transferring of existing asset data from a previous system or from a file maintained outside the accounting system. Normally, it is the first action that you do, after configuring (including classification of assets) FI-AA in SAP.

The legacy data transfer consists of transferring of (a) asset master records, (b) asset values and the accumulated prior-year acquisitions and (c) transactions, starting from the beginning of the fiscal year up to the time of the transfer, if legacy data transfer is during the year.

SAP provides you with multiple options for asset data transfer, as shown in Figure 15.1. We shall discuss the following in this Chapter:

- Parameters for Data Transfer
- Manual Data Transfer
- Legacy Data Transfer using Microsoft® Excel

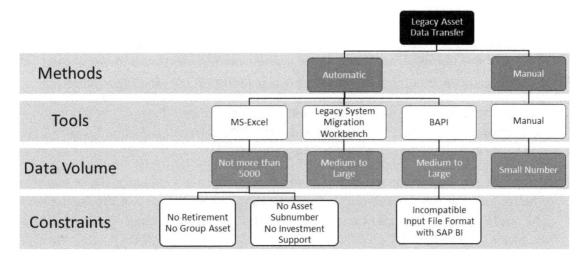

Figure 15.1: Legacy Data Transfer – Methods, Tools, Data Volume & Constraints

Let us now discuss the various settings that you need to make in Customizing in FI-AA, for legacy data transfer. Let us start with the parameters for data transfer.

15.1 Parameters for Data Transfer

Let us specify the various parameters for data transfer. This includes (a) defining the data transfer date and the associated parameters, (b) specifying the offsetting G/L account for legacy data transfer and (c) defining the transaction types for transferring open items.

The first activity is to define the transfer date and the additional parameters.

15.1.1 Define Transfer Date and Additional Parameters

The *'transfer date'* is the cut-off date for the transfer of legacy asset data. The transfer will only include data up to this point in time. There are two scenarios: (a) transfer at the end of the fiscal year – here, the transfer date is the end of the last closed fiscal year; when you transfer at the end of the year (YYYY-1), then, you can only open the fiscal year (YYYY) after the transfer date, and (b) transfer during the fiscal year – here, the transfer date can be in the fiscal year that directly follows the last closed fiscal year; when you transfer during the year, in year YYYY, then, you can open only the fiscal year of the transfer (YYYY). The system adopts the transfer date in the master record of the legacy asset as the value date. Once you have created the first legacy fixed asset, in SAP, you will not be able to change the transfer date in the segment.

The transfer date is, generally, not the same date in which you actually enter the data. Normally, you create legacy data after the transfer date. This could be due to the fact that you may have to perform a closing in your legacy system, between the transfer date and the date of the actual transfer. You can also transfer legacy assets to the SAP System before the transfer date: you, then, have to make sure that the transactions that you posted in your legacy system, up until the transfer date, are also later posted in the FI-AA in SAP.

Use the menu path: SAP Customizing Implementation Guide > Financial Accounting > Asset Accounting > Asset Data Transfer > Parameters for Data Transfer> Define Transfer Date and Additional Parameters, or Transaction FAA_CMP_LDT.

Upon entering the Transaction, you will see a tree structure on the left of the screen showing asset accounting company codes, and the relevant ledgers for each of the company codes. SAP displays only the representative ledgers for the various accounting principles and not the extension ledgers.

To define settings for a company code or ledger, you need to select the company code/ledger below the company code from the left-hand side tree structure. Here, in this Transaction, you can configure three different group of settings for company codes and ledgers that are relevant for FI-AA:

i.   Select the required company code (say, 1110) on the left-hand side 'FI-AA Company Codes' tree-structure. Highlight 'General Settings' tab on the right-hand side screen. Here, you set the company code status as to whether the company code is in testing status ('For Testing') or 'Productive' or 'Deactivated' (Figure 15.2). Since company code 1110 is still in testing phase, select the value 'For Testing' for 'Company Code Status'. You can also specify if the company code is locked, using the 'Company Code Locked' flag; when locked, you will not be able to make postings on fixed asset accounts or changes to the asset master record in that particular company code.

General Information

Company Code	1110	BESTM Farm Machinery	Chart of Accounts	BEUS BESTM - US !
Country Key	US			

General Settings   Legacy Data Transfer

General Settings for Company Code

Company Code Status	For Testing
Company Code Locked	☐

Figure 15.2: General Settings for FI-AA Company Code Status

ii. The second group of settings, you can make here, relates to year-end closing. By selecting the appropriate ledger (say, 0L), on the left-hand side tree structure, under the company code, you can close or re-open a fiscal year. You will be doing these settings in 'Ledger Settings' tab (Figure 15.3). Refer Section 16.5.1 for more details on closing / re-opening a fiscal year.

General Information

Company Code	1110	BESTM Farm Machinery	Chart of Accounts	BEUS BESTM - US
Country Key	US		Ledger	0L Ledger 0L

Ledger Settings

Ledger Settings

Ledger	0L	Ledger 0L
Highest F.Year	2020	

Depreciation Area Settings

Close   Reopen

Select Entry	De...	Name of Depreciation Area	Clsd.FY
☐	1	Book Depreciation	2019

Figure 15.3: Fiscal Year Settings for FI-AA Company Code

iii.   You can specify transfer date and other parameters, for legacy data transfer. Highlight the company code (say, 1110) on the left-hand side tree structure. In 'Legacy Data Transfer' tab, click on 'Create legacy transfer segment' and create the segment. Then, enter the details under 'Current Settings for Legacy Data Transfer' data block: specify the 'Transfer Date', select the appropriate value for 'Legacy Data Transfer Status' and select the appropriate 'Document Type' (Figure 15.4).

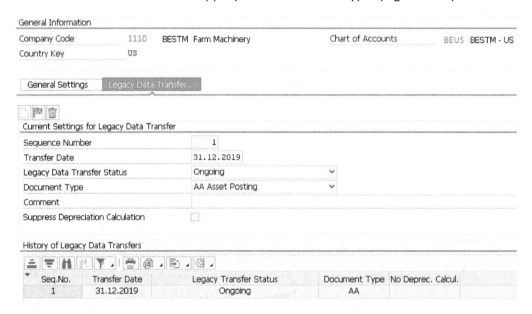

Figure 15.4: Legacy Data Transfer Settings for FI-AA Company Code

For 'Legacy Data Transfer Status', you can have three possible values: 'In Preparation' – here the system allows incomplete Customizing settings for legacy data transfer, 'Ongoing' - only legacy data transfer postings are permitted; other postings (like, acquisition, asset retirement etc) are not permitted, and 'Ongoing (Other Postings Allowed)' - both legacy data transfer and other postings are permitted; you will select this when you perform further legacy data transfers in a company code that is already productive. Select 'Ongoing' if your company code status is 'For Testing', and 'Ongoing (Other Postings Allowed)' when the company code status is 'Productive'.

You need to select 'Suppress Depreciation Calculation' check-box, to supress the calculation of planned values for depreciation, during legacy data transfer, purely on performance reasons. However, you need to perform this calculation, separately, using Transaction AFAR, later, once you have completed the legacy data transfer.

> **i** You should set the 'Suppress Depreciation Calculation' indicator only during mass data transfers. If you are transferring individual assets, manually, then, you should not set this.

The next configuration step is to specify the offsetting G/L account for legacy data transfer.

15.1.2 Specify Offsetting Account for Legacy Data Transfer

Here, you need to specify a G/L account that you will use with legacy data transfer, for transferring the asset balances. You need to make sure that you have defined this G/L as B/S account with line item management. Ensure that you use this account only for data transfer purposes, and the balance of this account is zero, once you complete the data transfer.

Use the menu path: SAP Customizing Implementation Guide > Financial Accounting > Asset Accounting > Asset Data Transfer > Parameters for Data Transfer> Specify Offsetting Account for Legacy Data Transfer. Enter the offsetting G/L account number, for legacy data transfer, against the chart of accounts (BEUS) as in Figure 15.5.

Change View "Offsetting Account for Legacy Data Transfer": Overview

Offsetting Account for Legac...

ChAc	G/L Account	
BEUS	39913000	

Figure 15.5: Offsetting G/L Account for Legacy Data Transfer

With this, we are ready to define the transaction types for transfer of open items.

15.1.3 Define Transaction Types for Transfer of Open Items

Here, you define the transaction types for the takeover of asset open items from a previous system. If you do not have AuC with line item management, you do not need this kind of transaction type. As in other cases of transaction types, go along with the SAP-supplied transaction types without defining your own.

Use the menu path: SAP Customizing Implementation Guide > Financial Accounting > Asset Accounting > Asset Data Transfer > Parameters for Data Transfer> Define Transaction Types for Transfer of Open Items, or Transaction AO79, to view the standard transaction types for transfer of open items (Figure 15.6).

Figure 15.6: Standard Transaction Types for Transfer of Open Items

With this, we are now ready to discuss the manual asset data transfer.

15.2 Manual Data Transfer

You will normally resort to manual data transfer when the volume is small, mainly in case of individual assets and for subsequent maintenance. When you transfer the asset values and transactions, the system updates the balances in G/L and hence no separate balance transfer is required. You can use various functions, under this Customizing node in the IMG, to manually create legacy assets in the system.

Though you create master data for legacy assets exactly the same way as you create regular asset master data, you need to consider the following special features of legacy assets:

- The 'Capitalization date' is always a required entry. Using the capitalization date, the system determines the depreciation start date and the expired useful life, based on the period control in the depreciation key. If you had acquired an asset, previously at a time when the company code had a different fiscal year variant, the system's determination of the useful life will be correct only if the period calendar assignments have been maintained historically.

- The 'Planned useful life' is a required entry when a depreciation key for automatic depreciation calculation has been entered. You can also account for increased wear and tear on an asset, in the past, as the result of multiple shift use. You can do this, by manually correcting the expired useful life that was automatically calculated by the system.

- You can only transfer the current values of time-dependent data (such as the assignment to a cost center) as on the transfer date. To create new time intervals, you have to use the function for changing master data.

There are separate functions for creating normal legacy fixed assets and legacy group assets:

15.2.1 Legacy Fixed Assets

Let us see the various Transactions associated with the creation / change of master data for legacy assets, posting transfer values etc in the following Table 15.1.

Menu Path: **SAP Customizing Implementation Guide > Financial Accounting > Asset Accounting > Asset Data Transfer > Manual Data Transfer > Legacy Fixed Asset >**	Transaction
Create Master Data for Legacy Asset	AS91
Change Master Data for Legacy Asset	AS92
Display Master Data for Legacy Asset	AS93
Create Master Data for Subnumber for Legacy Asset	AS94
Post Transfer Values*	ABLDT
Data Transfer During the Fiscal Year: Transfer Line Items**	AB01L
AUC with Line Item Management: Transfer Line Items***	ABLDT_OI

Table 15:1 Legacy Fixed Assets -Manual Data Transfer – Transactions

Post Transfer Values
The system posts a journal entry for the asset with this Transaction; it also updates the G/L accounts. The system creates, for each asset, a transfer document that posts the transfer values, for example, on the APC and accumulated depreciation account and against the offsetting account for the legacy data transfer

** *Data Transfer During the Fiscal Year: Transfer Line Items*
If you enter a posting date, in the current fiscal year, that is before the transfer date, the system recognizes this business transaction as a transfer document; it does not calculate depreciation, posts the document against the offsetting account for the legacy data transfer.

*** *AUC with Line Item Management: Transfer Line Items*
To ensure that the line item-managed AuC is included, the transfer values are not allowed to be entered as accumulated values, in Transaction ABLDT. Instead, you must enter the values individually using transaction ABLDT_OI. You must use the specific transaction types 900 and 910 for the transfer. If you have proportional depreciation on the AuC, then, enter this as proportional depreciation from the previous years' using the Transaction.

15.2.2 Legacy Group Assets

Similar to that of the legacy fixed assets, let us see the various Transactions associated with the creation / change of master data for legacy group assets, posting transfer values etc in the following Table 15.2.

Menu Path: **SAP Customizing Implementation Guide > Financial Accounting > Asset Accounting > Asset Data Transfer > Manual Data Transfer > Legacy Group Asset >**	Transaction
Create Master Data for Legacy Group Asset	AS81
Change Master Data for Legacy Group Asset	AS82
Display Master Data for Legacy Group Asset	AS83
Create Master Data for Subnumber for Legacy Group Asset	AS84
Post Transfer Values	ABLDT

Table 15:2 Legacy Fixed Assets -Manual Data Transfer – Transactions

With this, we can now move on to discuss the legacy data transfer using MS-Excel.

15.3 Legacy Data Transfer using Microsoft® Excel

You can use Microsoft® Excel, to transfer legacy asset data in combination with Transaction AS100. This Transaction is adjusted completely to be in line with the universal journal entry's logic. Using this Transaction, you can process about 5,000 assets in a single file upload. The amount of data, you transfer using this method, is limited by the maximum number of rows in your Excel version; you can, if necessary, split the data into several files.

ℹ️ You cannot use this method to transfer data relating to group assets, asset subnumbers, investment support and retirements.

The first step, when you use this method, is to load or manually enter the legacy asset data and values (from your legacy system) into an Excel sheet, in a pre-defined format. To ensure that you can transfer the data correctly, you need to adhere to certain guidelines when creating the Excel spreadsheet:

- Set the Excel format to 'General' for the entire document before you enter any data. You can, however, enter the dates, using the 'Custom' format.
- The Excel spreadsheet consists of two parts:
  - Header section: here, you specify the type of data you want to transfer for all the assets (for example, company code, description, and so on).
  - Asset section, you enter the information relating to individual assets and their values.

The Excel worksheet needs to contain cells for the legacy asset number, company code, asset class and capitalization date, and you need to supply the values in these cells for each asset. The same applies for any 'required' entry fields that are defined in the asset class in the system.

Header Section

In the 'header section', you need to specify the field descriptions that are to be transferred. The first 5 rows in the Excel worksheet are reserved for this header information. Do not to use them for asset master data or asset values.

The fields are organized in *record types*. Enter these record types in the first column of the worksheet. The next columns should contain the field descriptions assigned to these record types. SAP recommends that you follow the structure as shown in Table 15.3. If you do not need certain record types (for example, record type 4 – Transactions), then, you can omit them when creating your worksheet.

Record Type	Explanation	Remarks
0	Identifier (legacy asset number); record type 0 is reserved solely for the number of the asset from the legacy system, and is not allowed to be used for any other purpose. The system needs this identifier, in order to assign them to the correct assets, if there are errors.	Header data
1	Asset master data, general data and inventory data	Header data
2	Posting information, time-dependent data	Time-dependent data
3	Depreciation areas, cumulative values, posted values	Depreciation areas, cumulative values, posted values
4	Transactions	Transactions

Table 15:3 Legacy Asset Transfer using MS- Excel – Header Section

Asset Section

In the 'asset section', you will be entering the asset values, below the header data, in the Excel worksheet. Enter the asset data, as per the structure of the field descriptions in the header.

> **i** For example, you specify in the header for record type 1 that the company code is in column B and the asset class is in column C. The system, then, will recognize the field contents of all fields of record type 1 in column B as company codes and in column C as asset classes. Hence, you have to make sure that for each asset, which is in a row specified as record type 1, that its company code is always in column B and its asset class in column C. The fields with leading zeroes in the system (for example, company code 0001), should have leading zeroes in the format. Always enter the asset class with 8 places and leading zeroes (for example, asset class 1000 needs to entered as 00001000). You need enter all values specifying if they

are positive or negative (unlike when you create legacy asset data manually); for example, enter accumulated ordinary depreciation in the Excel worksheet with a negative sign.

The Figure 15.7 shows an example of a MS-Excel spreadsheet with header and asset data.

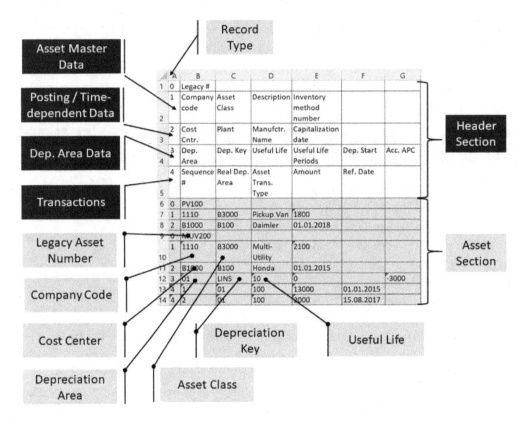

Figure 15.7: Sample Microsoft Excel Worksheet with Legacy Asset Data

You will notice, in Figure 15.7, that:

- Column A represents the record type: 0, 1, 2 etc.
- Rows 1 to 5 (records 0 to 4) represents the header data that contains the details of field for each of the cells; Record 0 (row 1) identifies the legacy or old asset number, record 1 (row 2) represents the asset master data including the company code, asset class and so on.
- From row number 6, you have the asset details.
- Rows 6, 7 and 8 together denotes a single asset record: row 6 has the legacy asset number in cell B6 (value = PV100).
- Rows 9 to 14 represent another asset data (the legacy asset number MUV200 is shown in cell B9). For this asset, the 'Company Code' (1110) value is in cell B10, Cell C10 denotes the 'Asset Class' (B3000), Cell B11 indicates the 'Cost Center' (B1000),

Cell B12 denotes the 'Depreciation Area' (01), Cell C12 is the 'Depreciation Key' (LINS), Cell D12 shows the 'Useful Life' and so on.

- Rows 13 and 14(record 4) represent the transaction details: 'Sequence #' denotes the sequence number of transaction (1, for example), 'Real Dep. Area' is the depreciation area (say, 01), 'Asset Trans. Type' is the asset transaction type (say, 100) and so on.

With this background on using MS-Excel for legacy data transfer, let us, now, understand how you can transfer legacy data in the system:

Use the menu path: SAP Customizing Implementation Guide > Financial Accounting > Asset Accounting > Asset Data Transfer > Legacy Data Transfer using Microsoft® Excel. You may also use Transaction AS100.

i. On the resulting screen (Figure 15.8), select the 'Input file' and click on 'Start'.

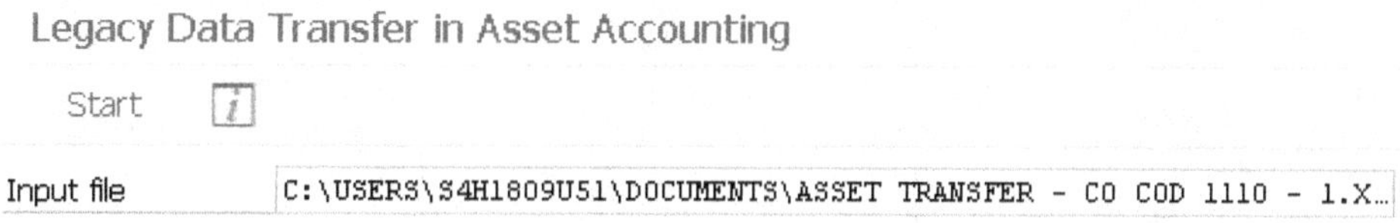

Legacy Data Transfer in Asset Accounting

Start   [i]

Input file   C:\USERS\S4H1809U51\DOCUMENTS\ASSET TRANSFER - CO COD 1110 - 1.X...

Figure 15.8: Legacy Data Transfer using Microsoft Excel – Initial Screen

ii. On the next screen (Figure 15.9), you will see the details for mapping the fields of your input Excel file to the fields of asset master record in SAP. Under 'Assignment of table fields', you will see two tables on the screen: on the left-hand side, you will see the fields from the input file ('Field of file') and on the right, you will see a table with 'Fields of asset master record' as it appears in SAP with the fields arranged in various tabs like 'Header Data', 'General Data' Inventory' and so on. At the bottom of the screen, you will see table that will show the 'Results of assignment'.

To start assigning the fields from your Excel input file to that of SAP's asset master record fields, you need to highlight a row on the left-hand side input table (say, 'Cost Cntr') and highlight the corresponding field on the right-hand side SAP table (say, 'Cost Center' on 'Time-dependent' tab), and click on the 'Assign' button located at the middle of these two tables. Now, the system will populate the bottom table ('Results of assignment') with this assignment. Continue to make all the assignments (you may need to search the fields on various tabs on the SAP table).

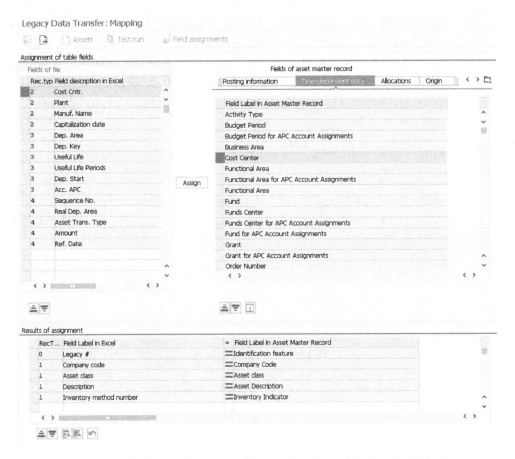

Figure 15.9: Legacy Data Transfer using Microsoft Excel – Field Mapping & Assignment

iii.   Once completed, you may 'Save' the assignments. Enter the details on the ensuing 'Field Assignments: Maintain Attributes' pop-up screen. This way you do not need to do assignments every time to make a transfer, using a similar file format but for uploading, say, another tranche of legacy assets.

iv.   Now, click on the 'Next screen (create assets)' button at the top of the 'Legacy Data Transfer: Mapping' screen. The system takes you to the 'Legacy Date Transfer: Creation of Assets' screen. Here, go to 'Settings > Date format…' and set the appropriate date format (European, American, SAP format). Unless you do this, you may encounter an error (like, 'Fiscal year of legacy data transfer could not be determined'), later, when you do the 'Test run' or the actual 'Creation of asset(s)'.

v.   Now, while on this screen, you may click on 'Test run' (before actually creating the assets using the 'Creation of asset(s)' button). At this point, the system will bring up errors, if any, without transferring the legacy data. At any time, you can click on 'Field assignments' to view or modify the assignments that you have already made.

vi. When satisfied, you can create the assets in SAP system by clicking on the 'Creation of asset(s)' button). The system issues suitable confirmations, on the table under 'Creation of asset(s)'. You can display incomplete or incorrect data that could not be processed; export them to a new MS-Excel file that you can correct and use for upload, later.

vii. Next time, when you start the Transaction, you will see the existing assignment of fields with the previous 'Assignment' name (Figure 15.10). You can use the same assignments or modify later when you do another transfer, by selecting another 'Input file'. This way, you can save your time on making new assignments every time you do a legacy data transfer using MS-Excel.

Legacy Data Transfer in Asset Accounting

Field assignment

Input file

Existing field assignments

Assignment	LongText	User	Created	Changed
1110-1	Test-Tranche1	S4H1909U01	12.05.2020	12.05.2020

Figure 15.10: Legacy Data Transfer using Microsoft Excel – Existing Field Assignment

This completes our discussion on asset data transfer.

15.4 Conclusion

You learned that the '(legacy) asset data transfer' refers to transferring of existing asset data from a previous system or from a file maintained outside the accounting system, and that will be first action you will do, after configuring FI-AA in SAP. You learned that the legacy data transfer consists of transferring of (a) asset master records, (b) asset values and the accumulated prior-year acquisitions and (c) transactions. You learned that SAP provides both manual and automatic methods for asset data transfer.

You learned that you need to configure various parameters for data transfer including (a) defining the data 'transfer date' and the associated parameters, (b) specifying the offsetting G/L account for legacy data transfer and (c) defining the transaction types for transferring open items, before you can actually undertake asset transfer.

You learned that the 'transfer date' is the cut-off date for the transfer of legacy asset data, and that the transfer will only include data up to this point in time. You learned that you can either transfer at the end of the fiscal year or transfer during the fiscal year. You understood that the system adopts the transfer date, in the master record of the legacy asset, as the value date.

You learned that you will normally resort to manual data transfer when the volume is small, mainly in case of individual assets and for subsequent maintenance. You learned that you create master data for legacy assets exactly the same way as you create regular asset master, in the manual method of asset data transfer.

You learned that you can use Microsoft® Excel, to transfer legacy asset data and that you can process about 5,000 assets in a single file upload. You also learned that the amount of data, you transfer using this method, is limited by the maximum number of rows in your Excel version, and that you can, if necessary, split the data into several files, for uploading.

With this, we are now ready to discuss the preparations required for 'going live' with FI-AA, in the next Chapter.

16 Preparations for Going Live

In the previous Chapters (Chapter 5 to 15), you have configured the system to meet your functional requirements of FI-AA, in SAP. You can, now, carry out the more technically-oriented activities that are necessary for 'going live' with FI-AA. In this Chapter, we shall discuss:

- Authorization Management
- Check Consistency
- Reset Company Code
- Production Startup

The first activity is to take care of the authorization management in the system.

16.1 Authorization Management

SAP's authorization protection is based on 'authorization objects' defined in the system. Using these objects, you can define 'authorizations'. Later, you can group these authorizations into 'authorization profiles' and assign the same to individual users. Here, in this Section, we shall be discussing the following configuration tasks for authorization management:

- Maintain Authorizations
- Assign Workflow Tasks
- Process Asset Views

Let us start with the first task of maintaining authorizations.

16.1.1 Maintain Authorizations

SAP comes delivered with several standard authorization objects (Table 16.1) that you can straightaway use in authorization management. However, should you decide to maintain your own authorizations, you may do so by using the menu path: SAP Customizing Implementation Guide > Financial Accounting > Asset Accounting > Asset Data Transfer > Preparations for Going Live > Authorization Management > Maintain Authorizations. You may also use Transaction PFCG.

Authorization Objects	Functions
Asset View	Assets in General
Company Code/Asset Class	Asset Postings
Asset Class/Transaction Type	
Asset Classes	Asset Class Maintenance
Authorizations for Periodic Processing	Asset Accounting
Company Code, Asset Class	Asset Master Record Maintenance
Company Code, Business Area	
Company Code, Cost Center	
Company Code, Plant	
Group Asset	Group Asset Maintenance
Chart of Depreciation, Company Code	Asset Customizing

Table 16:1 Standard Authorization Objects for FI-AA

Project Dolphin

BESTM will not be creating any new authorizations; rather, they will be using the standard ones supplied by SAP.

The next task is to assign the workflow tasks to appropriate organizational objects, and then to the required users.

16.1.2 Assign Workflow Tasks

Here, in this configuration task, you will be making the system settings for workflow control. You will need these settings for taking up some of the activities in FI-AA including (a) making mass changes to master data using workflow, (b) posting mass retirement using workflow and (c) completing assets that were not fully created.

However, you can carry out the above three activities without using workflow. For example, you can complete the activities (a) and (b) through mass changes and mass retirements; and you can complete activity (c) by processing incomplete assets using normal asset reporting. In such a situation, you do not need to complete this configuration task.

When you want to use workflow, then, you need to (a) assign the task by linking the same with an organizational object (like, asset accountant), (b) link the organizational objects (from you company's organization structure) to appropriate user (as owner) and finally (c) activate the event linkage for the standard tasks.

> **i** You can also assign a Workflow task directly to a user, but this option is available if you use workflow only in FI-AA, and when you have not defined your organizational plan in the system. Then, in this case, you do not need any other organizational objects.

Use the menu path: SAP Customizing Implementation Guide > Financial Accounting > Asset Accounting > Asset Data Transfer > Preparations for Going Live > Authorization Management > Assign Workflow Tasks. You may also use Transaction OAWF.

i. On the next screen, you will see various application components for FI-AA (Figure 16.1).

Figure 16.1: Initial Screen for Assigning Workflow Tasks

ii. Click on 'Assign Agents', and on the next screen (Figure 16.2), you will see the standard catalog of workflow tasks associated with FI-AA.

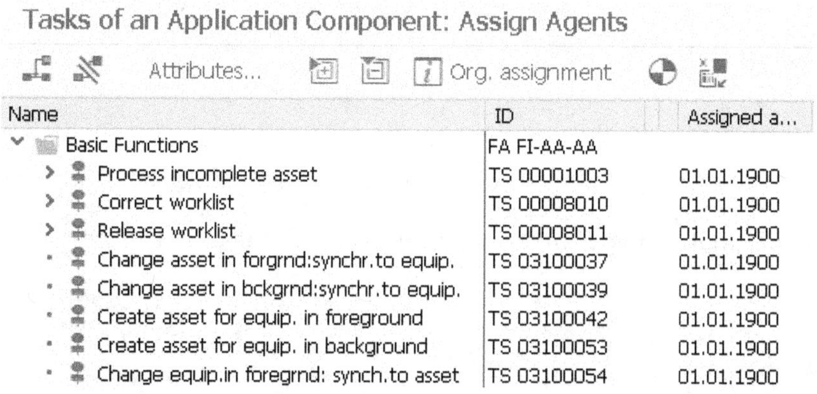

Figure 16.2: Workflow Tasks Catalog

iii.   Select the task (say, 'Process incomplete asset') and click on 'Create agent assignment' button (on the left corner of the screen, just above 'Name').

iv.   On the resulting 'Choose agent type' pop-up screen (Figure 16.3), highlight the object type (say, 'Role') and assign the appropriate object (say, 'Asset Accountant') to the task.

Figure 16.3: 'Choose agent type' Pop-Up Screen

v.   Now, assign the appropriate user(s) to the 'Role' ('Asset Accountant') that you have just linked with the task (Figure 16.4).

vi.   Repeat and link all the required tasks with the appropriate object, and assign the appropriate users in each case.

vii.   Once you have assigned the users, you need to 'activate' (Figure 16.4) the same.

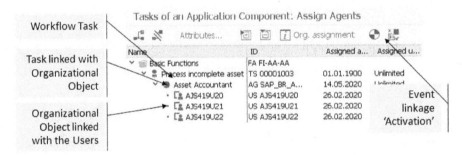

Figure 16.4: 'Workflow Task – Organization Object – User' Linkage and Activation

The final configuration activity, under authorization management, is to process the asset views.

16.1.3 Process Asset Views

Besides the standard SAP authorization functions, FI-AA component provides you with the *'asset view'* for additional authorization protection. The asset view authorization object (A_A_VIEW) controls master data maintenance to a certain extent. You can use this object to assign users limited views of asset data and asset values. We have already discussed asset views, in detail in Chapter 12.3.

With this, we are now ready to discuss how to check consistency of the system settings that you have made so far, in the next Section.

16.2 Check Consistency

Now that you have completed the configuration settings for FI-AA, you should carry out this step for checking the consistency of your system as to the settings that you have made under various configuration activities and tasks.

Use the menu path: SAP Customizing Implementation Guide > Financial Accounting > Asset Accounting > Asset Data Transfer > Preparations for Going Live > Check Consistency.

On the resulting pop-up screen (Figure 16.5), you will see several individual tasks to check for consistency of, say, asset class definition, chart of depreciation, company codes, depreciation area etc. At the end, you will see the activity 'Consistency Report: FI-AA Customizing' that will provide the overview of all the settings for FI-AA. Complete all the activities, as listed on the screen (Figure 16.5).

Select Activity:		
Activities		
Performed	Name of Activity	
✔	Overview Report: Asset Classes	
✔	Overview Report: Charts of Depreciation	
✔	Overview Report: Company Codes	
✔	Overview Report: Depreciation Areas	
✔	Consistency Report: Asset G/L Accounts	
✔	Consistency Report: FI-AA Customizing	

Figure 16.5: Consistency Check – Overview of Activities

For example, when you double-click on the activity 'Overview Report: Company Codes', you will get the details, on the next screen, for all your asset accounting company codes as shown in Figure 16.6.

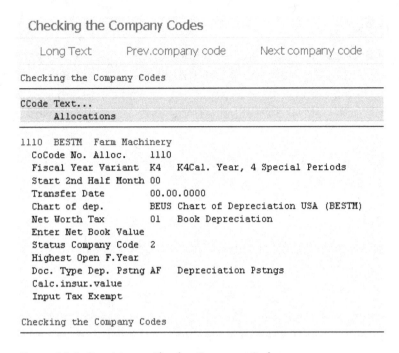

```
Checking the Company Codes

   Long Text       Prev.company code        Next company code

Checking the Company Codes

CCode Text...
      Allocations

1110  BESTM  Farm Machinery
   CoCode No. Alloc.     1110
   Fiscal Year Variant   K4    K4Cal. Year, 4 Special Periods
   Start 2nd Half Month  00
   Transfer Date         00.00.0000
   Chart of dep.         BEUS Chart of Depreciation USA (BESTM)
   Net Worth Tax         01    Book Depreciation
   Enter Net Book Value
   Status Company Code   2
   Highest Open F.Year
   Doc. Type Dep. Pstng  AF    Depreciation Pstngs
   Calc.insur.value
   Input Tax Exempt

Checking the Company Codes
```

Figure 16.6: Consistency Check – Company Codes

Instead of going through the menu path shown here, in this Section, you can also reach the individual screens directly using the corresponding Transactions as listed below, in Table 16.2:

Activity	Transaction
Overview Report: Asset Classes	ANKA
Overview Report: Charts of Depreciation	OAK1
Overview Report: Company Codes	OAK2
Overview Report: Depreciation Areas	OAK3
Consistency Report: Asset G/L Accounts	OAK4
Consistency Report: FI-AA Customizing	OAK6

Table 16:2 Transaction Codes for Consistency Check

The next activity is to reset the company code before making the settings for going live.

16.3 Reset Company Code

You can delete test data (asset master records and transactions) for a company code. You may need to do this activity, for example, following a test legacy data transfer. To reset, the 'Company Code Status' should be in 'For Testing' status (refer Chapter 15.1.1).

> ℹ️ Once deleted, you will not be able to retrieve the deleted data back. The system deletes data only in FI-AA component and not in any of the integrated applications. The system does not delete the configuration settings.

Use the menu path: SAP Customizing Implementation Guide > Financial Accounting > Asset Accounting > Asset Data Transfer > Preparations for Going Live > Tools > Reset Company Code. You may also use Transaction OABL:

i.   On the resulting screen, enter the 'Company Code' (say, 1110). If you select 'Line items only' check-box, then, the system deletes only the transactions and not the asset master data (Figure 16.7).

Reset Company Code

This transaction will reset all the application data from Asset Accoun
in one company code !!!
You can only use this company code in a test system !!!
When you carry out this action, it is logged with
your name!!!

User Name   S4H1909U01

Company Code   1110

☐ Line items only

Figure 16.7: Reset Company Code (in FI-AA) – Initial Screen

ii.   Press 'Yes' on the 'Reset company code' pop-up screen. Now, the system deletes all the test data in the selected company code for FI-AA and resets the company code. The system displays a message on the status bar informing that the company code has been reset (Figure 16.8).

iii.   Repeat for all other company codes.

✅ Company code 1110 was reset (terminal)

Figure 16.8: Reset Company Code (in FI-AA) - Confirmation

With this, we are now ready for making the settings for production startup.

16.4 Production Startup

Towards making the settings for production startup, you need to complete three configuration steps:

- Accounts Approach: Set/Reset Reconciliation Accounts for Parallel Valuation
- Define Settings for Company Code
- Activate New Asset Accounting (New Customers)

Let us start with the first step of setting / resetting reconciliation accounts for parallel valuation if you use account approach.

16.4.1 Accounts Approach: Set/Reset Reconciliation Accounts for Parallel Valuation

You need to complete this setting only if you use accounts approach (instead of ledger approach) for parallel accounting. In that case, you can define G/L accounts, as reconciliation accounts, for depreciation areas of a parallel valuation of FI-AA, or define them again as accounts for normal posting.

Use the menu path: SAP Customizing Implementation Guide > Financial Accounting > Asset Accounting > Asset Data Transfer > Preparations for Going Live > Production Startup > Accounts Approach: Set/Reset Reconciliation Accounts for Parallel Valuation, to set /reset the required reconciliation account(s) for parallel valuation.

On the resulting screen, select the required 'Company code' and double-click on 'Change Control of Reconciliation Accounts' on the left-hand side 'Dialog Structure'. On the next screen, set / reset the required G/L account(s) as the reconciliation accounts for parallel valuation. Since BESTM uses ledger approach for parallel accounting, we will not be configuring this step.

The next step is to assign the 'Productive' status to the asset accounting company codes as you have completed all the configuration and also reset the company code to delete all the test data.

16.4.2 Define Settings for Company Code

To change the status from 'For Testing' to 'Productive' for the required asset accounting company codes, use the menu path: SAP Customizing Implementation Guide > Financial Accounting > Asset Accounting > Asset Data Transfer > Preparations for Going Live > Production Startup > Define Settings for Company Code, or Transaction FAA_CMP. You will notice that this is the same Transaction that we have already discussed in Chapter 15.1.1, when we defined the transfer date and other parameters for asset data transfer.

You need to select the required company code on the tree-structure on the left, and change the 'Company Code Status' to 'Productive' on the 'General Settings' tab (Figure 16.9).

General Information

Company Code	1110	BESTM Farm Machinery	Chart of Accounts	BEUS BESTM - US Standard Chart of Accou
Country Key	US			

General Settings   Legacy Data Transfer

General Settings for Company Code

Company Code Status	Productive	⌄
Company Code Locked	☐	

Figure 16.9: Making the Company Code 'Productive'

Repeat and change the status to all other company codes, one by one.

> **i** You may also change the 'Legacy Data Transfer Status' (on the 'Legacy Data Transfer' tab) to 'Ongoing (Other Postings Allowed)' to allow both legacy data transfer postings and other postings. You will need this kind of status if you plan to perform further legacy data transfers the company code that is already productive.
>
> When you have completed legacy data transfer, you can set this status to 'Completed'.

With this, we are ready complete the final step in production startup, namely, activating the new Asset Accounting, in case you are a new customer for SAP.

16.4.3 Activate New Asset Accounting (New Customers)

You need to complete this activity if you have not yet used FI-AA in SAP S/4HANA. You will use this configuration step to activate new Asset Accounting in SAP S/4HANA. You must perform this activation per client. Before activating, you must first make the relevant settings in Customizing for new Asset Accounting. When activated, the system checks whether the settings in Customizing have been made correctly.

When you activate, the system activates the new Asset Accounting in downstream systems (test system and production system) by importing the active Customizing switch and the normal Customizing settings. Once the import to the downstream system has been carried out, the system performs the same checks here as in the Customizing system with the activation. If these checks are not successful, the switch for this activity gets the status 'Active (Posting in client not possible)'.

Use the menu path: SAP Customizing Implementation Guide > Financial Accounting > Asset Accounting > Asset Data Transfer > Preparations for Going Live > Production Startup > Activate

New Asset Accounting (New Customers). On the resulting screen, select the value '2 Active' to activate new Asset Accounting in the client (Figure 16.10).

Change View "New Asset Accounting: Activation": Details

New Asset Accounting

2 Active	∨

Figure 16.10: Activating New Asset Accounting

This completes our discussion on the settings required for production startup. Let us, now, understand the tools that are available for preparing the system for go-live.

16.5 Tools

There are two tools that are made available for preparations for go-live:

- Reset Company Code
- Execute/Undo Year-End Closing

As we have already discussed 'Reset Company Code' activity vide Section 16.3, let us look at the other activity that you can use for executing year end closing.

16.5.1 Execute/Undo Year-End Closing

You can use this configuration step to close / re-open a fiscal year. We have already touched upon this configuration activity in Chapter 15.1.1, when we were discussing the transfer date (and the related parameters) for legacy asset transfer.

16.5.1.1. Closing a Fiscal Year

You can close a fiscal year from an accounting view for a ledger or for a depreciation area. Then, you will not be able to make postings or change values (for example, by recalculating depreciation) in FI-AA for that closed fiscal year.

Let us understand the difference between closing a fiscal year at the ledger level and depreciation area level:

- *Year-End Closing at Ledger Level*
  The year-end closing at ledger level involves closing the fiscal year for all depreciation areas of the ledger. The prerequisite, for this, is that all depreciation areas have the last closed fiscal year.

- *Year-End Closing at the Level of Individual Depreciation Areas*
  If you want to do this, you must choose one or more depreciation areas and close it/them. If you choose all depreciation areas, it is the same as performing a year-end closing at ledger level. This option makes sense when you expect that you will have to re-open some depreciation areas and close them again later (for tax reasons, for example).

> **i** The fiscal year that is closed is always the year following the last closed fiscal year. You should not close current fiscal year unless you want to 'Deactivate' company code in FI-AA.

You will execute year-end closing only when (a) the system has found no errors (such as, incorrectly defined depreciation keys) during the calculation of depreciation, (b) all assets (excluding AuC) acquired in the fiscal year have already been capitalized and (c) all incomplete assets (master records) have been completed.

Use the menu path: SAP Customizing Implementation Guide > Financial Accounting > Asset Accounting > Asset Data Transfer > Preparations for Going Live > Production Startup > Define Settings for Company Code, or Transaction FAA_CMP to close a fiscal year. As you can close a fiscal year at the ledger level or at the depreciation area level, you need to decide at what level you want to close the fiscal year.

To close a fiscal year at the ledger level:

i.   On the resulting screen, select the company code (say, 1110) on the left-hand side tree structure.

General Information

Company Code	1110	BESTM Farm Machinery		Chart of Accounts	BEUS	BESTM - US Standard Chart of Accou
Country Key	US			Ledger	OL	Ledger OL

Ledger Settings

Ledger Settings

Ledger	OL	Ledger OL
Highest F.Year	2019	

Depreciation Area Settings

Close		Reopen

Select Entry	De..	Name of Depreciation Area	Clsd.FY
☐	1	Book Depreciation	2018

Figure 16.11: Closed Fiscal Year 2018

ii.   Select the appropriate ledger, below the selected company code (say, OL).

iii.   Now, on the right-hand side of the screen, on the 'Ledger Settings' tab (Figure 16.11), you will notice that the 'Highest F.Year' is 2019 with the fiscal year 2018 already closed (you can see that there is an entry under 'Depreciation Area Settings' block as to the closed fiscal year = 2018).

iv.   With the fiscal year 2018 already closed, if you want to close the next fiscal year (2019), select the check-box ('Select Entry') against the all the depreciation areas, and then click on 'Close' button.

v.   Now, you will see that the closed fiscal year ('ClsdFY') is 2019, and you can enter the highest fiscal year as 2020 (Figure 16.12).

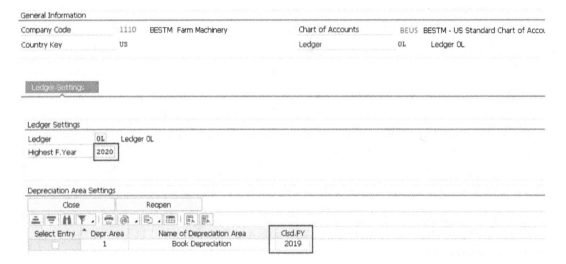

Figure 16.12: Closed Fiscal Year 2019

To close a fiscal year at the depreciation area level:

i.   On the resulting screen, select the company code (say, 1110) on the left-hand side tree structure.

ii.   Select the appropriate ledger, below the selected company code.

iii.   Now, on the right-hand side of the screen (Figure 16.11) on the 'Ledger Settings' tab, you will notice that the 'Highest F.Year' is 2019 with the fiscal year 2018 already closed (you may see entries under 'Depreciation Area Settings' block as to the closed fiscal year (2018), for various depreciation areas)

iv.   If you want to close the next fiscal year (2019), for a particular depreciation area(s), select the appropriate check-box(es) against the depreciation area(s) under 'Select Entry', and then click on 'Close' button.

v.   Now, the system closes the fiscal year 2019 for the selected depreciation area(s).

vi.   If you select all the check-boxes (meaning, all the depreciation areas) then it is as good as closing that fiscal year at the ledger level.

Let us now understand how to undo a year-end closing or re-open a closed fiscal year.

16.5.1.2. Re-open a Fiscal Year / Undo Year-end Closing

You may resort to re-open the last closed fiscal in FI-AA, if you have closed it by mistake. This way, you open that fiscal year, again, for postings. As in the case of closing a fiscal year, you can re-open the fiscal year, for individual depreciation areas of a ledger or for all depreciation areas of the ledger.

> **i** You cannot, in general, open a fiscal year that is already closed from an accounting point of view if that has already been certified by an external auditor.

Use the menu path: SAP Customizing Implementation Guide > Financial Accounting > Asset Accounting > Asset Data Transfer > Preparations for Going Live > Production Startup > Define Settings for Company Code, or Transaction FAA_CMP, to re-open a fiscal year.

As in the case of closing a fiscal year, select the company code, and select the ledger (one or more depreciation areas if the fiscal year is to be re-opened only for selected depreciation area(s) and not for the entire ledger). You will, then, select appropriate check box(es) under the 'Depreciation Area Settings' data block, and click on 'Reopen' button. Here, as shown in Figure 13.198, we are trying to re-open the last closed FY (2019). Now, the system brings up a pop-up screen confirming that the closed fiscal year is reset to 2018, from 2019 (Figure 16.13).

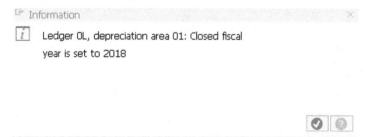

Figure 16.13: Closed Fiscal Year set to 2018

Press 'Continue' and you can see now that closed fiscal year is se to 2018, fiscal year 2019 is re-opened and the highest fiscal year at 2020 (Figure 16.14).

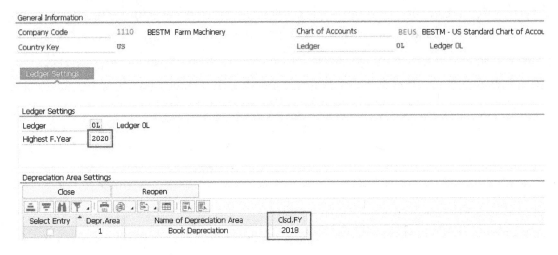

Figure 16.14: Closed Fiscal Year set to 2018, Fiscal Year 2019 Re-opened

> ℹ️ You can also perform the year-end closing by using the SAP Easy Access menu path: SAP Menu > Accounting > Financial Accounting > Fixed Assets >Periodic Processing > Year-End Closing > Execute/Undo, instead of using the Customizing activity using the IMG. The Transaction Code FAA_CMP is the same.

This completes our discussion on the preparations for going live.

16.6 Conclusion

You learned that though you have configured the system to meet your functional requirements of FI-AA, in SAP, you need to carry out the more technically-oriented activities for going live with FI-AA. You learned that such activities include authorization management, checking consistency of configuration, resetting the company code and production startup settings.

You learned that SAP's authorization protection is based on 'authorization objects' defined in the system, and that by using these objects, you can define 'authorizations'. You learned that you can group these authorizations into 'authorization profiles' and assign the same to individual users to manage access to transactions in FI-AA.

You learned how to carry out checking the consistency of your system settings that you have made under various IMG configuration activities and tasks. You learned that you can delete test data (asset master records and transactions) and reset the company code, making it ready for going live.

As a part of production startup, you learned that you need to (i) complete setting / resetting reconciliation accounts, if you use accounts approach (instead of ledger approach) for parallel accounting, (ii) change the status from 'For Testing' to 'Productive' for the required asset accounting company codes, and (iii) activate new Asset Accounting. You learned how to close a fiscal year and also learned how to re-open a closed fiscal year in the system.

With this, let us move on to discuss the overview for experts, in the next Chapter.

17 Overview for Experts

The *'overview for experts'* provides a one-stop review of the settings that you made in different sections of IMG while configuring the system for FI-AA. Using the various activities under this IMG node, you can re-check the configuration settings, at a glance; and, go back to the respective IMG node to correct, if necessary. The various activities include:

- Assign Accounts
- Assign Selected G/L Accounts per Chart of Accounts
- Check Depreciation Areas
- Check Real Depreciation Areas
- Check Active Charts of Depreciation for Asset Accounting
- Check Company Code
- Check Depreciation Areas of Company Codes
- Check Account Assignments
- Check Transaction Types
- Check Asset Classes

Let us see these activities one-by-one:

17.1 Assign Accounts

Here, you can display the G/L accounts that you have already determined for the write-off or allocation of special reserves.

Use the menu path: SAP Customizing Implementation Guide > Financial Accounting > Asset Accounting > Asset Data Transfer > Overview for Experts > Assign Accounts, or Transaction AO99.

On the resulting screen, for your chart of accounts, you can display the G/L accounts that have already been determined for special reserves per account determination.

17.2 Assign Selected G/L Accounts per Chart of Accounts

In this activity, you can display the G/L accounts that you have already determined for the following account assignments. If required, you may also maintain the same here.

- Offsetting of revenue from sale of asset
- Gain with sale of asset
- Acquisition offsetting account, acquisition value
- Offsetting account, revaluation APC
- Loss with sale of asset
- Loss from asset retirement without revenue (scrapping)

Use the menu path: SAP Customizing Implementation Guide > Financial Accounting > Asset Accounting > Asset Data Transfer > Overview for Experts > Assign Selected G/L Accounts per Chart of Accounts.

On the resulting screen, for your chart of accounts, you can display / maintain the G/L accounts for each of the account assignments listed above, per account determination and per depreciation area. This is very convenient as all these assignments are shown in a tabular format (Figure 17.1).

Figure 17.1: Determining G/L Accounts for Various Account Assignments

17.3 Check Depreciation Areas

Here, in this step, you can display depreciation areas that you have defined for your chart of depreciation. Besides, you can view the settings associated with the depreciation areas for ordinary depreciation, special depreciation, unplanned depreciation, transfer of reserves, interest, investment support and replacement values. You can also view the settings for cross-system depreciation area.

Use the menu path: SAP Customizing Implementation Guide > Financial Accounting > Asset Accounting > Asset Data Transfer > Overview for Experts > Check Depreciation Areas.

17.4 Check Real Depreciation Areas

Here, you can check the various settings like depreciation area type, currency type, value copy rules, copy rules for depreciation terms, gross transfer for intercompany asset transfer, sequence of depreciation calculation and capitalization version for the real depreciation areas.

Use the menu path: SAP Customizing Implementation Guide > Financial Accounting > Asset Accounting > Asset Data Transfer > Overview for Experts > Check Real Depreciation Areas.

17.5 Check Active Charts of Depreciation for Asset Accounting

You have already activated, vide Chapter 16.4.3, new Asset Accounting in Customizing in the IMG activity 'Activate New Asset Accounting (New Customers)'. Now, in this activity, you can check if the Customizing settings for your depreciation areas are correct for new Asset Accounting, as correct configuration (of the depreciation areas) is a prerequisite for activating the Customizing switch (FAA_PARALLEL_VAL) for new Asset Accounting. Of course, the individual checks of this program are already contained in the various IMG activities for the depreciation areas. Here, using this program, however, you can start the individual checks together. The check is carried out per chart of depreciation.

Use the menu path: SAP Customizing Implementation Guide > Financial Accounting > Asset Accounting > Asset Data Transfer > Overview for Experts > Check Active Charts of Depreciation for Asset Accounting. You may also use Transaction FAA_CHEK_AREA_4_PARV.

On the resulting screen, enter the chart of depreciation (say, BEUS) and click 'Execute'. On the next screen, the system brings up the log displaying the details (Figure 17.2). If everything is fine, you will see a green coloured square against the message 'No error found; requirements to activate Customizing switch have been met'.

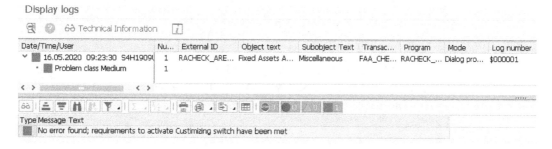

Figure 17.2: Checking Customizing for Depreciation Areas, for Chart of Depreciation BEUS

17.6 Check Company Code

Here, you can check the various settings like chart of depreciation, number range, posting of net value, fiscal year variant etc for an asset accounting company code (Figure 17.3).

Display View "Depreciation document type": Overview

Dialog Structure		CoCode	Company Name		Doc.Type	Description
Company codes		1110	BESTM	Farm Machinery	AF	Depreciation Pstngs
· Chart of depreciation						
· Number range						
· Depreciation document type						
· Posting of net value						
· Fiscal year variant						
· Entry of half months						
· Status of company code						
· Settlement profile						
· Cross-company-code cost accounting						
· Time-dependent managmt of org. units						
· Variant for determining asset value date						
· Default values for depreciation						
· Retention period for archiving						
· Technical specif.						

Figure 17.3: Company Code Check

Use the menu path: SAP Customizing Implementation Guide > Financial Accounting > Asset Accounting > Asset Data Transfer > Overview for Experts > Check Company Code.

17.7 Check Depreciation Areas of Company Codes

In this activity, you can check the various settings for depreciation areas of company codes.

Use the menu path: SAP Customizing Implementation Guide > Financial Accounting > Asset Accounting > Asset Data Transfer > Overview for Experts > Check Depreciation Areas of Company Codes.

Here, you can check the settings relating to period version, currency, memo value, changeover amount, LVA amount, period weighting, B/S version, capitalization of down payments, posting rules and net reserve for special depreciation (Figure 17.4).

Figure 17.4: Checking Depreciation Areas for Company Codes

17.8 Check Account Assignments

Here, you can check, for the given chart of accounts, the various account assignments (B/S accounts, depreciation accounts and accounts for special reserves), per account assignment and per depreciation area (Figure 17.5).

Use the menu path: SAP Customizing Implementation Guide > Financial Accounting > Asset Accounting > Asset Data Transfer > Overview for Experts > Check Account Assignments.

Figure 17.5: Checking Account Assignments

17.9 Check Transaction Types

Here, you can check various settings associated with transaction types. You can also check, for example, if there is a limitation of depreciation areas that can used with specific transaction types, is there a need for special handling of transfer posting, for a given transaction type in a given depreciation area and so on (Figure 17.6).

Use menu path: SAP Customizing Implementation Guide > Financial Accounting > Asset Accounting > Asset Data Transfer > Overview for Experts > Check Transaction Types.

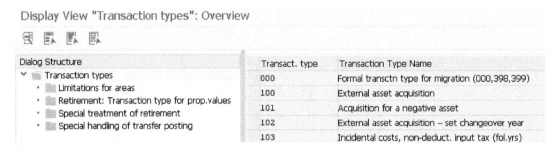

Figure 17.6: Checking Transaction Types

17.10 Check Asset Classes

In this activity you can see an overview of all settings that you have made, up to now, for asset classes. Per asset class, you can view the settings relating to net worth tax, leasing specifications, user fields, asset history form, group assets, memo value etc (Figure 17.7).

Use the menu path: SAP Customizing Implementation Guide > Financial Accounting > Asset Accounting > Asset Data Transfer > Overview for Experts > Check Asset Classes.

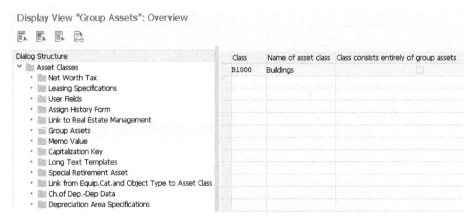

Figure 17.7: Checking Asset Classes

This completes our discussion on overview for experts.

17.11 Conclusion

You learned that you can use *'overview for experts'* as a one-stop review of the settings that you have made in different sections of IMG while configuring the system for FI-AA. You learned that, using the various activities under this IMG node, you can re-check the configuration settings, at a glance, and, go back to the respective IMG node to correct, if necessary.

With this we have come to the end of this book.

In this book:

- You learned about SAP HANA, SAP S/4HANA and SAP S/4HANA Finance. You went through the case study and understood about the enterprise structure, and other FI global settings of the fictious corporate, before looking at the business requirements that need to be configured for implementing SAP FI-AA for this corporate.
- Towards configuring SAP FI-AA:
  - ✓ You learned that you can use SAP Asset Accounting (FI-AA) to manage your business entity's fixed assets internationally, in any country and in any industry. You learned that you need to portray your organizational structure in FI-AA - by defining organizational objects like chart of depreciation, FI company code, asset class etc - to classify your fixed assets according to asset accounting criteria. For this, you learned that the starting point is to define the chart of depreciation.
  - ✓ You understood that the 'chart of depreciation' is a list of 'depreciation areas' arranged according to business and legal requirements, to manage the rules for depreciation and valuation of assets in a particular country. You also understood that, once defined, you can assign the chart of depreciation to the appropriate company codes, so as to make them available for asset accounting.
  - ✓ You learned that you can structure fixed assets, in FI-AA, at three different levels: at balance sheet (B/S) structure level, at classification structure level and at asset-related structure level. For example, at 'classification structure level', you learned that you can use the 'asset classes' (like buildings, vehicles, AuC, machinery etc) in structuring the fixed assets. With every asset belonging to an asset class, you noticed, that the asset class establishes the link (through the account determination key) between asset master records and the G/L accounts in SAP FI.
  - ✓ You learned that FI-AA is tightly integrated with other application components like SAP MM (Materials Management), PM (Plant Maintenance), SAP PP (Production Planning) and IM (Investment Management). With its integration with SAP G/L Accounting, you learned, that you can automatically update all asset accounting transactions including depreciation, to SAP G/L, in real-time for the leading depreciation areas of an accounting principle.

✓ You learned that you can manage valuation of fixed assets through 'depreciation areas'. You learned that you need different depreciation areas for valuation according to local laws (book depreciation), tax depreciation, cost-accounting depreciation, special reserves and investment support. You also learned about the differences between a 'real depreciation area' and a 'derived depreciation area', and how to derive the values for the derived area.

✓ You learned that SAP supports both automatically calculated depreciation (ordinary & special depreciation) and manually planned depreciation (unplanned depreciation & transfer of reserves / reduction in APC). You understood that the depreciation calculation is based on the 'valuation method' and the 'planned useful life' of the asset. You further understood that the valuation methods are based on two variables: the depreciation key and the cutoff value. You learned that the 'depreciation key' (defined at the level of the chart of depreciation) contains all the control indicators for depreciation calculation, besides the calculation methods. You learned that the 'calculation methods' - defined within the depreciation key - supply the required parameters to the 'Depreciation Calculation Program' (DCP).

✓ You learned that you will use 'special valuations' for special value adjustments to assets (like, investment support, special depreciation reserves etc) and for meeting some of the special valuation purposes like, cost-accounting replacement values, interest, revaluation for the balance sheet etc.

✓ You learned that an asset master record, in SAP, consists of two data areas: (a) general master data and (b) data for calculating asset values. You further learned that while the 'general master data', contains the concrete information about the fixed asset, the 'data for calculating asset values', contains the depreciation terms in the asset master record, for each depreciation area.

✓ You learned that the system makes use of asset 'transaction types', for carrying out all accounting / business transactions that occur during the life of a fixed asset (like acquisitions, retirements, intracompany / intercompany transfers, capitalization of AuC etc). You also learned that each transaction type is assigned exactly to one 'transaction type group', with the group determining the characteristics and parameters for a transaction.

✓ Later, you learned how to configure the FI-AA Information system to suit your own reporting requirements. You learned about the sort versions, simulation variants and SAP Queries in asset reporting. You also learned about the key figures / key figure groups for some of the SAP Fiori apps relating to assets. You finally learned about configuring asset history sheets, especially the history sheet versions and history sheet groups.

✓ In asset data transfer, you learned about the parameters for data transfer including the definition of transfer date, offsetting account for legacy data transfer and the associated transaction types. You also learned about manual data transfer of legacy fixed assets and legacy group assets. You understood how to carry out legacy asset transfer using Microsoft Excel.

✓ As a part of preparations for going live, you learned about maintenance of authorizations, assignment of workflow tasks and processing asset views. You learned how to check the consistency of FI-AA configuration settings. You learned how to reset the company codes and how to make them 'productive' in the system. You also learned that you can use the 'overview for experts' functionality to check and verify the configuration settings at a glance.

With this, we are confident that you will be able to configure FI-AA to meet the business requirements of a company, in a real-life situation.

About the Author

Narayanan Veeriah is a Chartered Financial Analyst (CFA), a PMP (from Project Management Institute), and IBM Certified Executive Project Management Professional, having more than 35 years of work experience, in finance, project management and information technology (IT), including 20+ years of experience in SAP implementation and consulting. A member of Certified Associate of Indian Institute of Bankers (CAIIB), he brings along with him a strong domain expertise in Banking and Finance with core competencies in retail banking and credit management, along with SAP.

Narayanan has worked with several multi-national clients for consulting, implementing and supporting SAP, across industries including automotive, banking & finance, electronics, manufacturing, multimedia, pharmaceuticals etc. He has worked with several versions of SAP right from SAP R/3 3.1H to the latest SAP S/4HANA, in new implementations, upgrades and support.

Till recently, he was leading SAP practice, for a couple of industry verticals in a leading multinational IT consulting company. He has authored several books on SAP Finance, besides being a regular guest faculty at management institutions for ERP, SAP, banking & finance and project management.

He is currently a freelance SAP consultant.

You can reach him at vdotn@yahoo.com.

Index

Latest Book by the Author

Configuring Financial Accounting in SAP ® ERP
(3rd Edition)

This is your comprehensive guide to configuring Financial Accounting in SAP ERP! Brush up on the old standbys—Accounts Payable, Account Receivable, SAP General Ledger, and Asset Accounting—and then dive in to Contract Accounts Receivable and Payable, Consolidation, Lease Accounting, Travel Management, SAP Fiori, and much more. You'll learn to set up your enterprise structure, use maintenance tools, and ensure your implementation works for your unique business.

916 pages, 3rd, updated edition 2018
E-book formats: EPUB, MOBI, PDF, online
ISBN 978-1-4932-1723-6

https://www.sap-press.com/configuring-financial-accounting-in-sap-erp_4674/

Other Books by the Author

Title: **SAP ERP: Quick Reference Guide**
Edition: 2
Publisher: Mercury Learning & Information, 2020
ISBN: 1683920961, 9781683920960
Length: 500 pages

Title: **SAP FI: Financial Accounting ERP ECC6, R/3 4.70**
Edition: 2
Publisher: Mercury Learning & Information, 2017
ISBN: 1683921003, 9781683921004
Length: 350 pages

Title: **SAP CO: Controlling**
Edition: 2
Publisher: Mercury Learning & Information, 2017
ISBN: 168392102X, 9781683921028
Length: 350 pages

Title: **Configuring Financial Accounting in SAP**
Edition 2, illustrated
Publisher: Galileo Press, 2014 (SAP Press)
ISBN: 1493210424, 9781493210428
Length: 907 pages

Title: **Implementing SAP ERP Financials: A Configuration Guide**
Edition: 2
Publisher: Tata McGraw Hill Publishing Co Ltd, 2013
ISBN-13: 978-0-0701-4297-8
Length: 965 pages

Title: **SAP FI Financial Accounting: SAP ERP ECC 6.0, SAP R/3 4.70**
Author V. Narayanan
Edition: 1, illustrated, reprint
Publisher: Mercury Learning & Information, 2013
ISBN   1937585646, 9781937585648
Length 338 pages

Title: **Customizing Financial Accounting in SAP**
Edition: 1, illustrated
Publisher: Galileo Press, 2011 (SAP Press)
ISBN   1592293778, 9781592293773
Length   792 pages

Title: **Mastering SAP CO: Controlling**
Edition: 1, illustrated
Publisher: BPB Publications, 2007
ISBN: 9788183333344
Length: 297 pages

Title: **SAP FI**
Edition: 1, illustrated
Publisher: BPB Publications, 2010
ISBN: 9788183333238
Length: 302 pages

Title: **SAP FI/CO Demystified**
Edition: 1, illustrated
Publisher: BPB Publications, 2008
ISBN: 8183332315, 9788183332316
Length: 370 pages

Title: **SAP® R/3® FI Transactions**
Edition: 1, illustrated
Publisher: Jones & Bartlett Learning, 2007
ISBN: 1934015016, 9781934015018
Length: 530 pages

Title: **Mastering SAP R/3 FI: Transaction Made Easy**
Edition: 1, illustrated
Publisher: BPB Publications, 2007
ISBN: 8183331319, 9788183331319
Length: 472 pages